SCIENCE.
BAD.

JONATHAN HICKMAN
WRITER

NICK PITARRA
ARTIST

JORDIE BELLAIRE
COLORS

RUS WOOTON
LETTERS

WITH

RYAN BROWNE
ARTIST (CHAPTER 10)

IMAGE COMICS, INC.
Robert Kirkman - chief operating officer
Erik Larsen - chief financial officer
Todd McFarlane - president
Marc Silvestri - chief executive officer
Jim Valentino - vice-president
Eric Stephenson - publisher
Ron Richards - director of business development
Jennifer de Guzman - pr & marketing director
Branwyn Bigglestone - accounts manager
Emily Miller - accounting assistant
Jamie Parreno - marketing assistant
Jenna Savage - administrative assistant
Kevin Yuen - digital rights coordinator
Jonathan Chan - production manager
Drew Gill - art director
Tyler Shainline - print manager
Monica Garcia - production artist
Vincent Kukua - production artist
Jana Cook - production artist
www.imagecomics.com

THE MANHATTAN PROJECTS, VOLUME 2
First Printing / April 2013 / ISBN: 978-1-60706-726-9

Published by Image Comics, Inc. Office of publication: 2001 Center Street, Sixth Floor, Berkeley, CA 94704. Copyright © 2013 Jonathan Hickman & Nick Pitarra. Originally published in single magazine form as THE MANHATTAN PROJECTS #6-10. All rights reserved. THE MANHATTAN PROJECTS (including all prominent characters featured herein), its logo and all character likenesses are trademarks of Jonathan Hickman & Nick Pitarra, unless otherwise noted. Image Comics® and its logos are registered trademarks of Image Comics, Inc. No part of this publication may be reproduced or transmitted, in any form or by any means (except for short excerpts for review purposes) without the express written permission of Jonathan Hickman, Nick Pitarra, or Image Comics, Inc. All names, characters, events and locales in this publication are entirely fictional. Any resemblance to actual persons (living or dead), events or places, without satiric intent, is coincidental. Printed in the U.S.A. For information regarding the CPSIA on this printed material call: 203-595 3636 and provide reference # RICH – 477193 For international licensing inquiries, write to: foreignlicensing@imagecomics.com

MP

THE MANHATTAN PROJECTS

2

HE BELIEVED
THE LIE

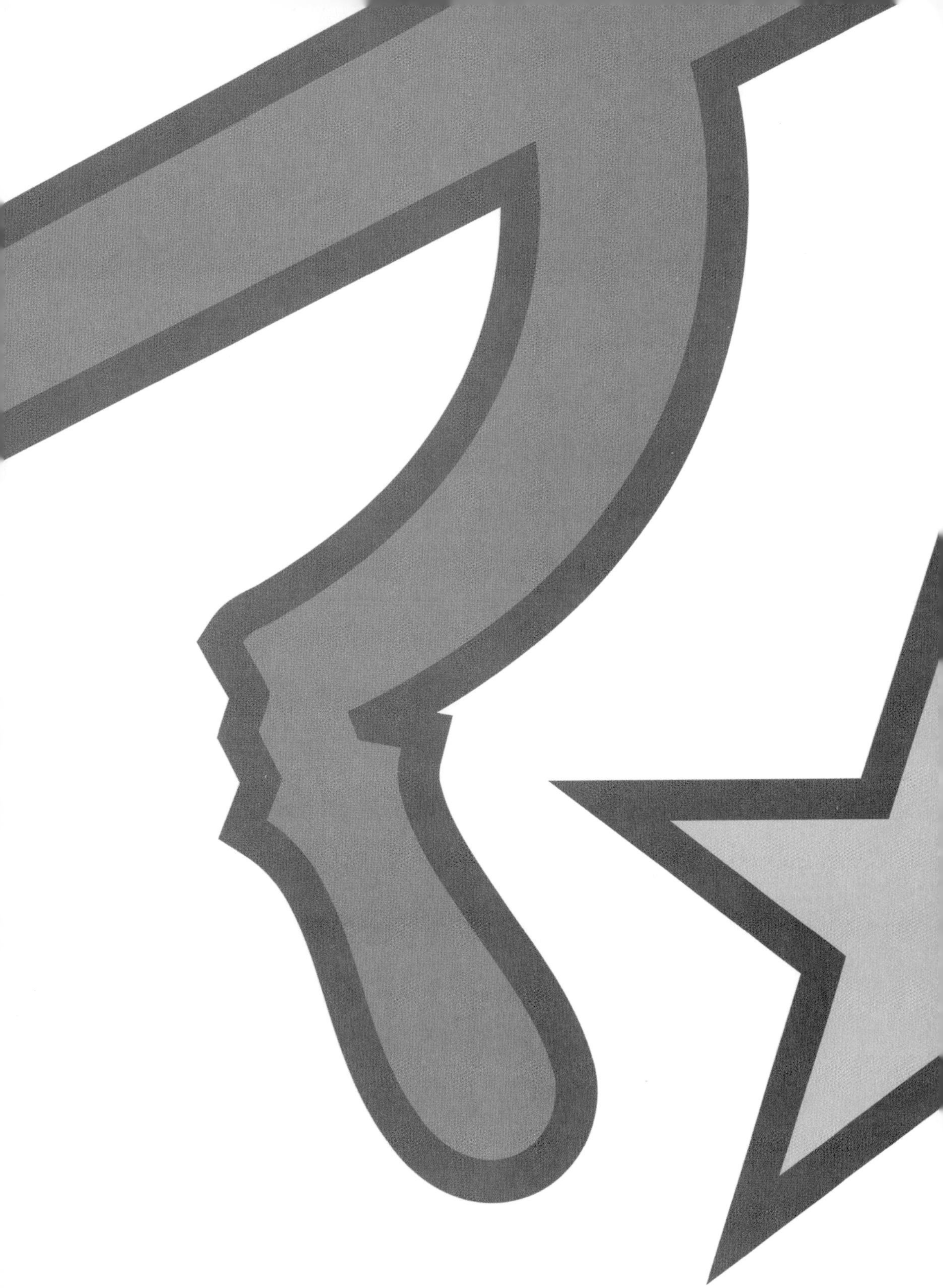

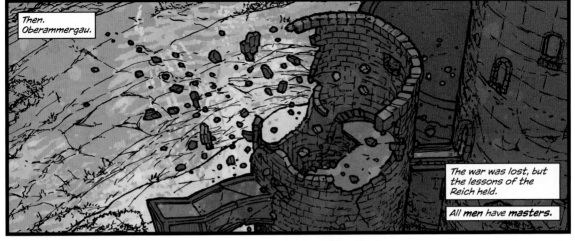

Then.
Oberammergau.

The war was lost, but the lessons of the Reich held.

All *men* have *masters.*

Achtung, gentlemen.

What now, Sturmbannführer? The Americans are almost upon us...

We must not let --

No one here needs you to remind us of responsibility, Dr. Schmidt. We are all --

Wait...

Where is Helmutt?

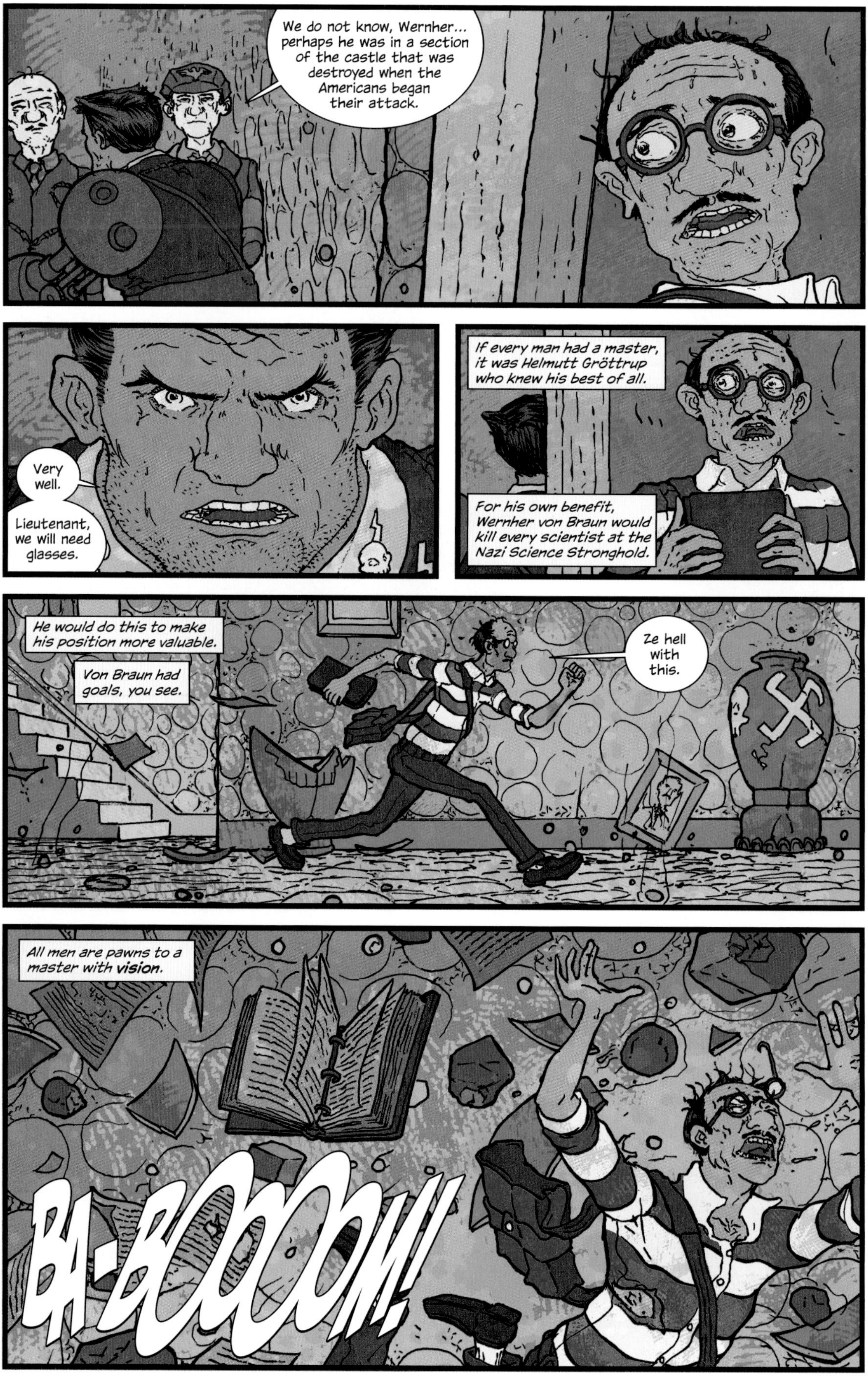
We do not know, Wernher... perhaps he was in a section of the castle that was destroyed when the Americans began their attack.
Very well.
Lieutenant, we will need glasses.
If every man had a master, it was Helmutt Gröttrup who knew his best of all.
For his own benefit, Wernher von Braun would kill every scientist at the Nazi Science Stronghold.
He would do this to make his position more valuable.
Von Braun had goals, you see.
Ze hell with this.
All men are pawns to a master with **vision**.
BA-BOOOM!

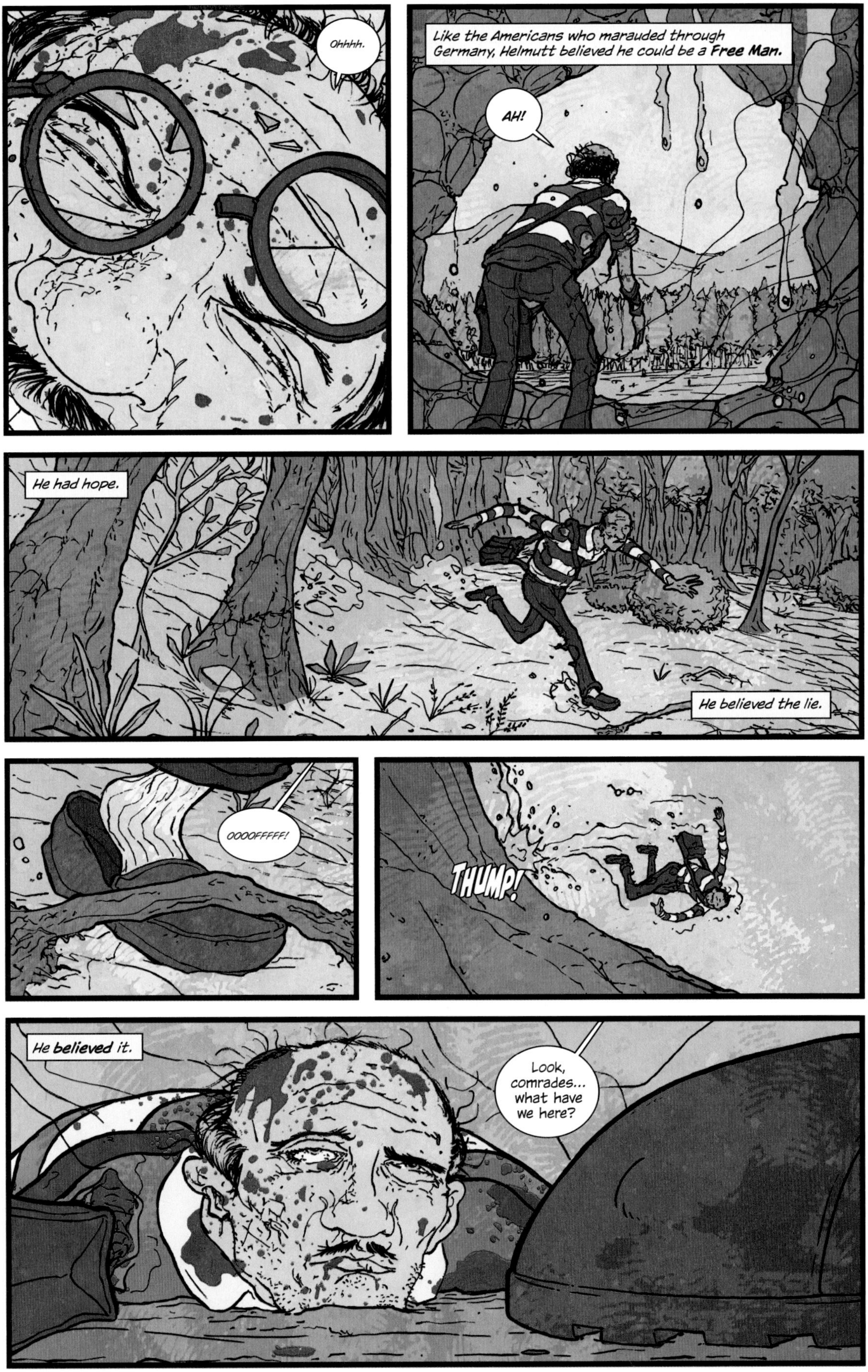
Ohhhh.
Like the Americans who marauded through Germany, Helmutt believed he could be a **Free Man.**
AH!
He had hope.
He believed the lie.
OOOOFFFFF!
THUMP!
He **believed** it.
Look, comrades... what have we here?

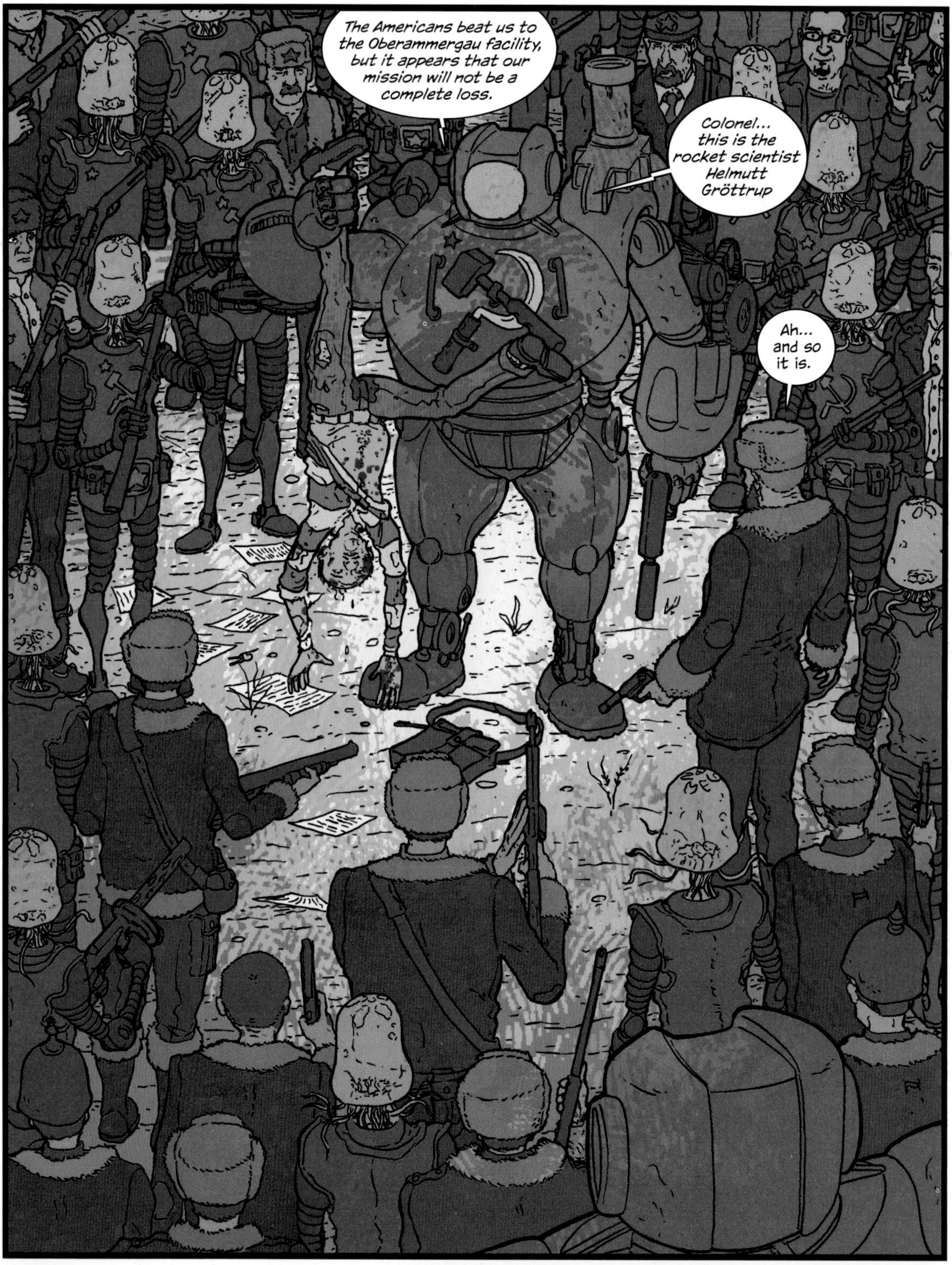
The Americans beat us to the Oberammergau facility, but it appears that our mission will not be a complete loss.
Colonel... this is the rocket scientist Helmutt Gröttrup
Ah... and so it is.

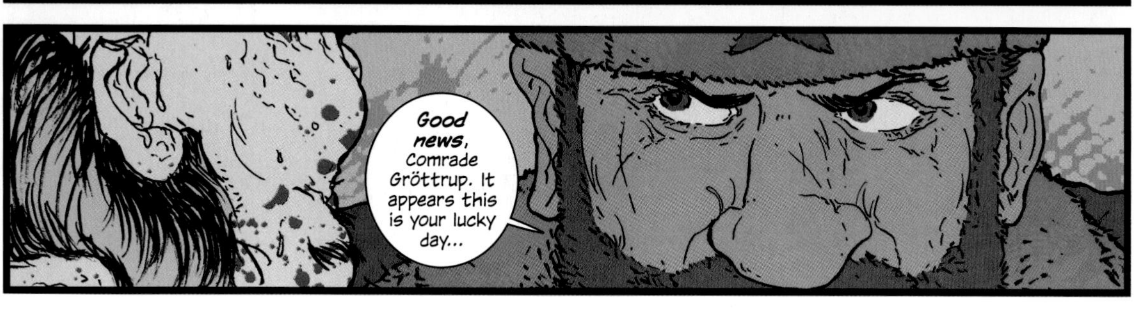
Good news, Comrade Gröttrup. It appears this is your lucky day...

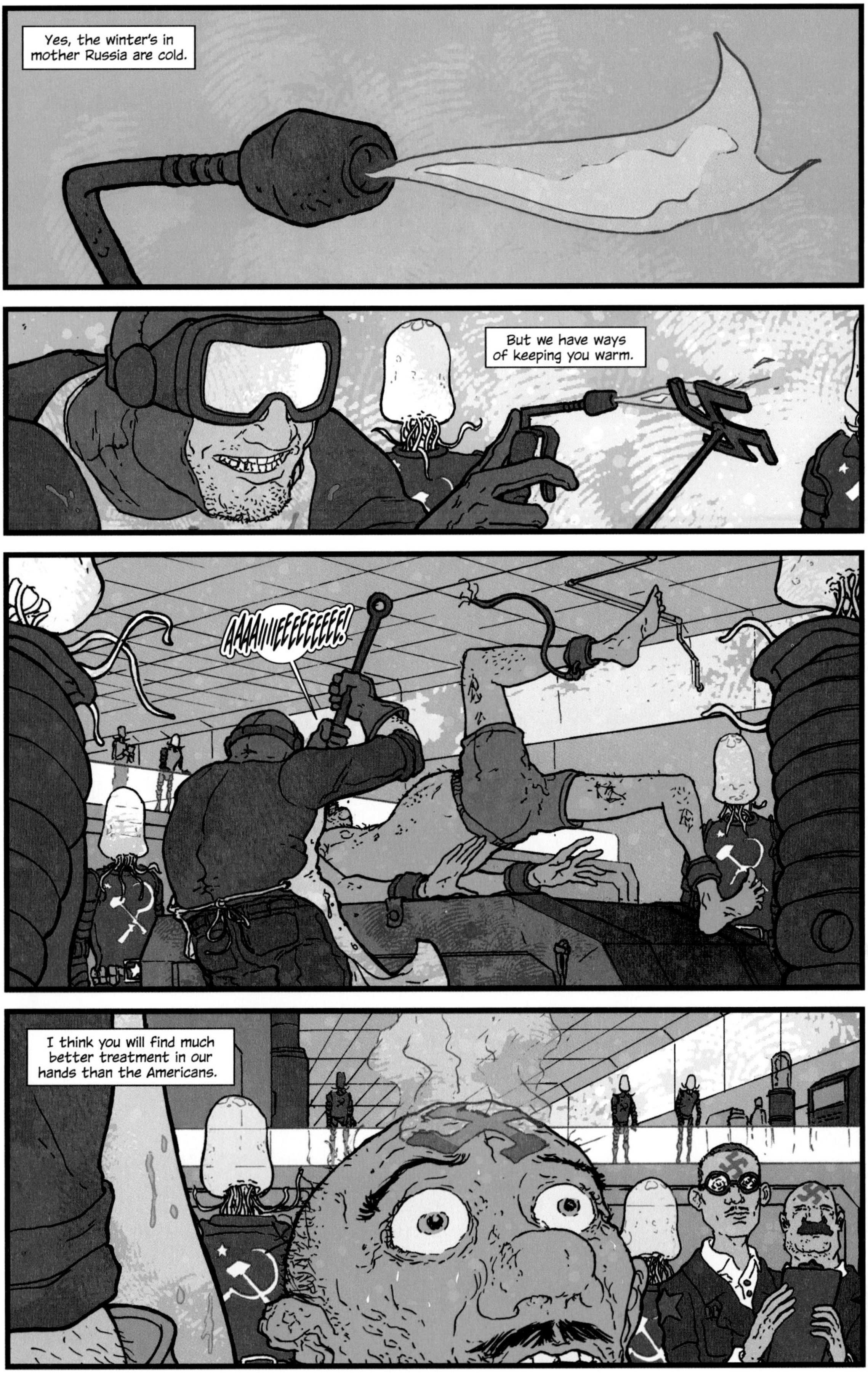

Yes, the winter's in mother Russia are cold.
But we have ways of keeping you warm.
AAAAIIIIEEEEEEEEE!
I think you will find much better treatment in our hands than the Americans.

06

STAR CITY

"WHAT MAN CAN SERVE TWO MASTERS?
WHO WOULD NOT BE TORN ASUNDER BY
TITANS?"

CLAVIS AUREA
THE RECORDED FEYNMAN

VOL. 2

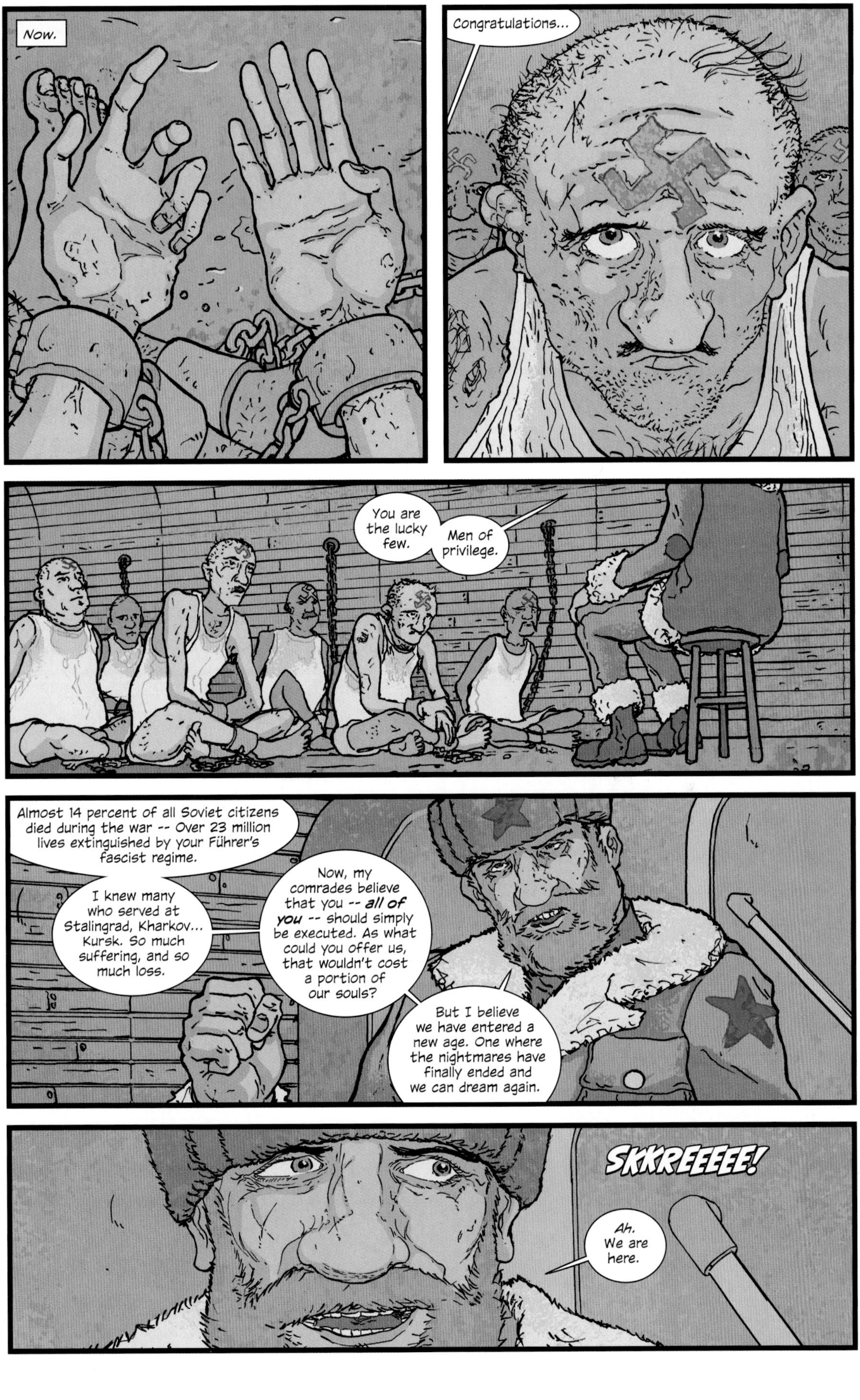

Now.
Congratulations...
You are the lucky few.
Men of privilege.
Almost 14 percent of all Soviet citizens died during the war -- Over 23 million lives extinguished by your Führer's fascist regime.
I knew many who served at Stalingrad, Kharkov... Kursk. So much suffering, and so much loss.
Now, my comrades believe that you -- ***all of you*** -- should simply be executed. As what could you offer us, that wouldn't cost a portion of our souls?
But I believe we have entered a new age. One where the nightmares have finally ended and we can dream again.
SKKREEEEE!
Ah. We are here.

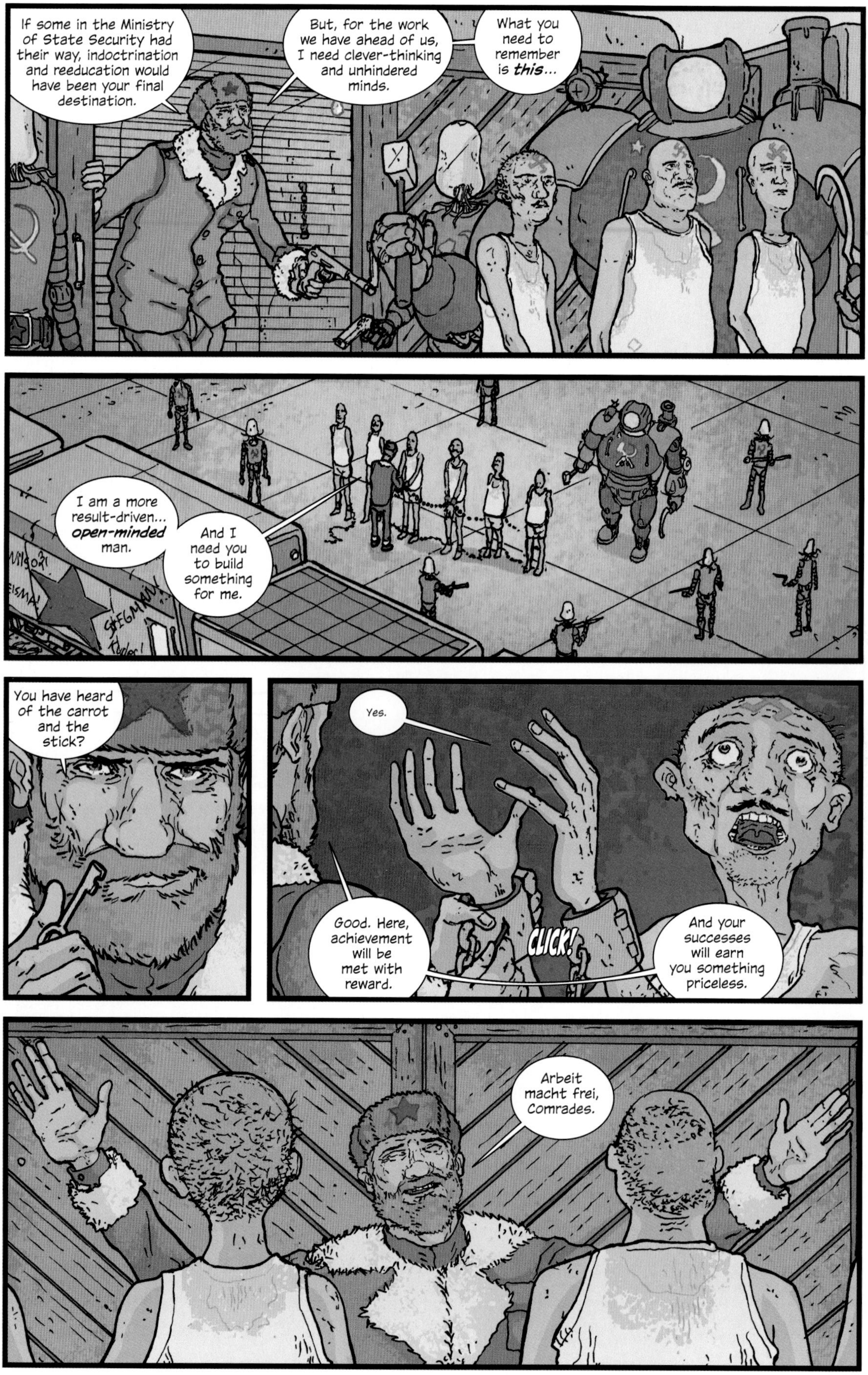
If some in the Ministry of State Security had their way, indoctrination and reeducation would have been your final destination.
But, for the work we have ahead of us, I need clever-thinking and unhindered minds.
What you need to remember is *this*...
I am a more result-driven... *open-minded* man.
And I need you to build something for me.
You have heard of the carrot and the stick?
Yes.
Good. Here, achievement will be met with reward.
CLICK!
And your successes will earn you something priceless.
Arbeit macht frei, Comrades.

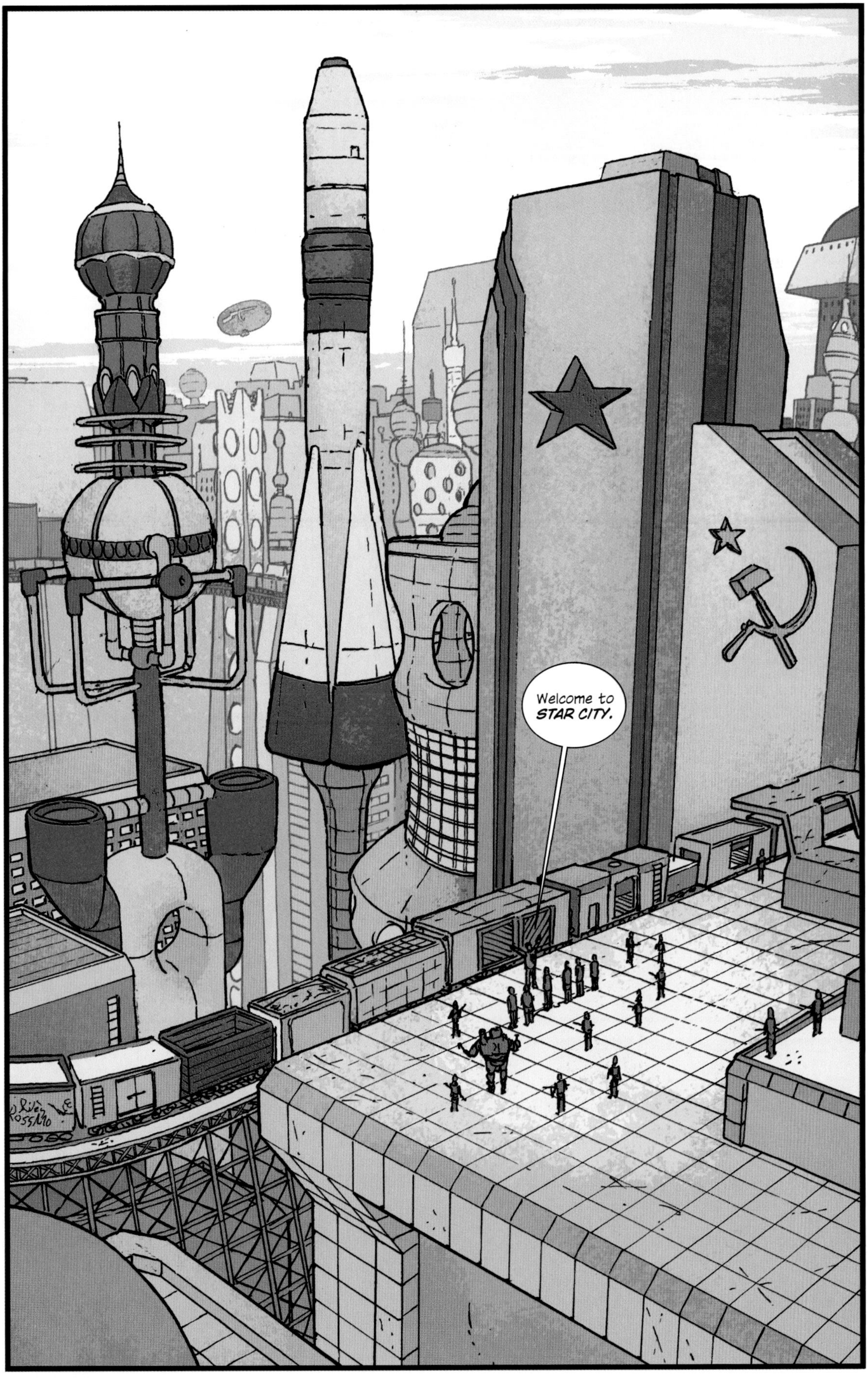
Welcome to STAR CITY.

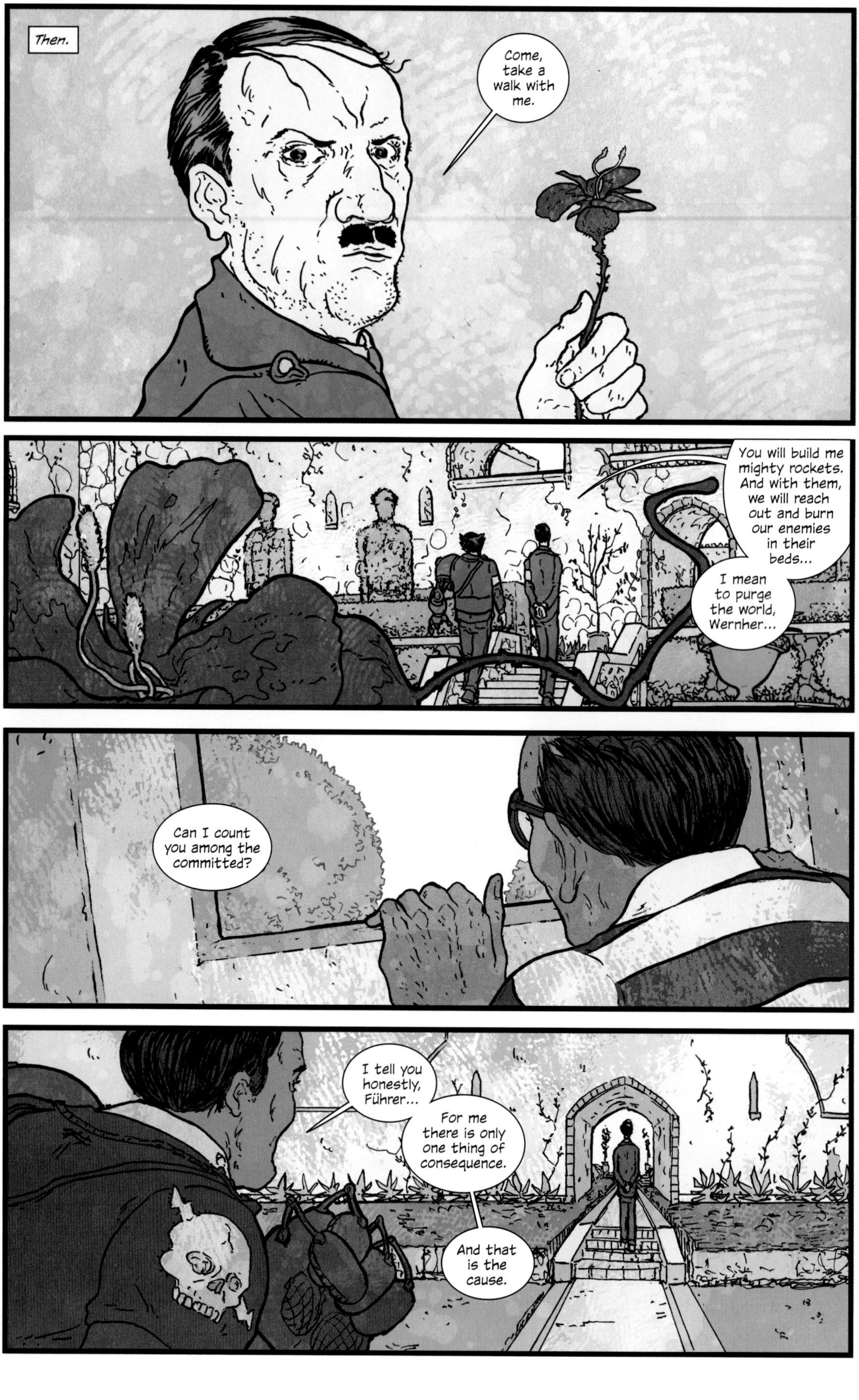
Then.
Come, take a walk with me.
You will build me mighty rockets. And with them, we will reach out and burn our enemies in their beds...
I mean to purge the world, Wernher...
Can I count you among the committed?
I tell you honestly, Führer...
For me there is only one thing of consequence.
And that is the cause.

That man is either going to conquer the world or kill us all.
I must work quickly.
Wernher!
I heard from the window...
We are going to BUILD ROCKETS!
ROCKETS, Wernher! **ROCKETS!**
Yes, Helmutt... rockets.
But what is this... ***We?***
This will be a challenge for the ages.
The greatest minds assembled for a singular task...
The ***greatest minds,*** Helmutt.
You cannot possibly count yourself among them.

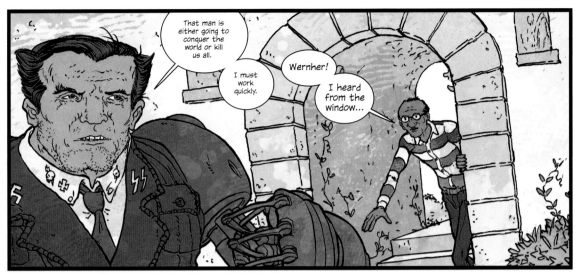

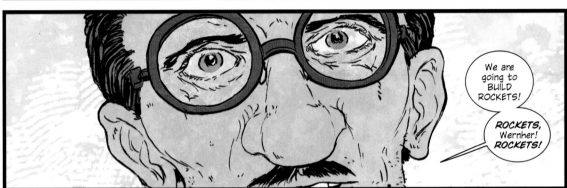

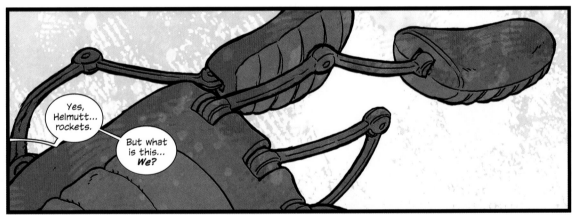

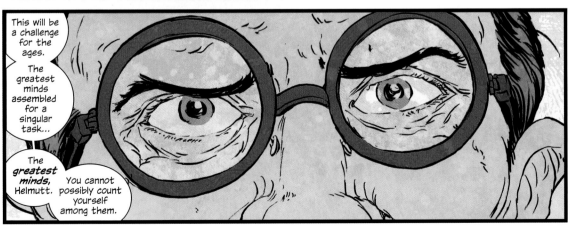

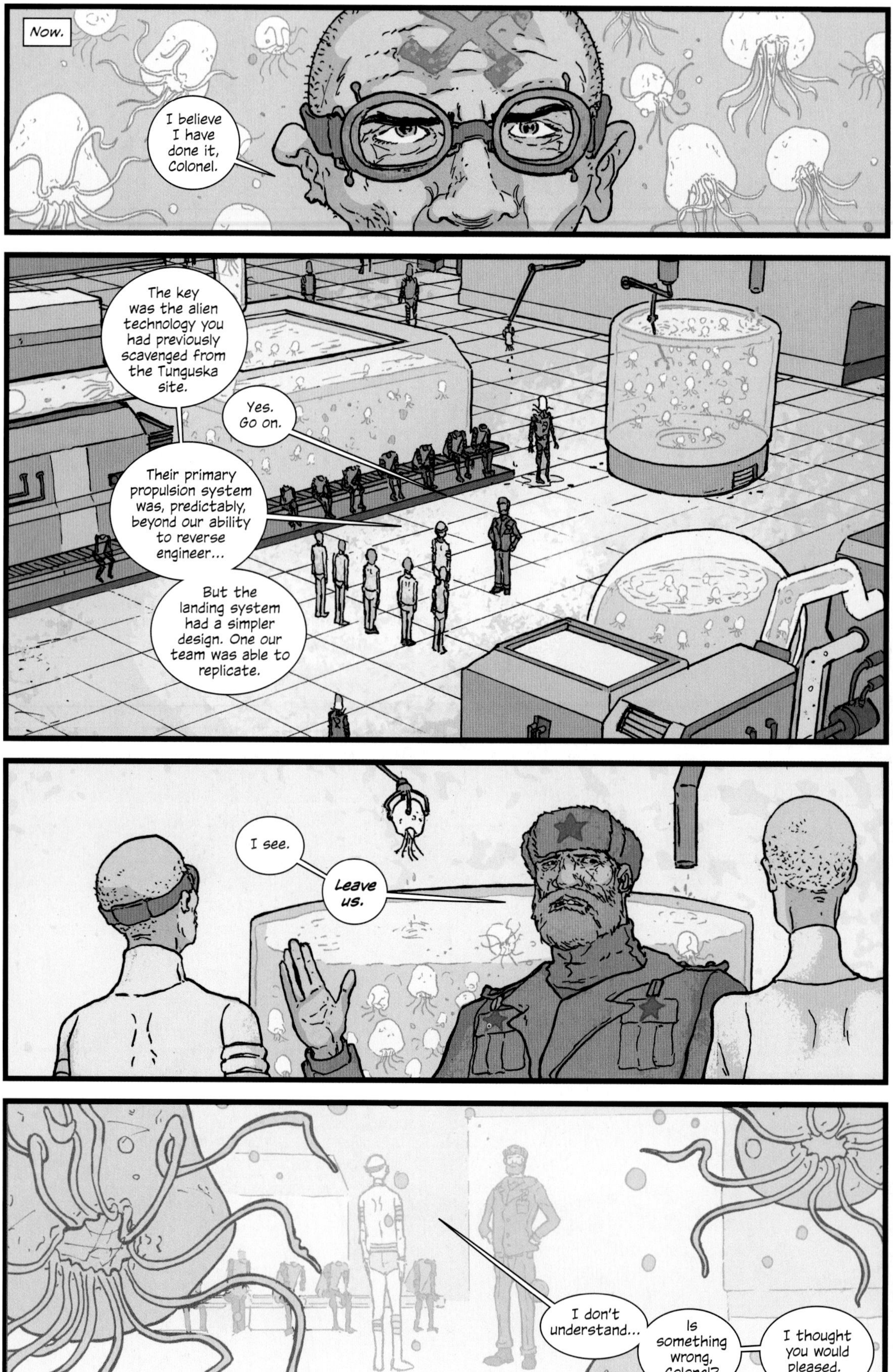
Now.
I believe I have done it, Colonel.
The key was the alien technology you had previously scavenged from the Tunguska site.
Yes. Go on.
Their primary propulsion system was, predictably, beyond our ability to reverse engineer...
But the landing system had a simpler design. One our team was able to replicate.
I see.
Leave us.
I don't understand...
Is something wrong, Colonel?
I thought you would pleased.

I was under the impression that, regardless of system, what powered the alien ship was beyond us.

Have you been keeping secrets, Helmutt?

No, Colonel. Never.

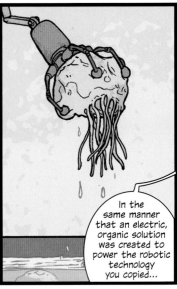

In the same manner that an electric, organic solution was created to power the robotic technology you copied...

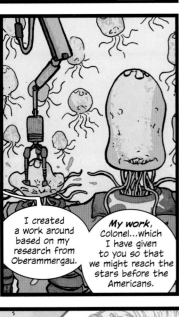

I created a work around based on my research from Oberammergau.

My work, Colonel...which I have given to you so that we might reach the stars before the Americans.

Then that would mean I am talking to a free man.

Ex-- excuse me?

Do this...and if it works, you will have what you have longed for, Helmutt.

Send our good Captain, Yuri Gagarin, into space -- bring him home safely...

And I will sign your papers, giving you your release.

You can go home, Helmutt.

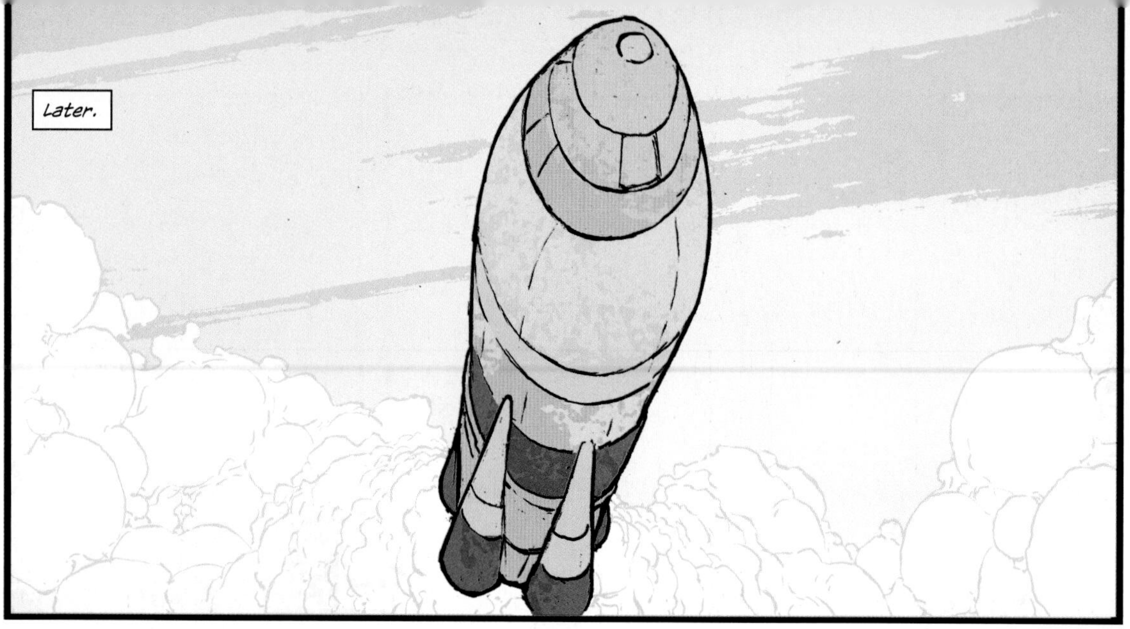
Later.

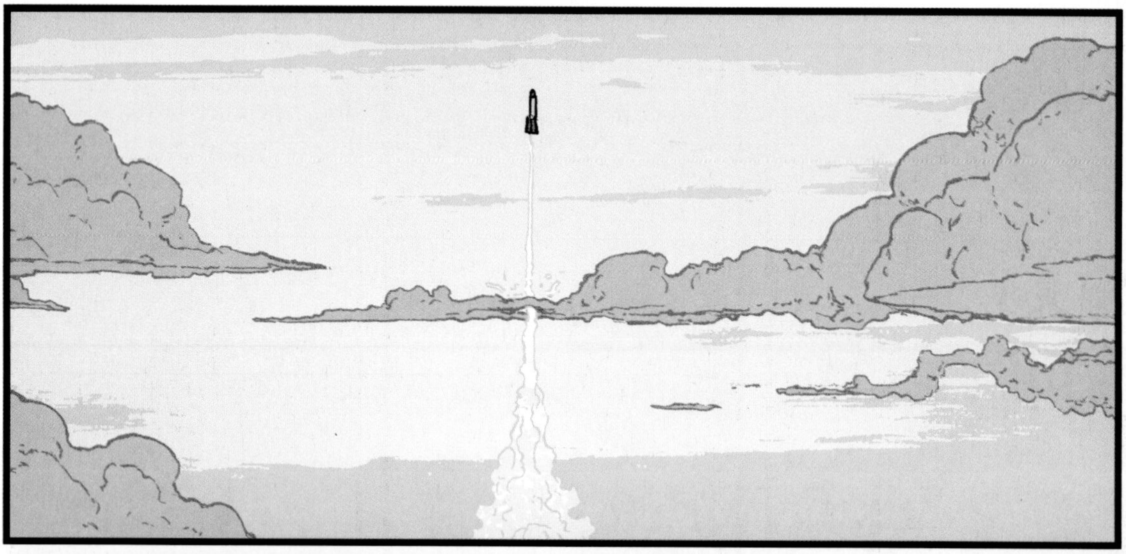

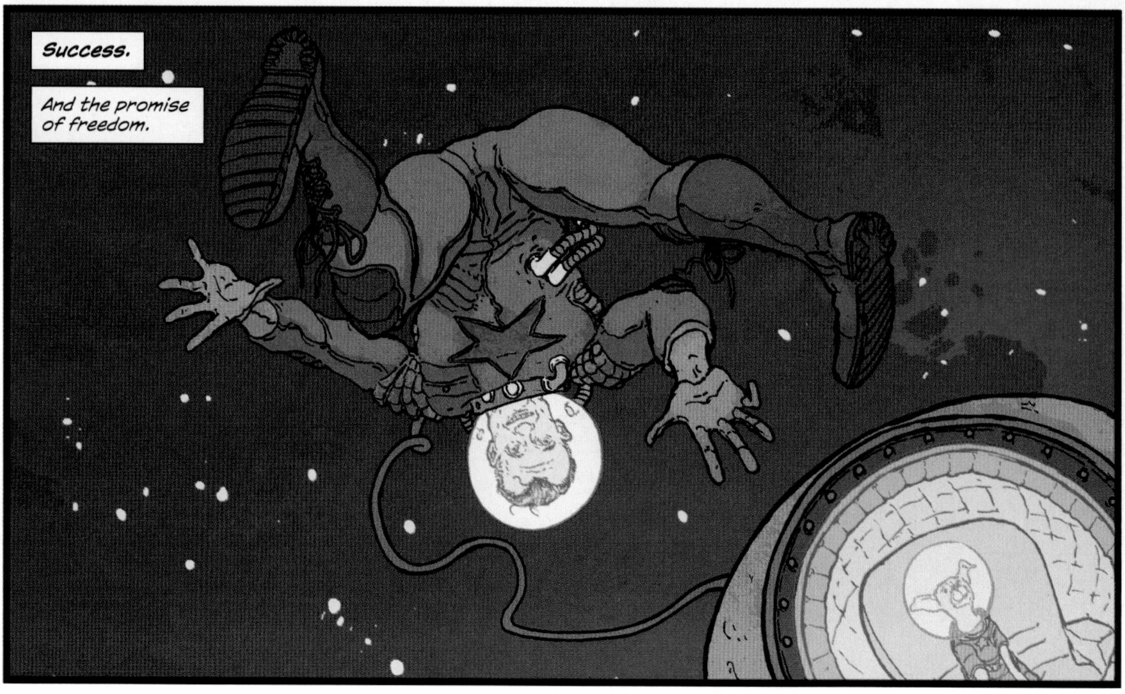
Success.
And the promise of freedom.

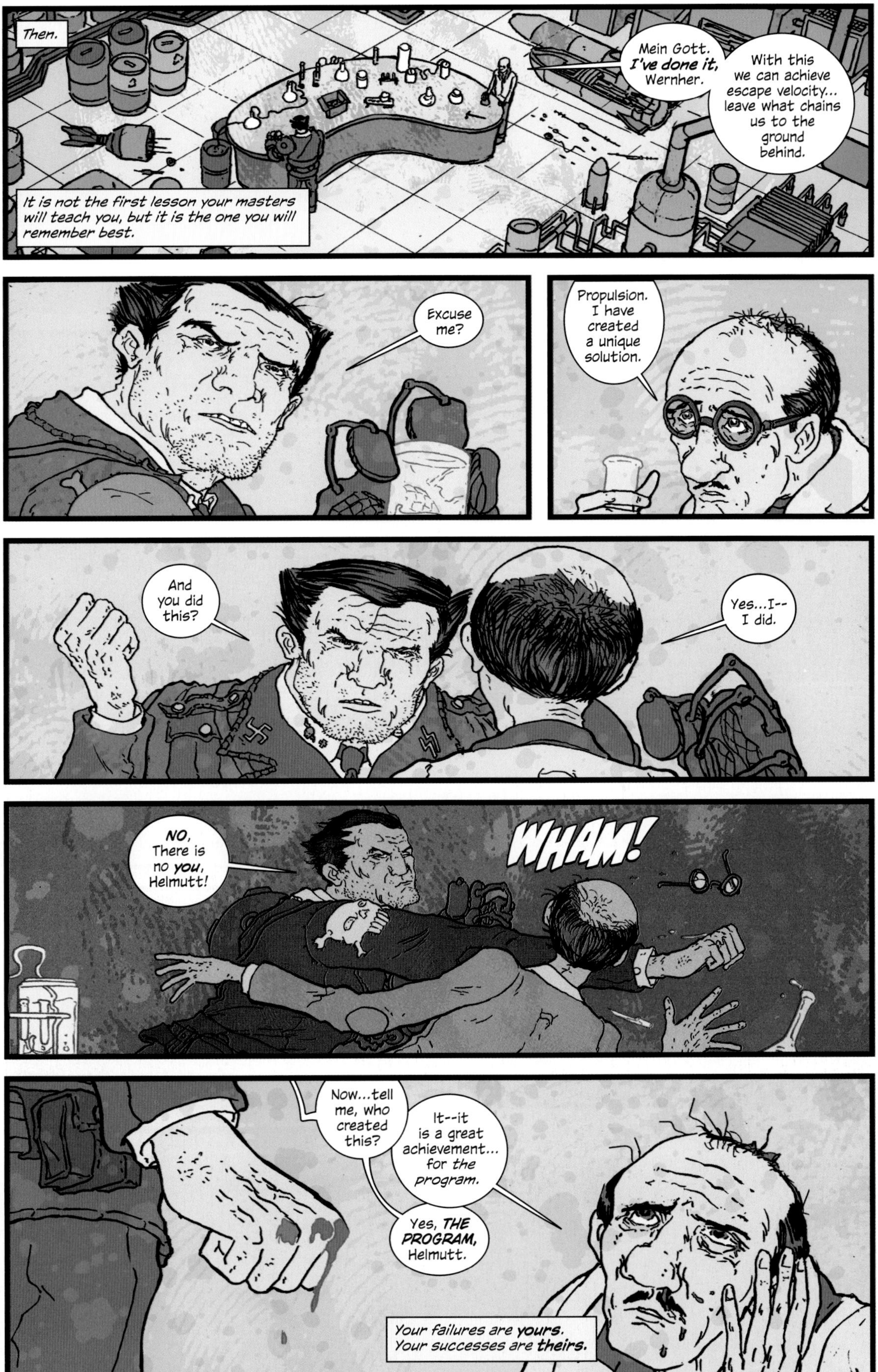
Then.
Mein Gott. I've done it, Wernher.
With this we can achieve escape velocity... leave what chains us to the ground behind.
It is not the first lesson your masters will teach you, but it is the one you will remember best.
Excuse me?
Propulsion. I have created a unique solution.
And you did this?
Yes...I-- I did.
NO, There is no you, Helmutt!
WHAM!
Now...tell me, who created this?
It--it is a great achievement... for the program.
Yes, THE PROGRAM, Helmutt.
Your failures are yours. Your successes are theirs.

Now.

A horrible thing has happened...

...Korolev is dead.

There was a secret meeting with the Americans in their New Mexico territory.

Something went wrong, and the Colonel was killed.

What?

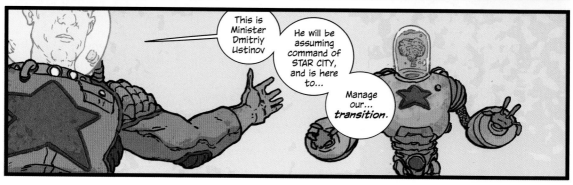

This is Minister Dmitriy Ustinov

He will be assuming command of STAR CITY, and is here to...

Manage our... *transition*.

Thank you, comrade Gagarin.
Da, this is a sad day... a tragic day.
But you must overcome your grief -- our great loss -- so that you can hear the words I am about to say...
Humans have now been to other worlds.
Tunguska, and your hard work, have given us a seat in a great game.
The greatest man has ever known.
But now I must ask for even more.
A redoubling of efforts.
RECOMMITMENT.
SACRIFICE.

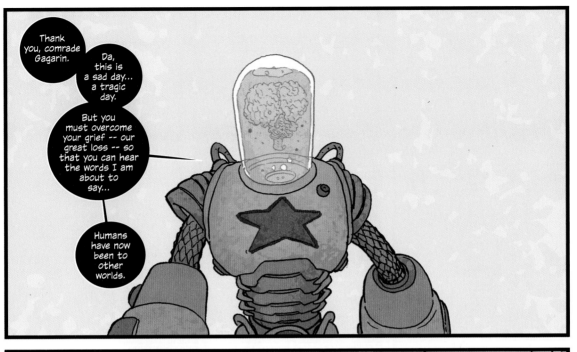

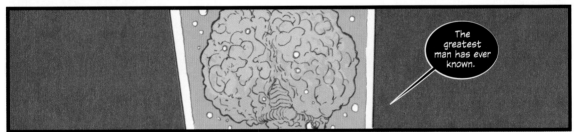

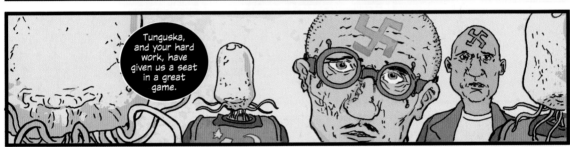

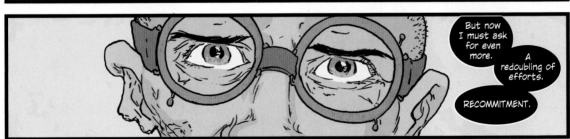

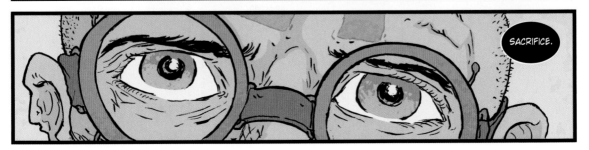

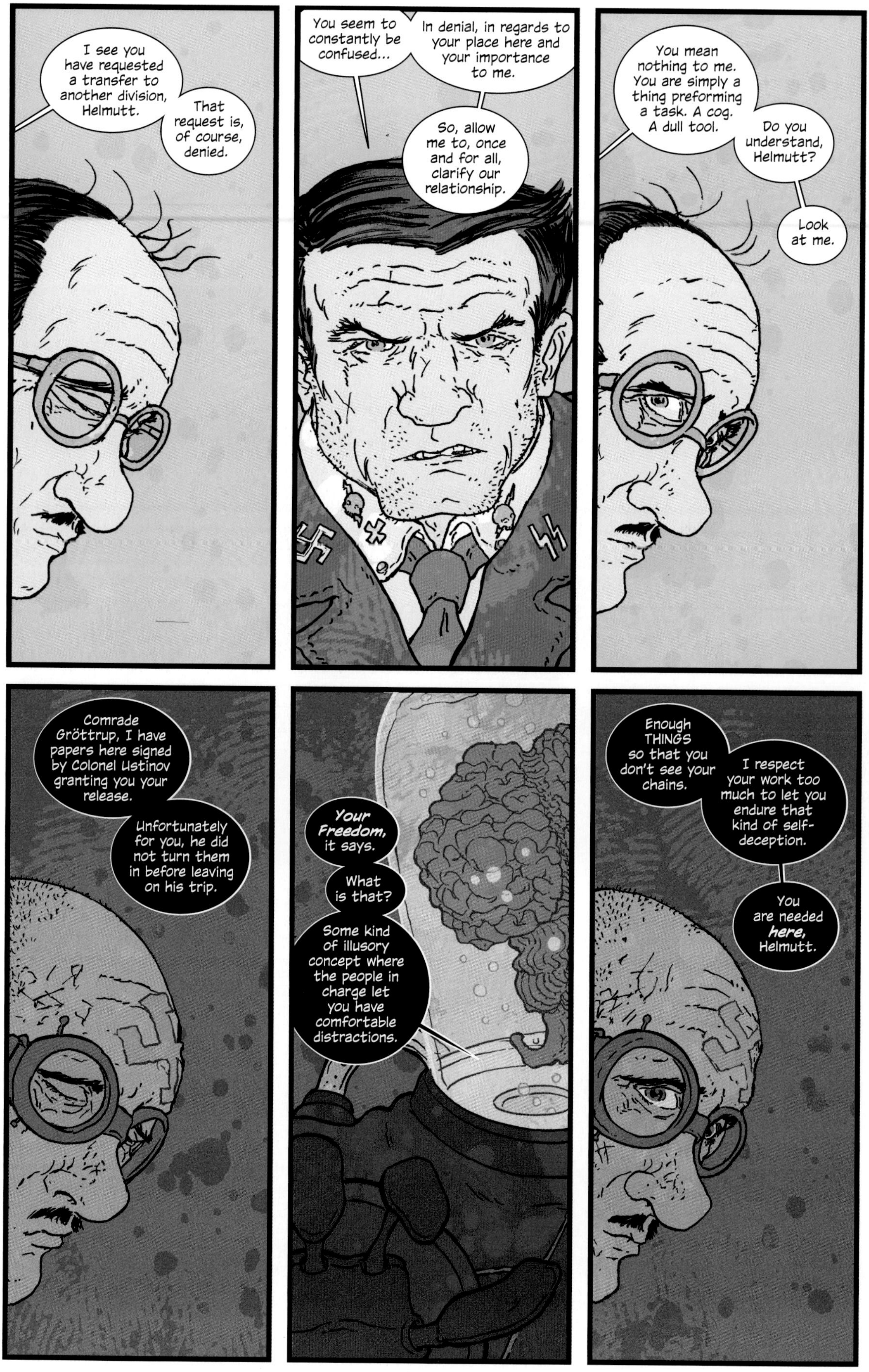

I see you have requested a transfer to another division, Helmutt.
That request is, of course, denied.
You seem to constantly be confused...
In denial, in regards to your place here and your importance to me.
So, allow me to, once and for all, clarify our relationship.
You mean nothing to me. You are simply a thing preforming a task. A cog. A dull tool.
Do you understand, Helmutt?
Look at me.
Comrade Gröttrup, I have papers here signed by Colonel Ustinov granting you your release.
Unfortunately for you, he did not turn them in before leaving on his trip.
Your Freedom, it says.
What is that?
Some kind of illusory concept where the people in charge let you have comfortable distractions.
Enough THINGS so that you don't see your chains.
I respect your work too much to let you endure that kind of self-deception.
You are needed *here,* Helmutt.

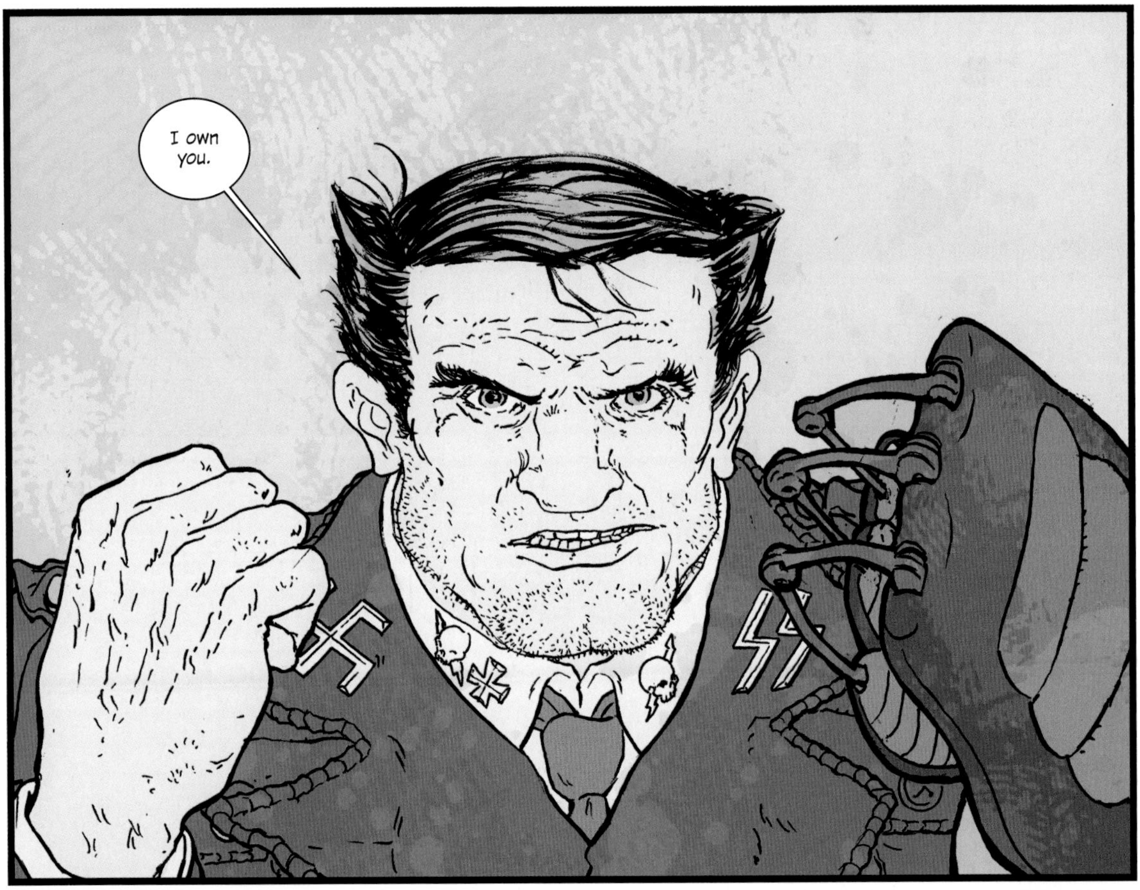
I own you.

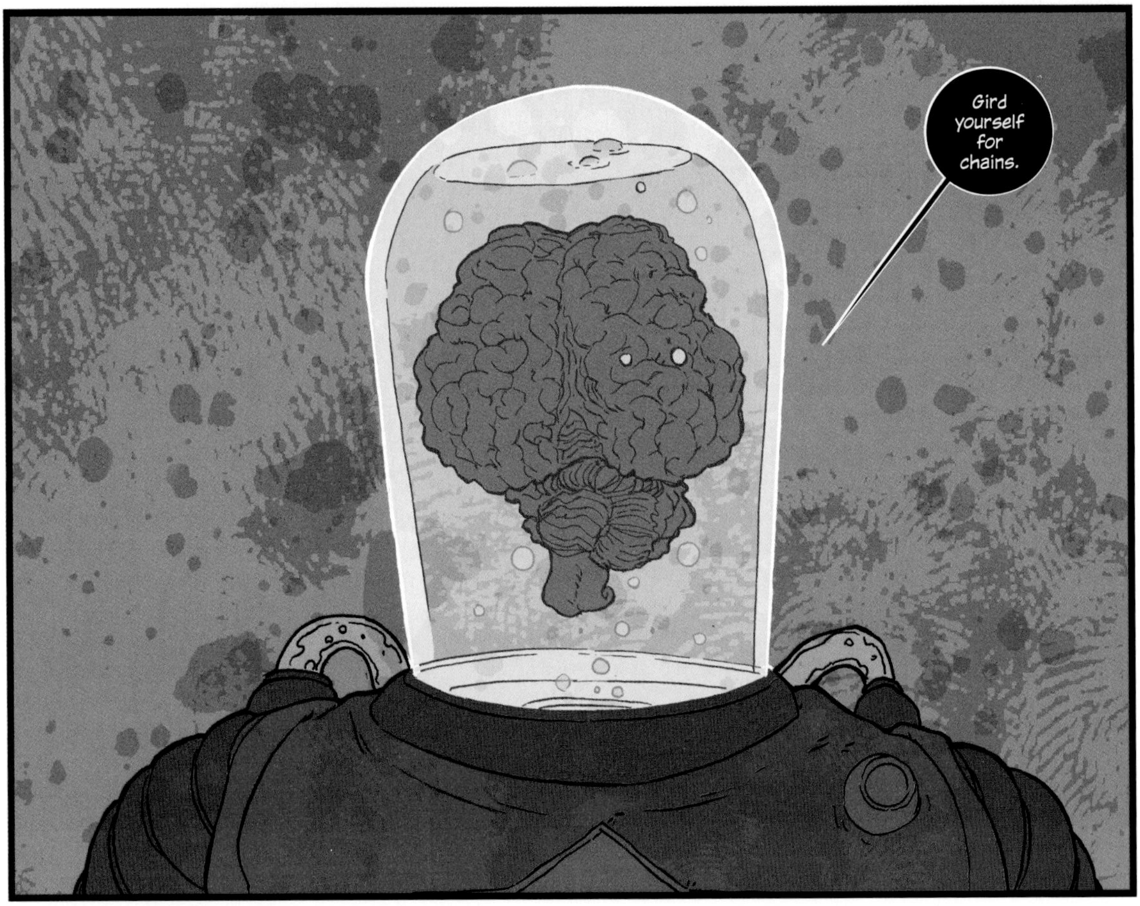
Gird yourself for chains.

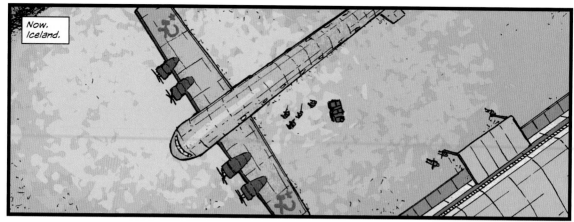

Now.
Iceland.

We arrived undetected, Minister.

Good.
Proceed.

They are waiting for you inside.

Helmutt Gröttrup believed the lie until he could believe it no more...

Until it broke him.

No.

Helmutt wanted to be free.

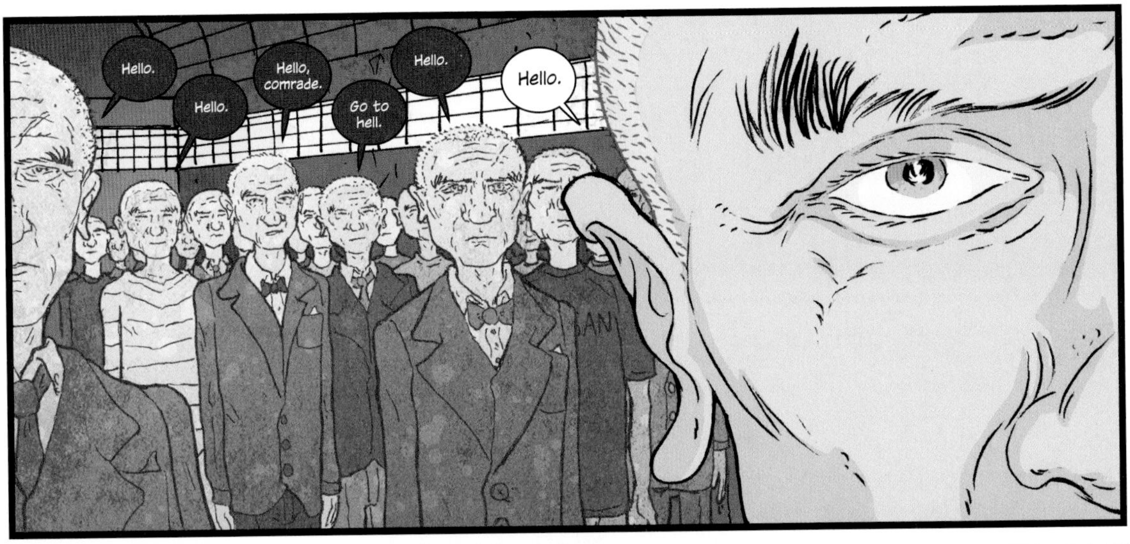
Hello.
Hello.
Hello, comrade.
Go to hell.
Hello.
Hello.

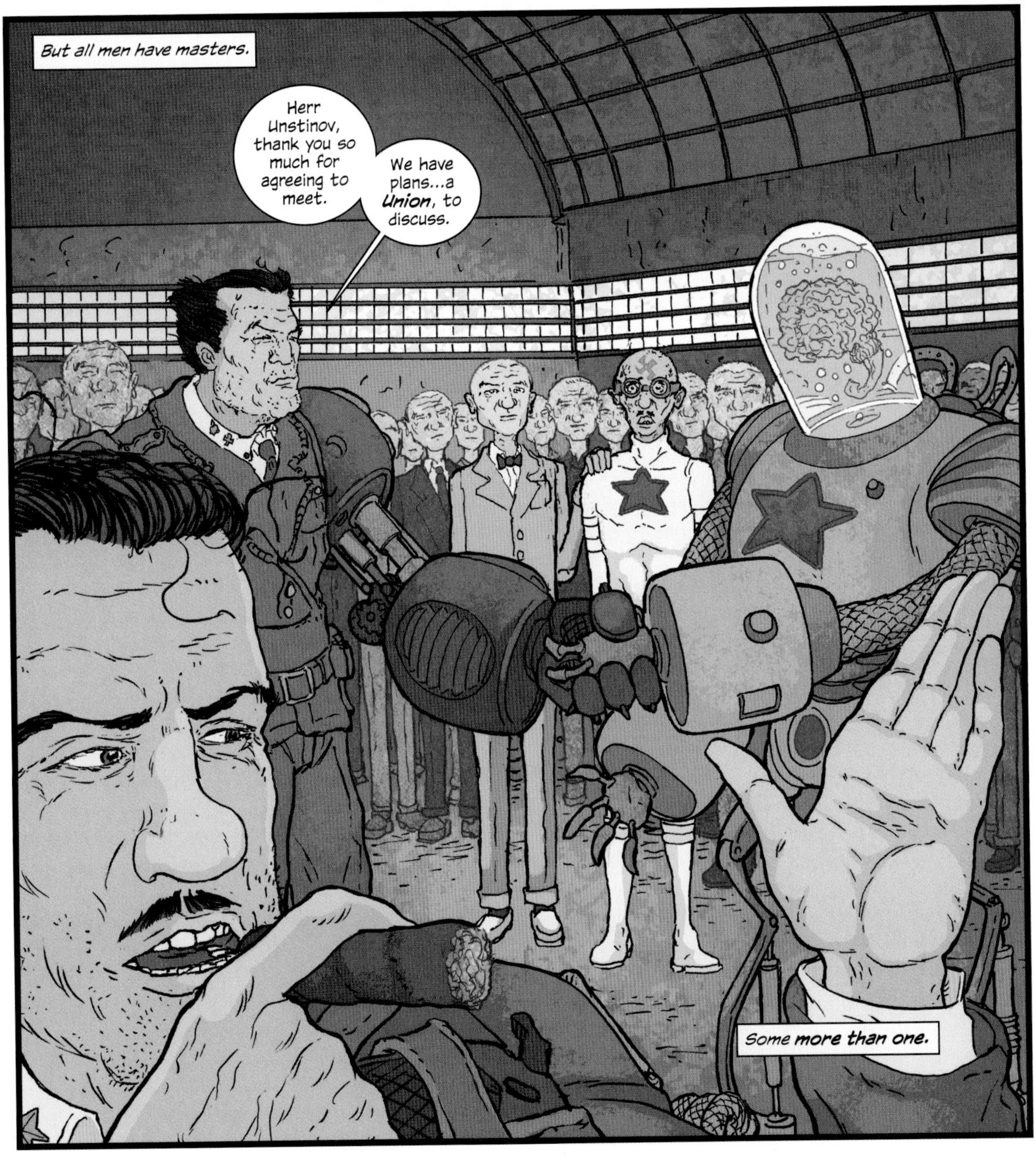
But all men have masters.
Herr Unstinov, thank you so much for agreeing to meet.
We have plans...a Union, to discuss.
Some more than one.

WHO'S GOING TO CALL
OUR BLUFF

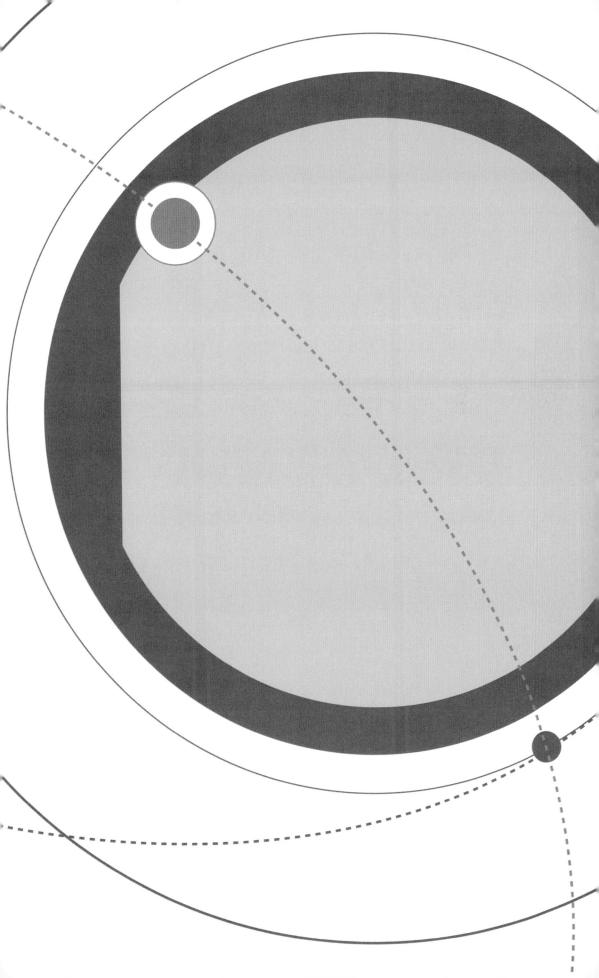

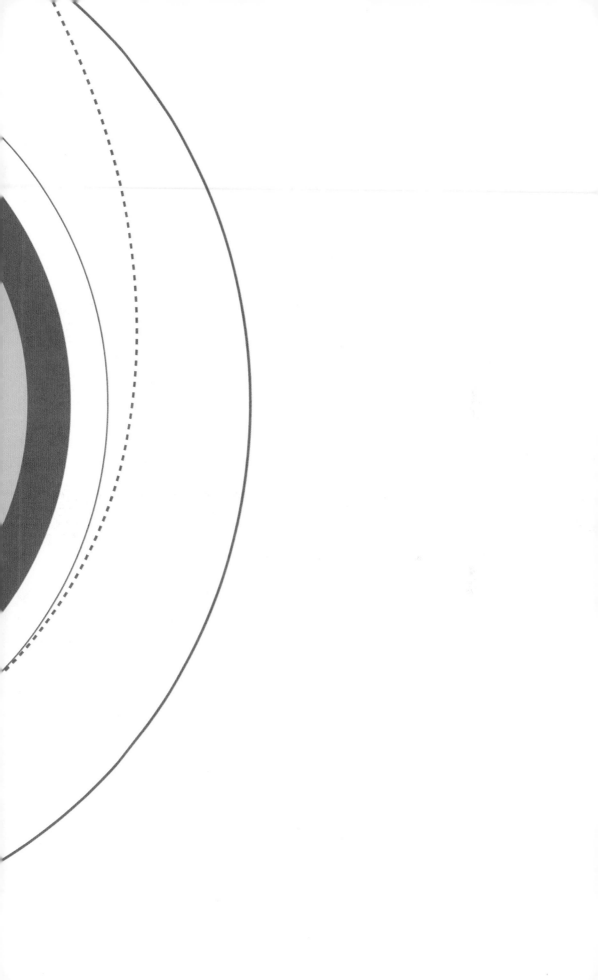

Now.

Star City.

Instructions say the final step is connecting the conduit to the coupling at the structure's base...

Good?

CLICK!

Ja.

It's completed, sir. We've assembled the device as directed.

Very well, Helmutt... Turn it on.

Let us see if this 'act of good faith' does what the Americans claim it can.

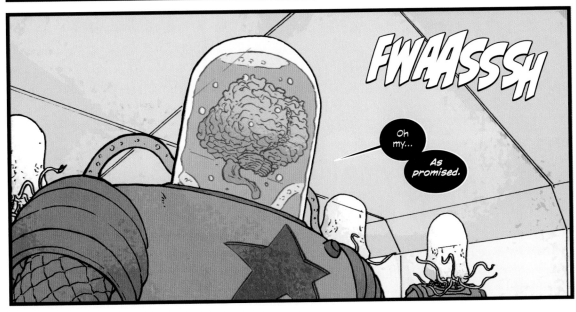

FWAASSSH

Oh my...

As promised.

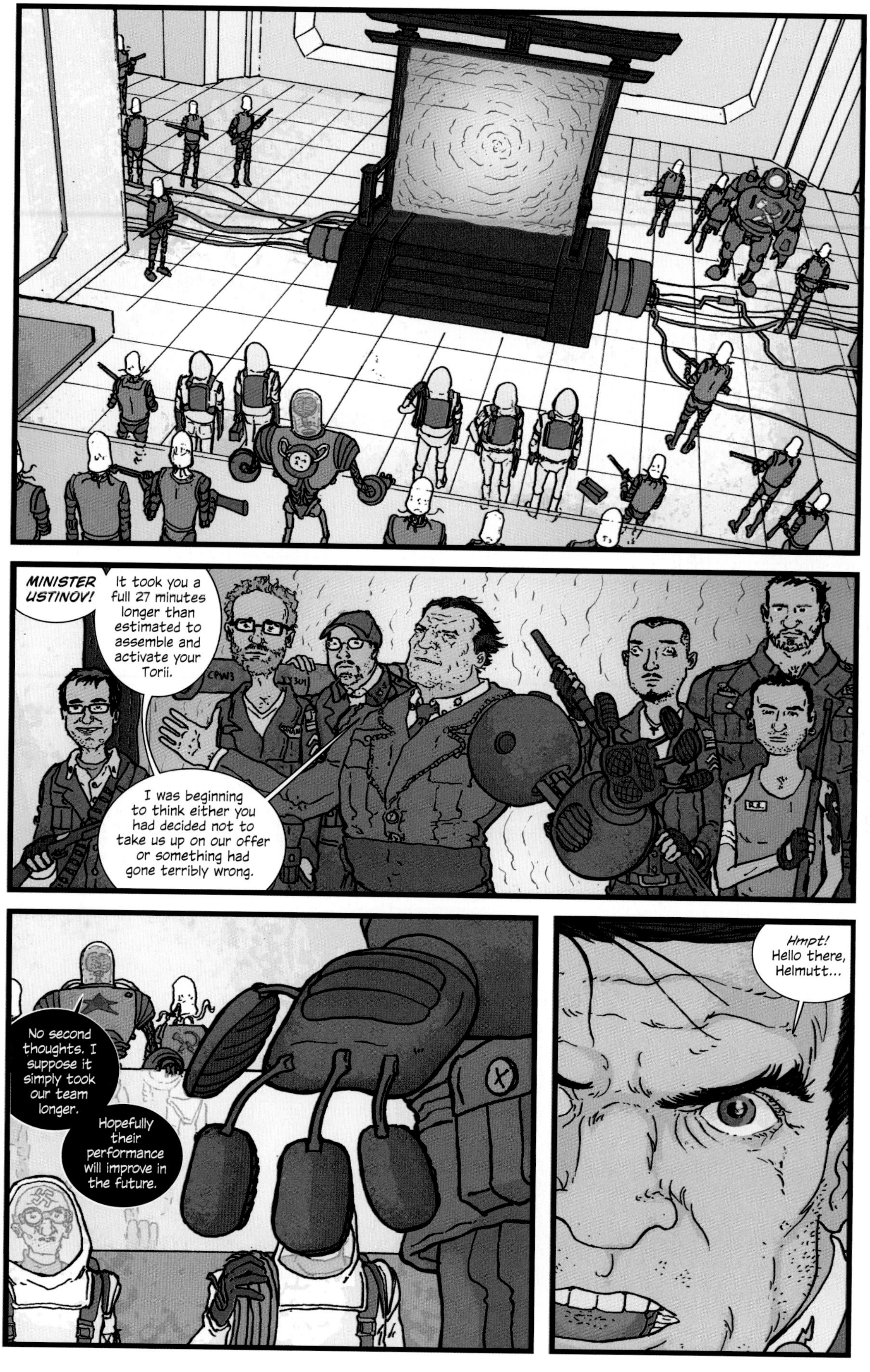

MINISTER USTINOV!
It took you a full 27 minutes longer than estimated to assemble and activate your Torii.
I was beginning to think either you had decided not to take us up on our offer or something had gone terribly wrong.
No second thoughts. I suppose it simply took our team longer.
Hopefully their performance will improve in the future.
Hmpt! Hello there, Helmutt...

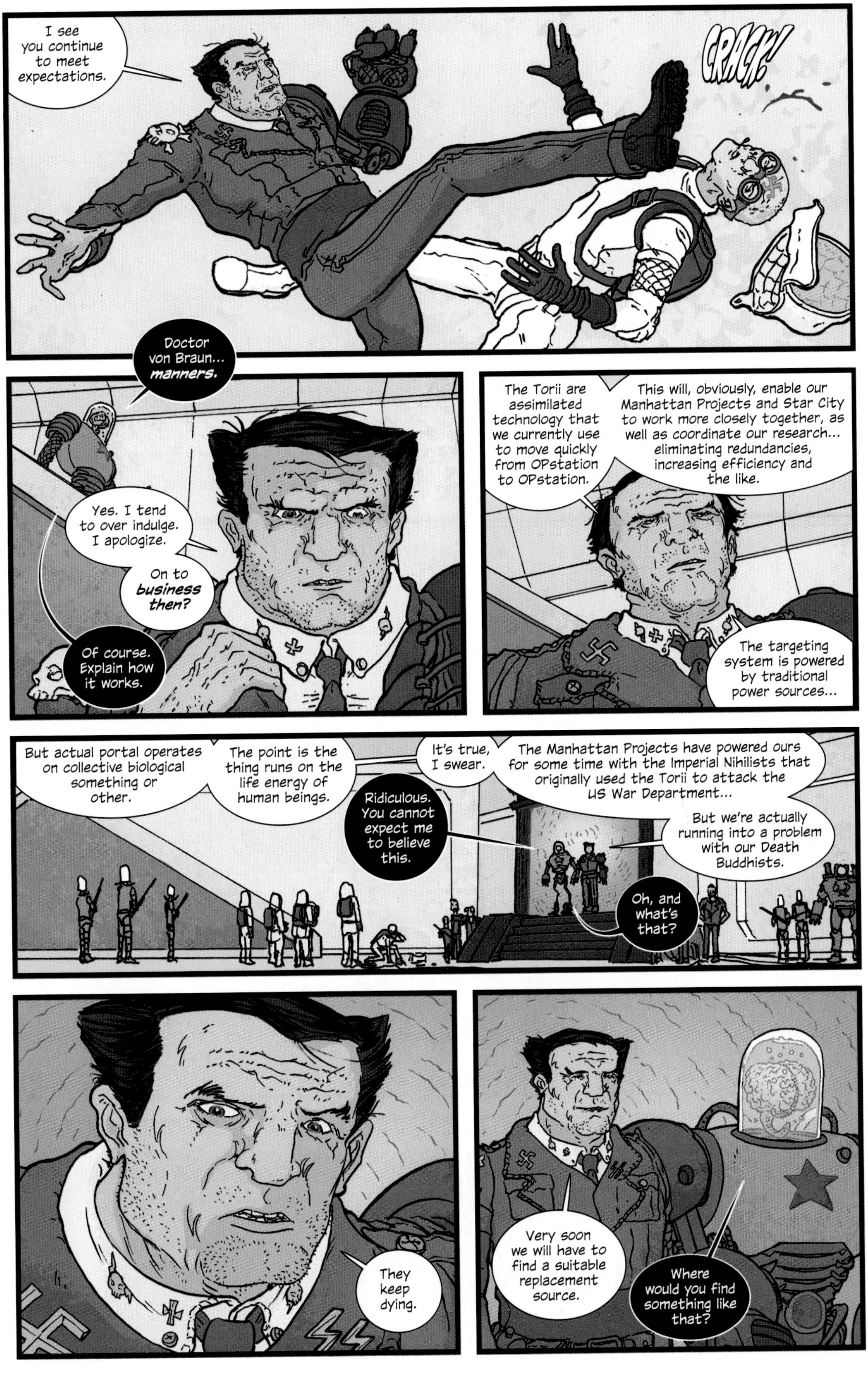
I see you continue to meet expectations.
CRACK!
Doctor von Braun... **manners.**
Yes. I tend to over indulge. I apologize.
On to **business then?**
Of course. Explain how it works.
The Torii are assimilated technology that we currently use to move quickly from OPstation to OPstation.
This will, obviously, enable our Manhattan Projects and Star City to work more closely together, as well as coordinate our research... eliminating redundancies, increasing efficiency and the like.
The targeting system is powered by traditional power sources...
But actual portal operates on collective biological something or other.
The point is the thing runs on the life energy of human beings.
Ridiculous. You cannot expect me to believe this.
It's true, I swear.
The Manhattan Projects have powered ours for some time with the Imperial Nihilists that originally used the Torii to attack the US War Department...
But we're actually running into a problem with our Death Buddhists.
Oh, and what's that?
They keep dying.
Very soon we will have to find a suitable replacement source.
Where would you find something like that?

Actually... I have some ideas.
Ah... I see.
Helmutt!
Yes, Minister?
Congratulations!
It's possible we have found a new job for you and your fellow workers.

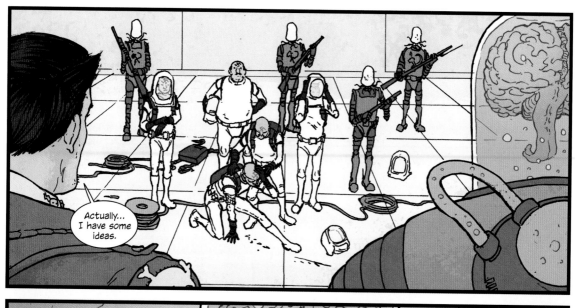

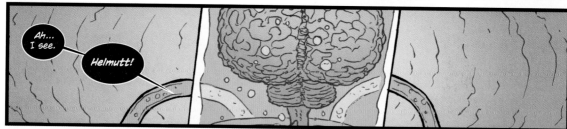

"WE PLANNED FOR BETRAYAL. THEY PLANNED FOR DECEIT. NO ONE EVER THOUGHT TO PLAN FOR HARMONY."

CLAVIS AUREA
THE RECORDED FEYNMAN | **VOL. 3**

07

ABOVE AND BEYOND

"LEGEND SAYS ROMULUS SLEW REMUS AND THEN BUILT ROME.

IMAGINE IF THEY HAD WORKED TOGETHER AND BUILT SOMETHING BETTER. "

CLAVIS AUREA
THE RECORDED FEYNMAN

VOL. 2

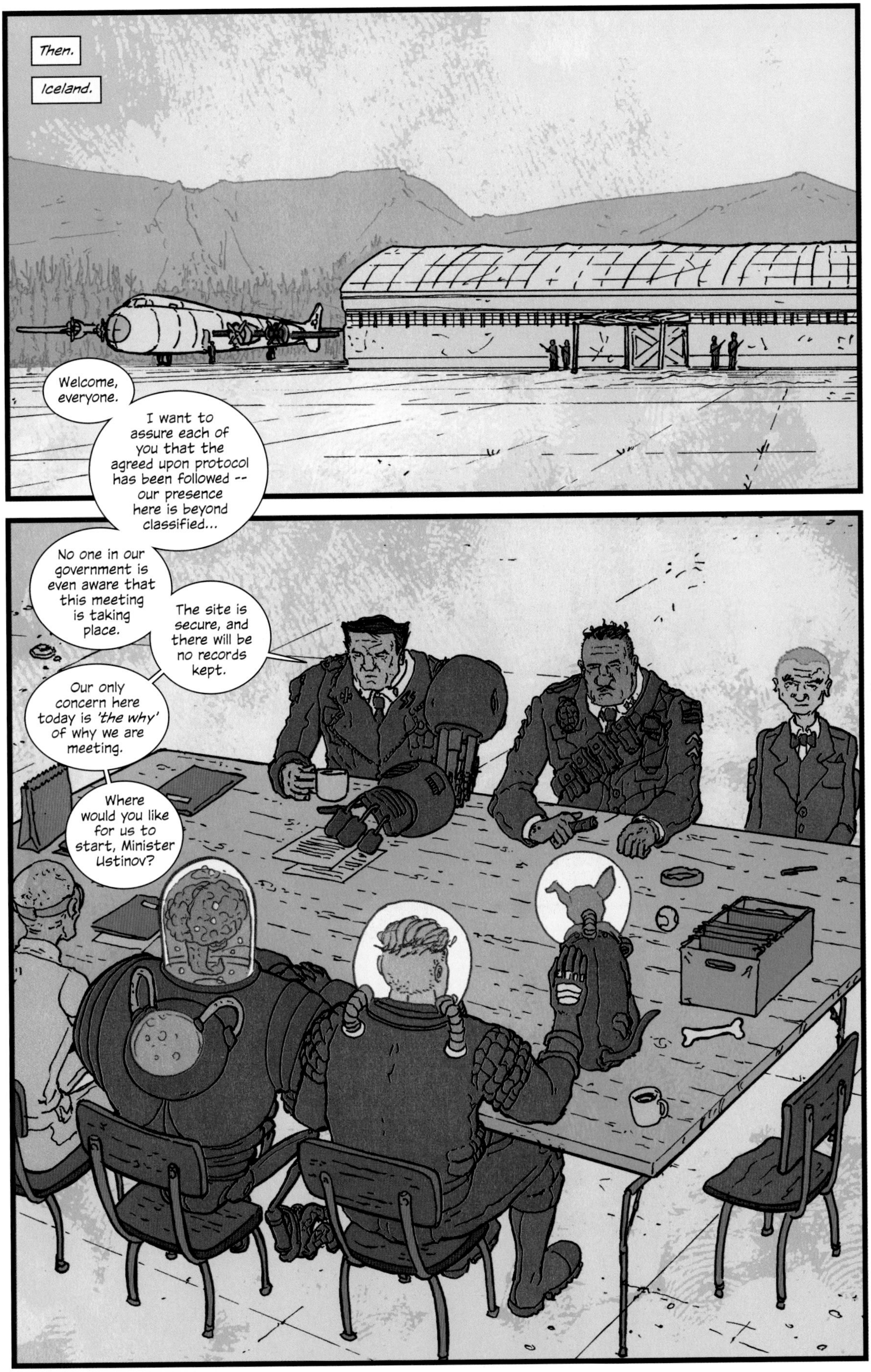

Then.
Iceland.
Welcome, everyone.
I want to assure each of you that the agreed upon protocol has been followed -- our presence here is beyond classified...
No one in our government is even aware that this meeting is taking place.
The site is secure, and there will be no records kept.
Our only concern here today is *'the why'* of why we are meeting.
Where would you like for us to start, Minister Ustinov?

You summoned us here, Comrade von Braun.

Lured us with fantastic stories, so...

Please, start at the beginning.

General, do you want to, or would you rather...

Oh, no. Enjoy yourself, Wernher.

Go right ahead and put on a goddamn show.

Very well.

Minister, if you don't mind, I'd like to start with your secret space program, Star City.

We know that much of the technology you've developed was derived from the Tunguska event, just as you know that we've made similar use of our Roswell incident.

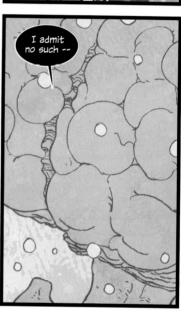

I admit no such --

Minister. These things were confirmed to me personally through your predecessor, Colonel Korolev.

Leave the old ways of thinking behind, son...none of those hoo-ha party tricks are worth paying attention to anyway.

What the General means is there's a greater point to focus on.

We are not alone.

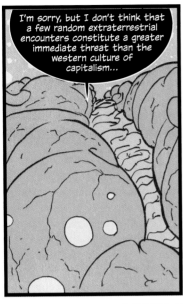

I'm sorry, but I don't think that a few random extraterrestrial encounters constitute a greater immediate threat than the western culture of capitalism...

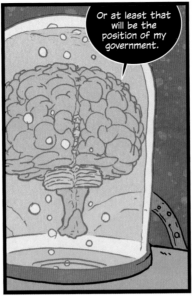

Or at least that will be the position of my government.

You're wrong. It is the greater threat...

The greatest threat.

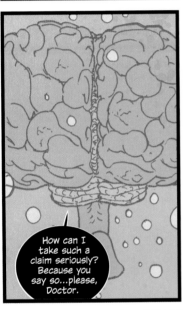

How can I take such a claim seriously? Because you say so...please, Doctor.

You believe it because we've gone out there. We've seen these things first hand.

We know.

Ah...excuse me. Hello.

My name is Yuri Gagarin, and I am the only man to have ventured into space...

I am.

Me.

The Yuri.

Well, Colonel... I'm afraid that's no longer true.

But I was still first, no?

Okay. Sure.

Good. And how exciting!

Tell us of your American space vessel.

Actually, we used a door.

I'm sure you've heard of our Torii from the Japanese -- it's like that...but much, much more powerful.

A wormhole?

You have the ability to tunnel space-time?

Minister Ustinov, this is... this is...

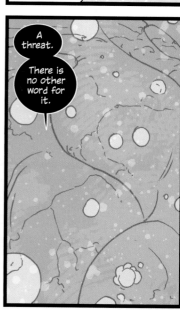

A threat.

There is no other word for it.

You seem to be missing the point, Minister.

This proxy propaganda war being fought through our science programs is a potential half-century distraction.

We are here today to ensure that doesn't happen.

And how do you propose to do that?

I was thinking, maybe, we join forces.

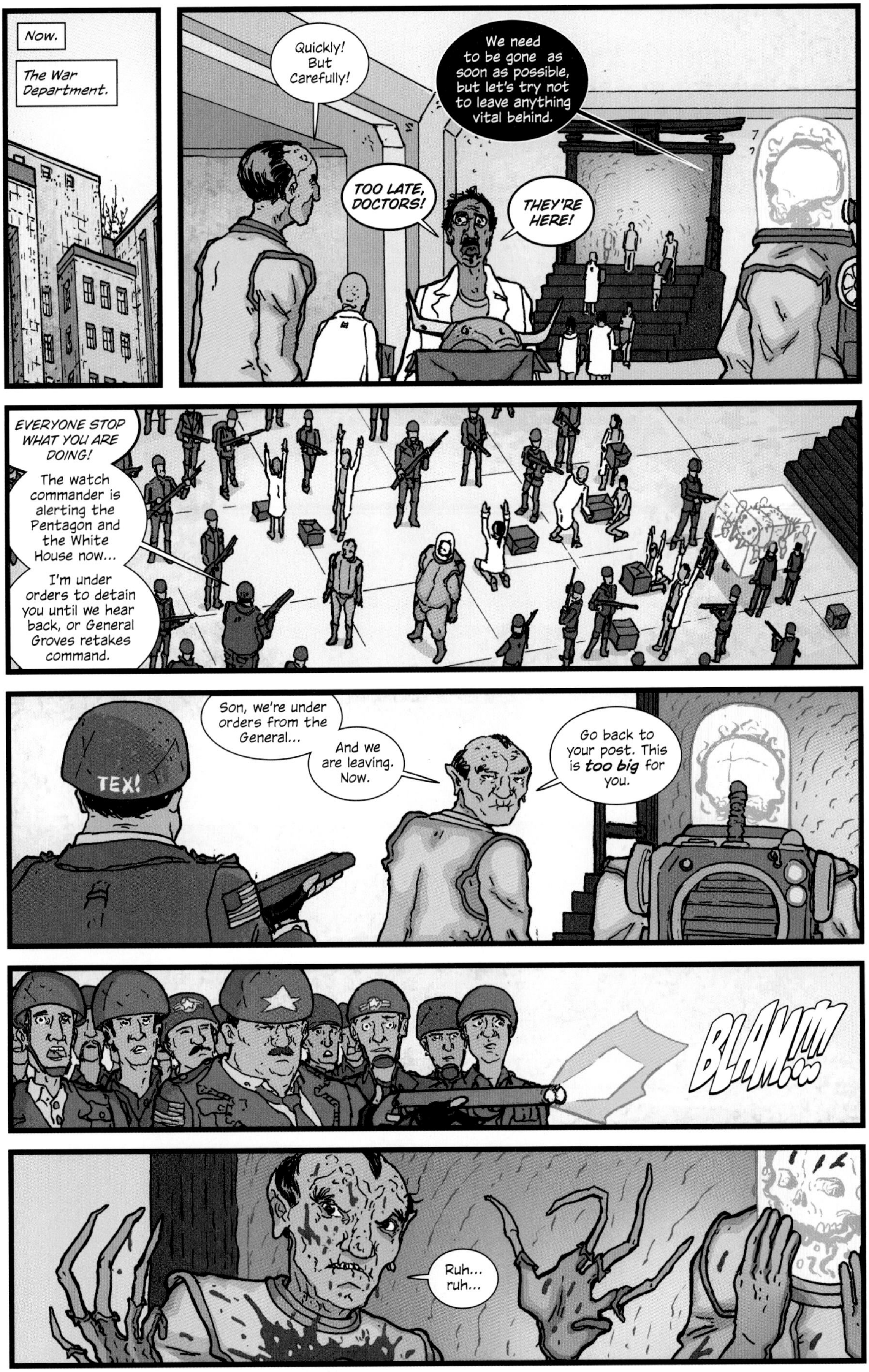
Now.
The War Department.
Quickly! But Carefully!
We need to be gone as soon as possible, but let's try not to leave anything vital behind.
TOO LATE, DOCTORS!
THEY'RE HERE!
EVERYONE STOP WHAT YOU ARE DOING!
The watch commander is alerting the Pentagon and the White House now...
I'm under orders to detain you until we hear back, or General Groves retakes command.
TEX!
Son, we're under orders from the General...
And we are leaving. Now.
Go back to your post. This is too big for you.
BLAM!!!
Ruh... ruh...

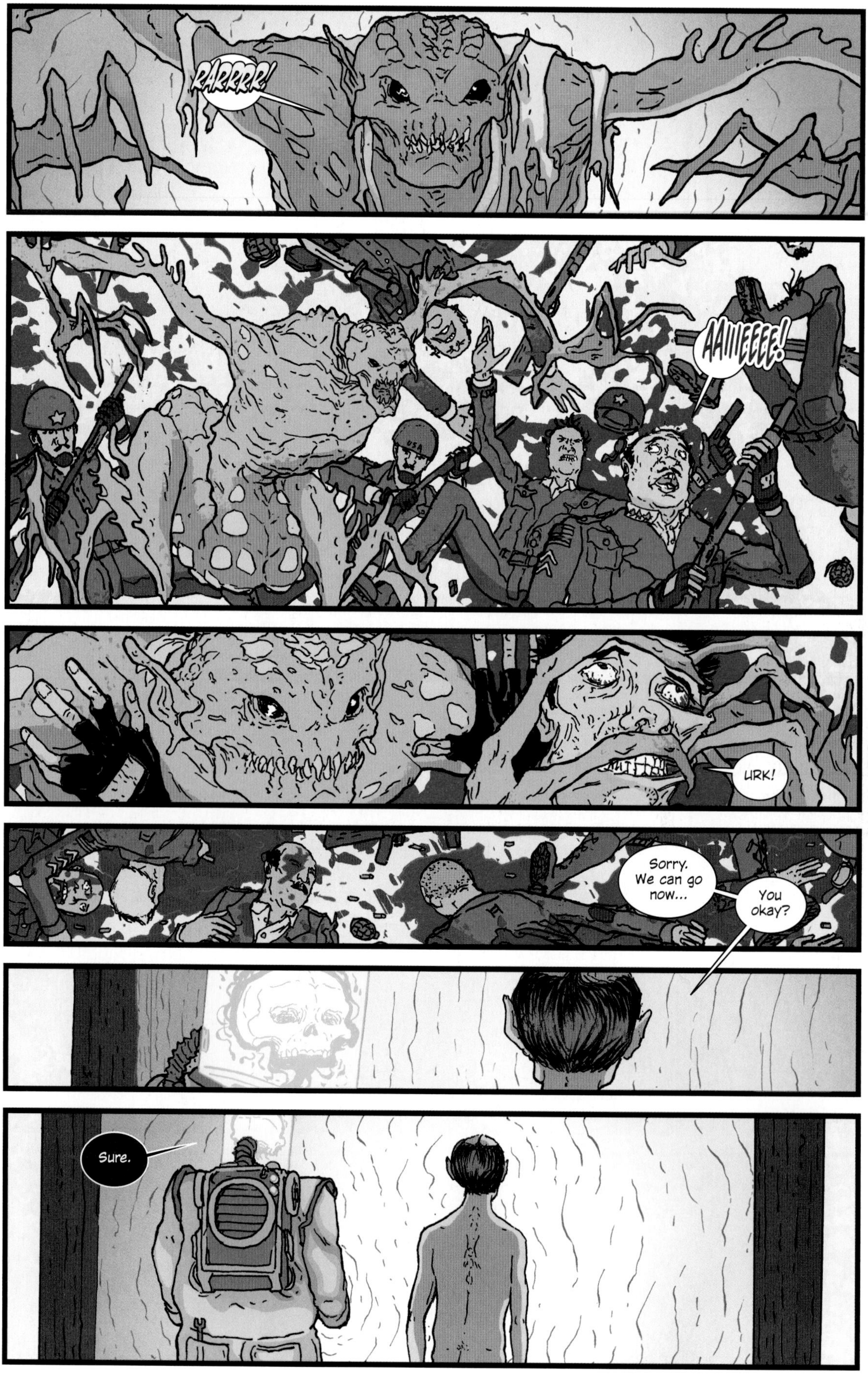
RARRRR!
AAIIIEEEE!
URK!
Sorry. We can go now...
You okay?
Sure.

Then.

Doctor von Braun...exactly what exactly do you mean by 'join forces?'

Exactly that. Star City and the Manhattan Projects will, as soon as possible, work in tandem towards a single goal.

That goal being, to protect the general welfare of our planet and to ensure the dominance of mankind in first our local sector and then the entirety of the Milky Way galaxy.

In short...

We rule.

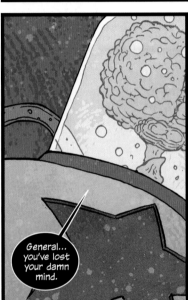

General... you've lost your damn mind.

He says this as if it's a bad thing.

Have you looked at the world, sir?

It's a shit hole. A total and complete shit hole.

I love it.

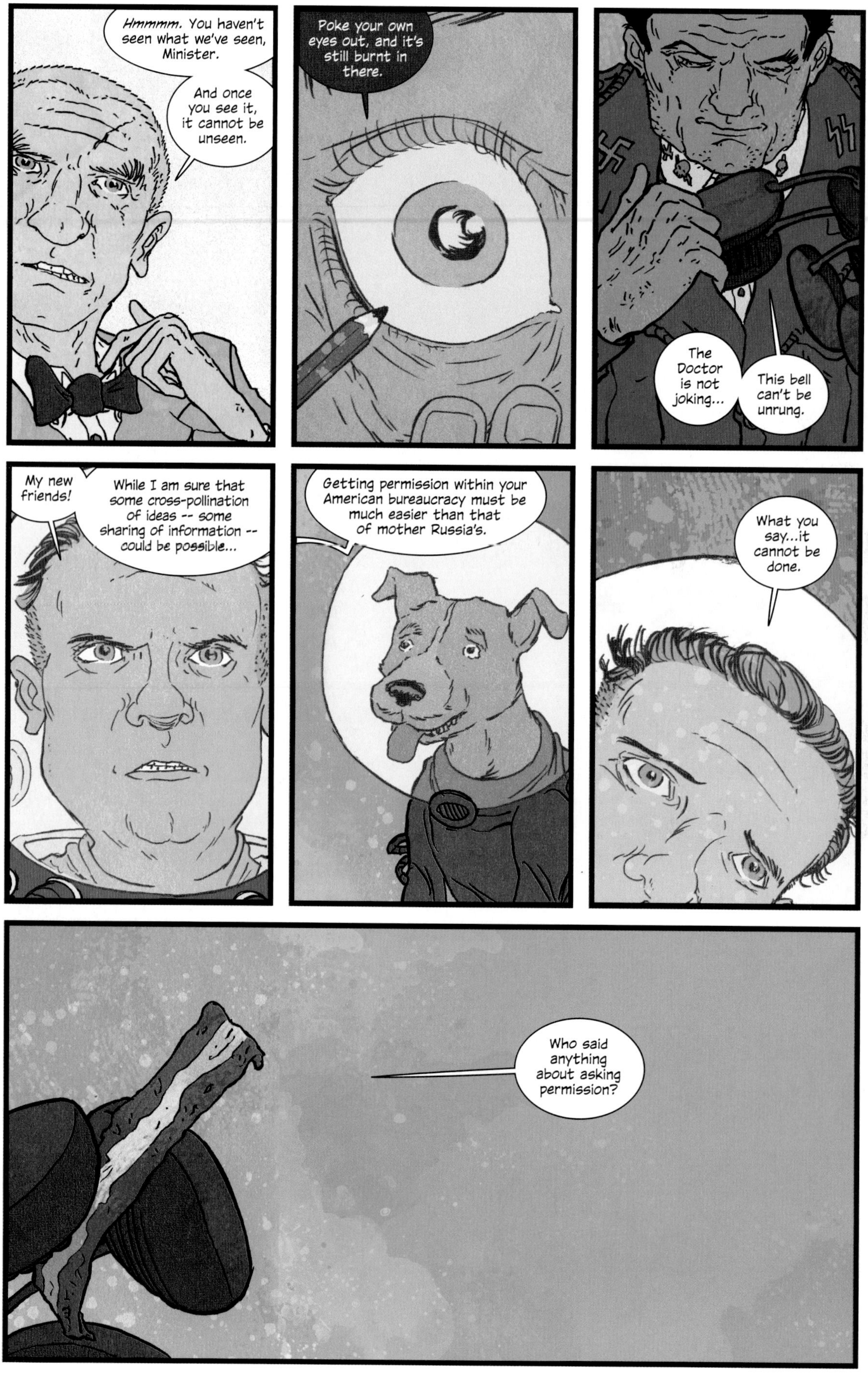
Hmmmm. You haven't seen what we've seen, Minister.
And once you see it, it cannot be unseen.
Poke your own eyes out, and it's still burnt in there.
The Doctor is not joking...
This bell can't be unrung.
My new friends!
While I am sure that some cross-pollination of ideas -- some sharing of information -- could be possible...
Getting permission within your American bureaucracy must be much easier than that of mother Russia's.
What you say...it cannot be done.
Who said anything about asking permission?

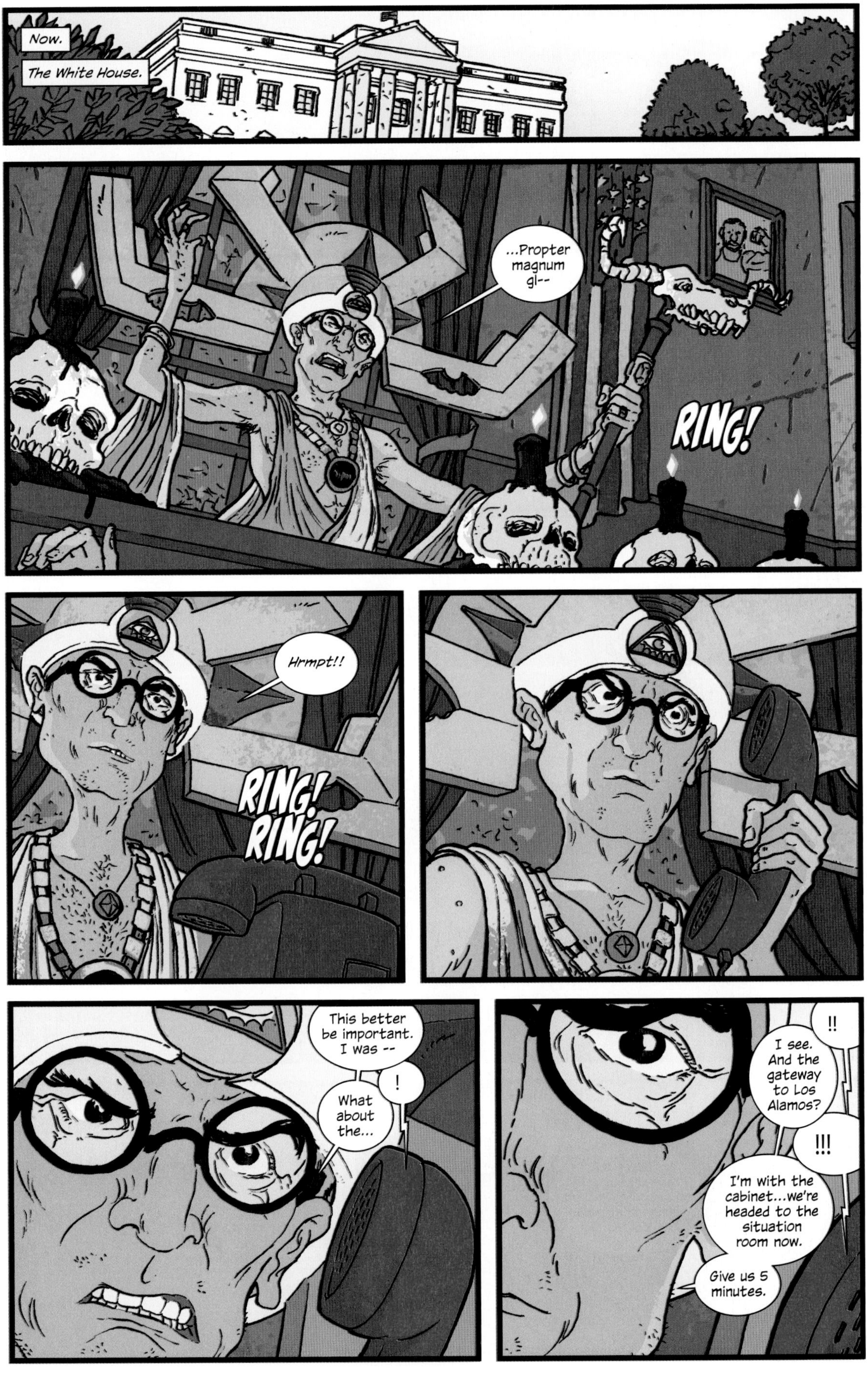
Now.
The White House.
...Propter magnum gl--
RING!
Hrmpt!!
RING! RING!
This better be important. I was --
!
What about the...
!!
I see. And the gateway to Los Alamos?
!!!
I'm with the cabinet...we're headed to the situation room now.
Give us 5 minutes.

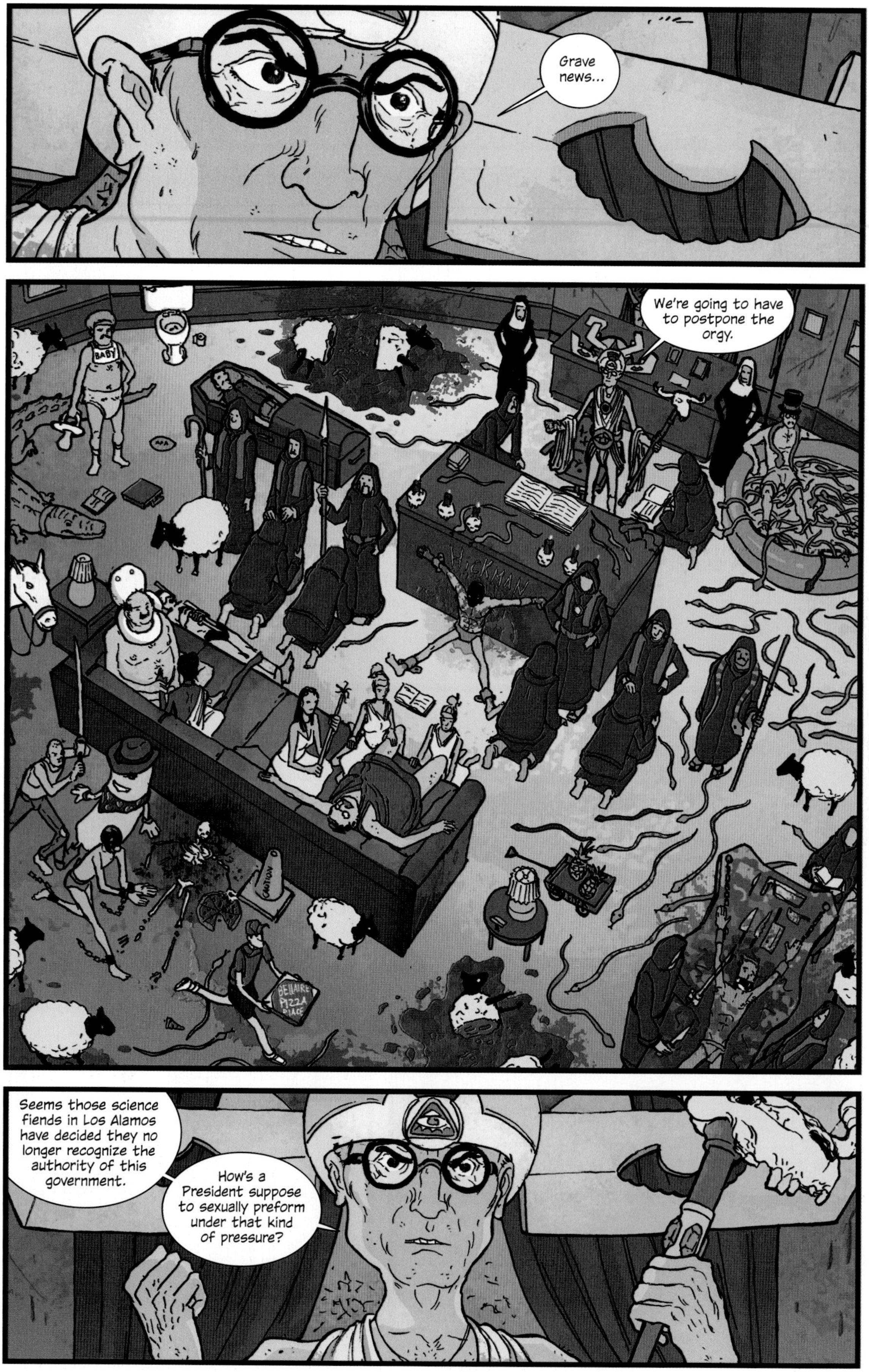
Grave news...
We're going to have to postpone the orgy.
BABY
HICKMAN
CAUTION
BELLAIRE PIZZA PLACE
Seems those science fiends in Los Alamos have decided they no longer recognize the authority of this government.
How's a President suppose to sexually preform under that kind of pressure?

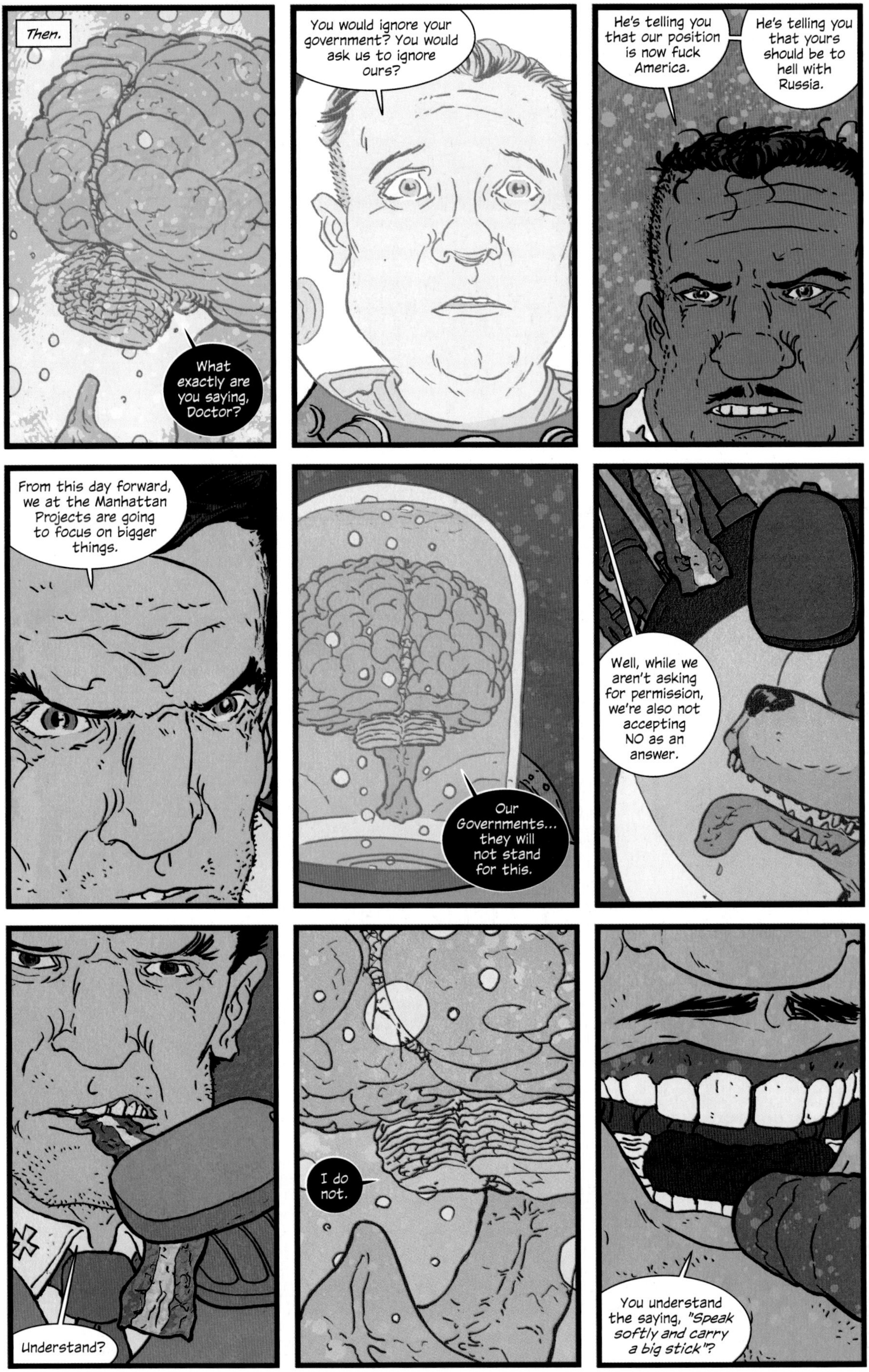
Then.
What exactly are you saying, Doctor?
You would ignore your government? You would ask us to ignore ours?
He's telling you that our position is now fuck America.
He's telling you that yours should be to hell with Russia.
From this day forward, we at the Manhattan Projects are going to focus on bigger things.
Our Governments... they will not stand for this.
Well, while we aren't asking for permission, we're also not accepting NO as an answer.
Understand?
I do not.
You understand the saying, "Speak softly and carry a big stick"?

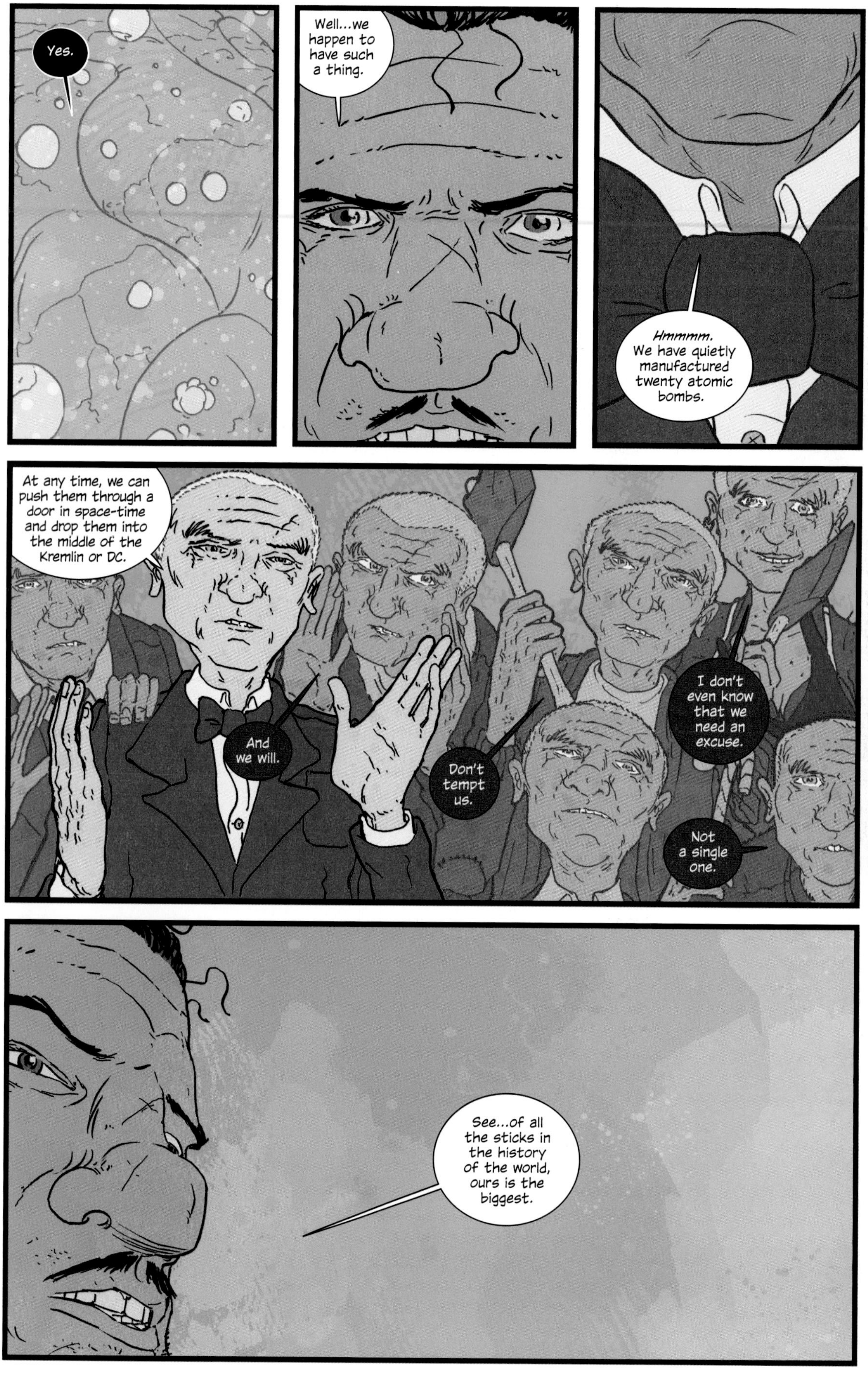
Yes.
Well...we happen to have such a thing.
Hmmmm. We have quietly manufactured twenty atomic bombs.
At any time, we can push them through a door in space-time and drop them into the middle of the Kremlin or DC.
And we will.
Don't tempt us.
I don't even know that we need an excuse.
Not a single one.
See...of all the sticks in the history of the world, ours is the biggest.

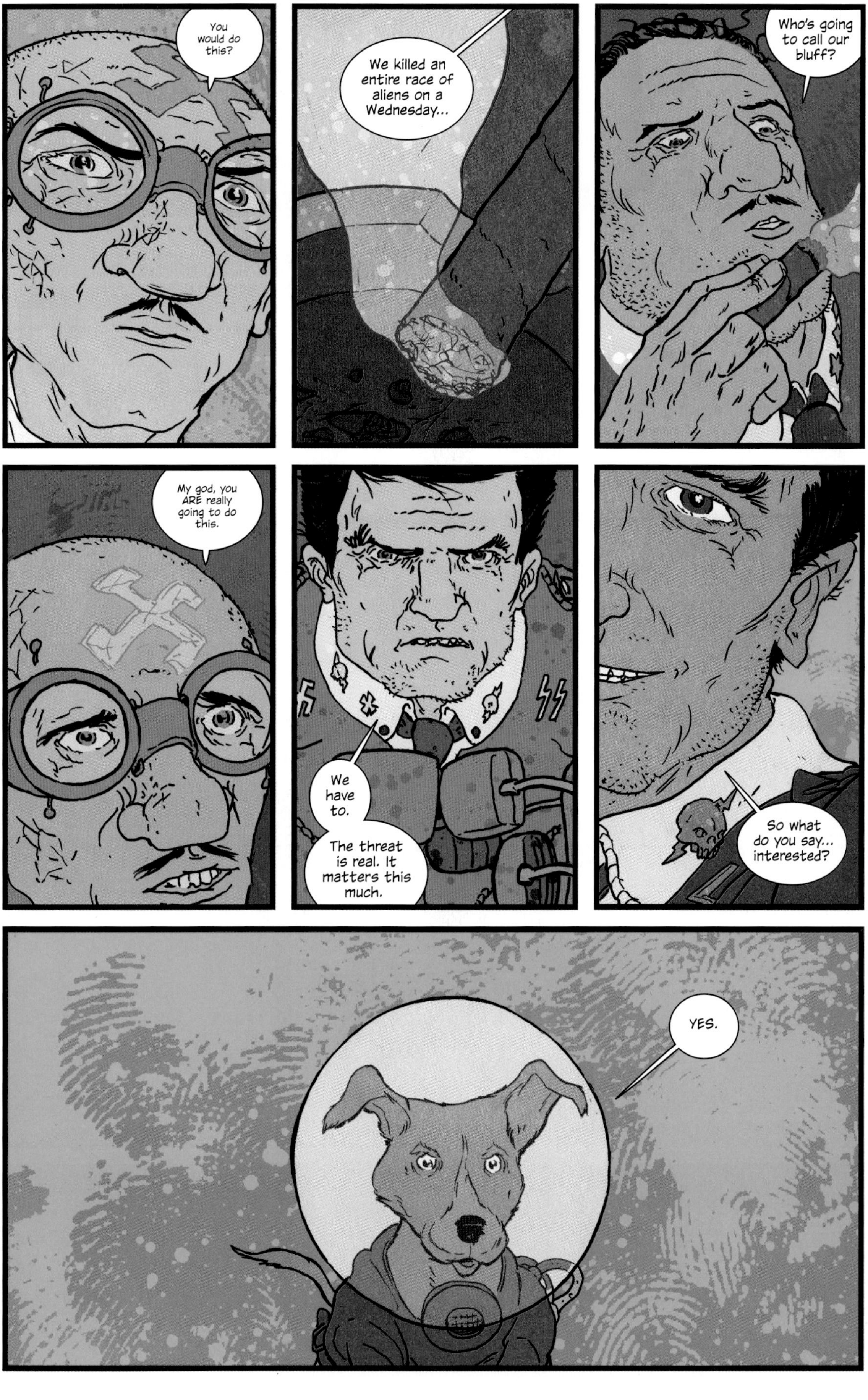
You would do this?
We killed an entire race of aliens on a Wednesday...
Who's going to call our bluff?
My god, you ARE really going to do this.
We have to.
The threat is real. It matters this much.
So what do you say... interested?
YES.

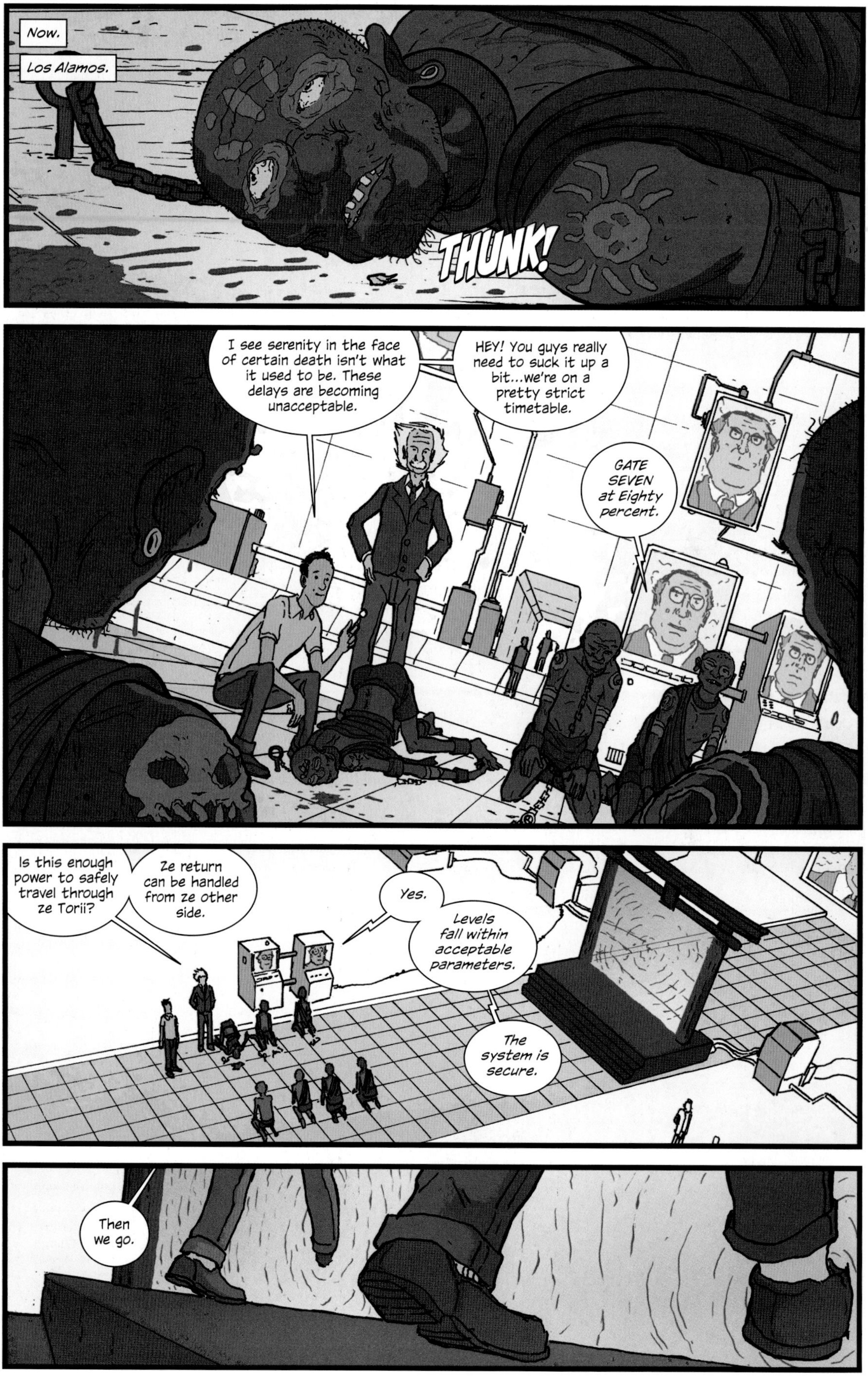
Now.
Los Alamos.
THUNK!
I see serenity in the face of certain death isn't what it used to be. These delays are becoming unacceptable.
HEY! You guys really need to suck it up a bit...we're on a pretty strict timetable.
GATE SEVEN at Eighty percent.
Is this enough power to safely travel through ze Torii?
Ze return can be handled from ze other side.
Yes.
Levels fall within acceptable parameters.
The system is secure.
Then we go.

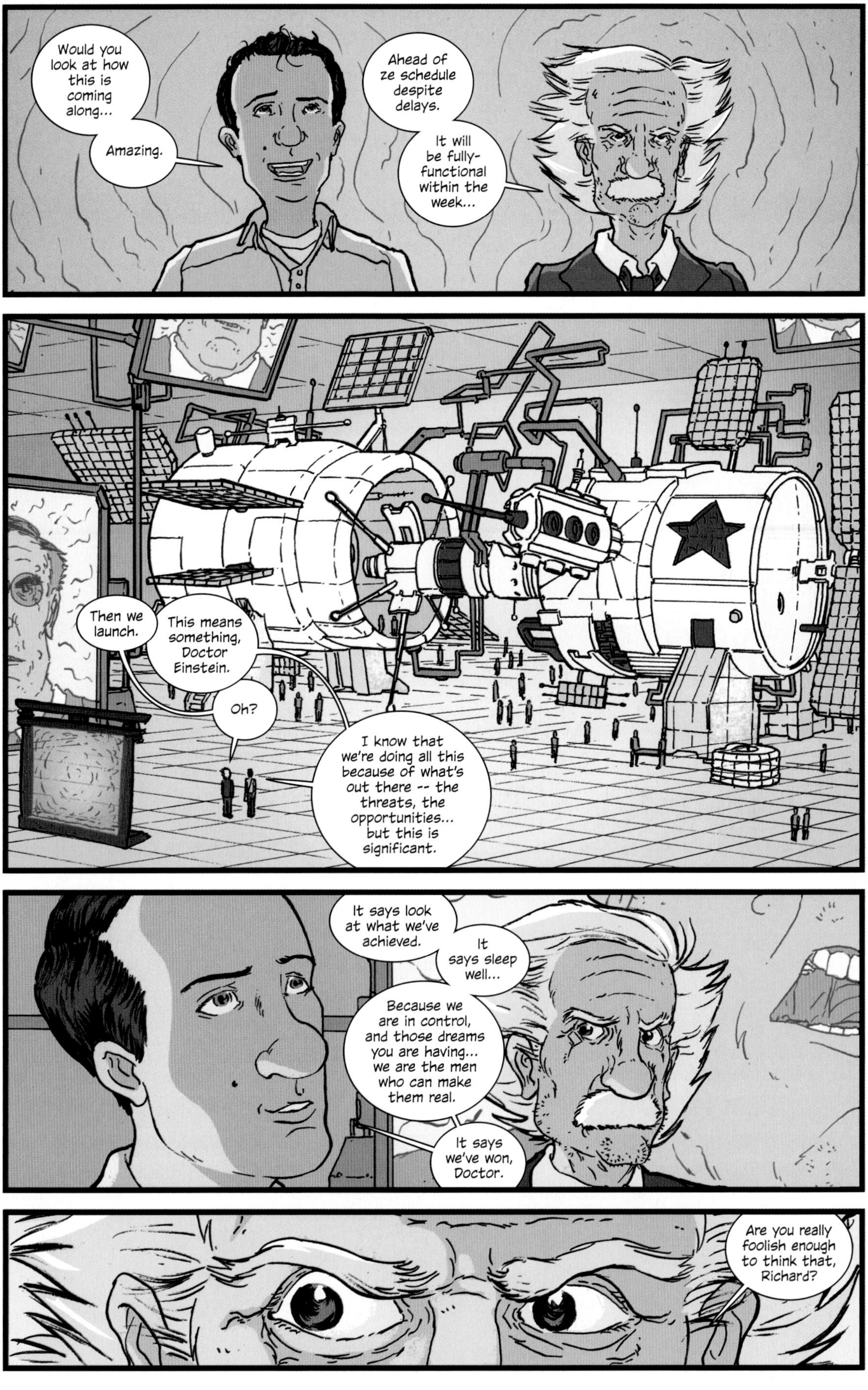
Would you look at how this is coming along...
Amazing.
Ahead of ze schedule despite delays.
It will be fully-functional within the week...
Then we launch.
This means something, Doctor Einstein.
Oh?
I know that we're doing all this because of what's out there -- the threats, the opportunities... but this is significant.
It says look at what we've achieved.
It says sleep well...
Because we are in control, and those dreams you are having... we are the men who can make them real.
It says we've won, Doctor.
Are you really foolish enough to think that, Richard?

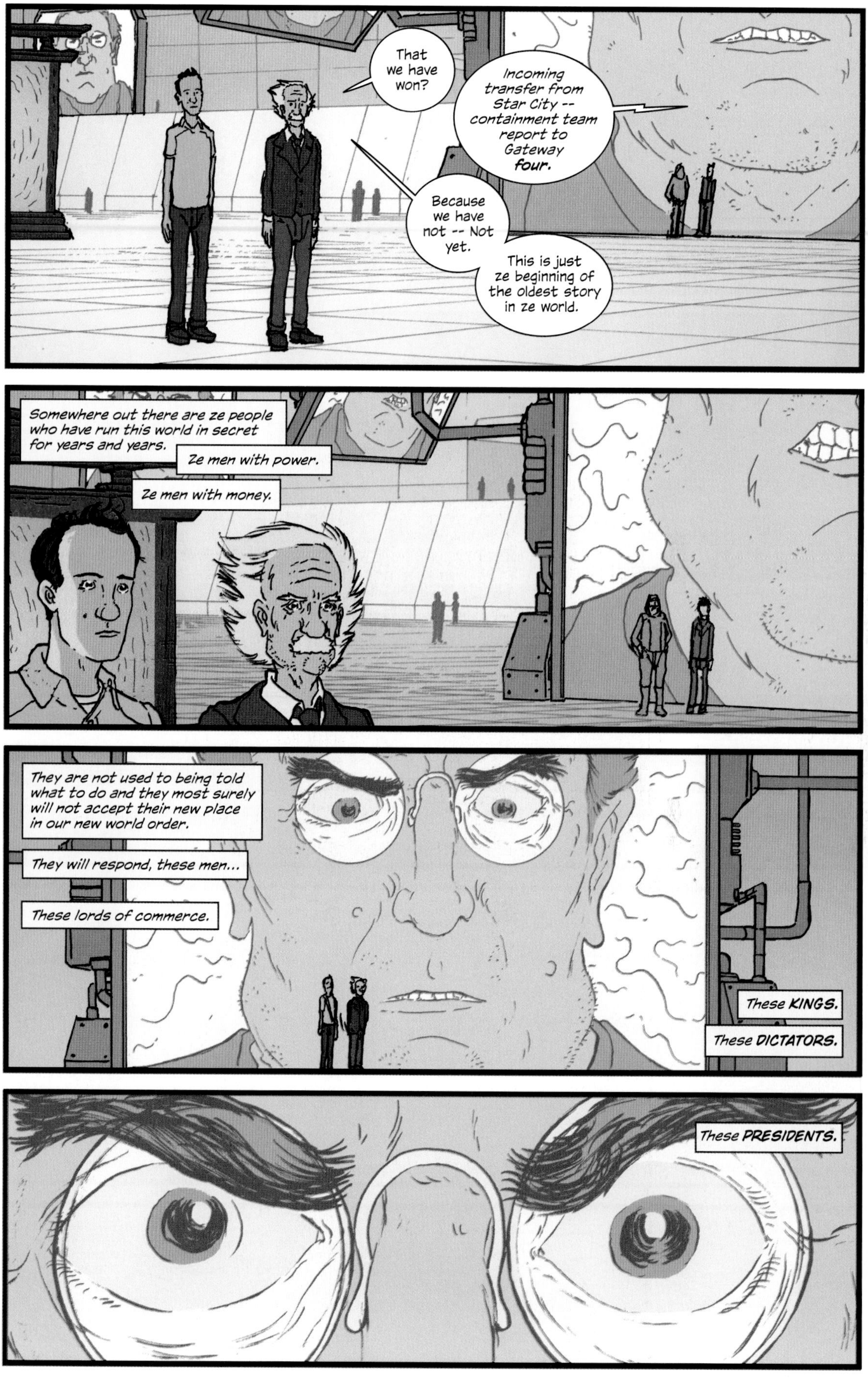
That we have won?
Incoming transfer from Star City -- containment team report to Gateway four.
Because we have not -- Not yet.
This is just ze beginning of the oldest story in ze world.
Somewhere out there are ze people who have run this world in secret for years and years.
Ze men with power.
Ze men with money.
They are not used to being told what to do and they most surely will not accept their new place in our new world order.
They will respond, these men...
These lords of commerce.
These KINGS.
These DICTATORS.
These PRESIDENTS.

"WHO STANDS ON A HILL AND DECLARES THEY ARE KING?

FOOLS."

CLAVIS AUREA
THE RECORDED FEYNMAN | **VOL. 3**

I WILL PAY IT
IN FULL

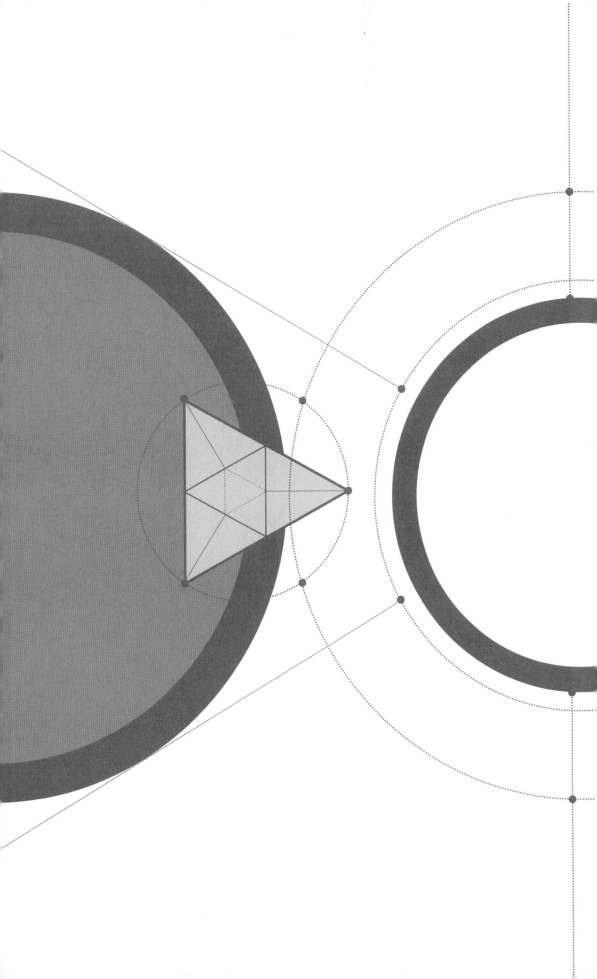

"TO FOLLOW IS TO YIELD. "

CLAVIS AUREA
THE RECORDED FEYNMAN

VOL. 2

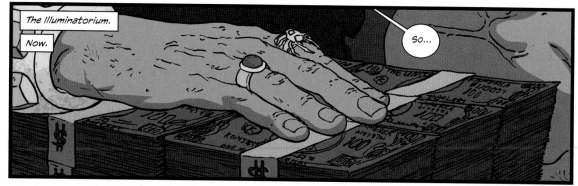

The Illuminatorium.

Now.

So...

Shall we put this to a vote?

Of course. Formalities are our true trade, aren't they?

The top scientists of the two world super powers have decided to remove the yoke of their betters -- They want independence from those who rule this world...

From us.

So, yes... by all means, let's vote.

We observe the forms because the forms predate us.

Abandon the forms and lose every right we assume.

Who here holds themselves above history? **No one.**

I will vote yes.

Yes.

Agreed.

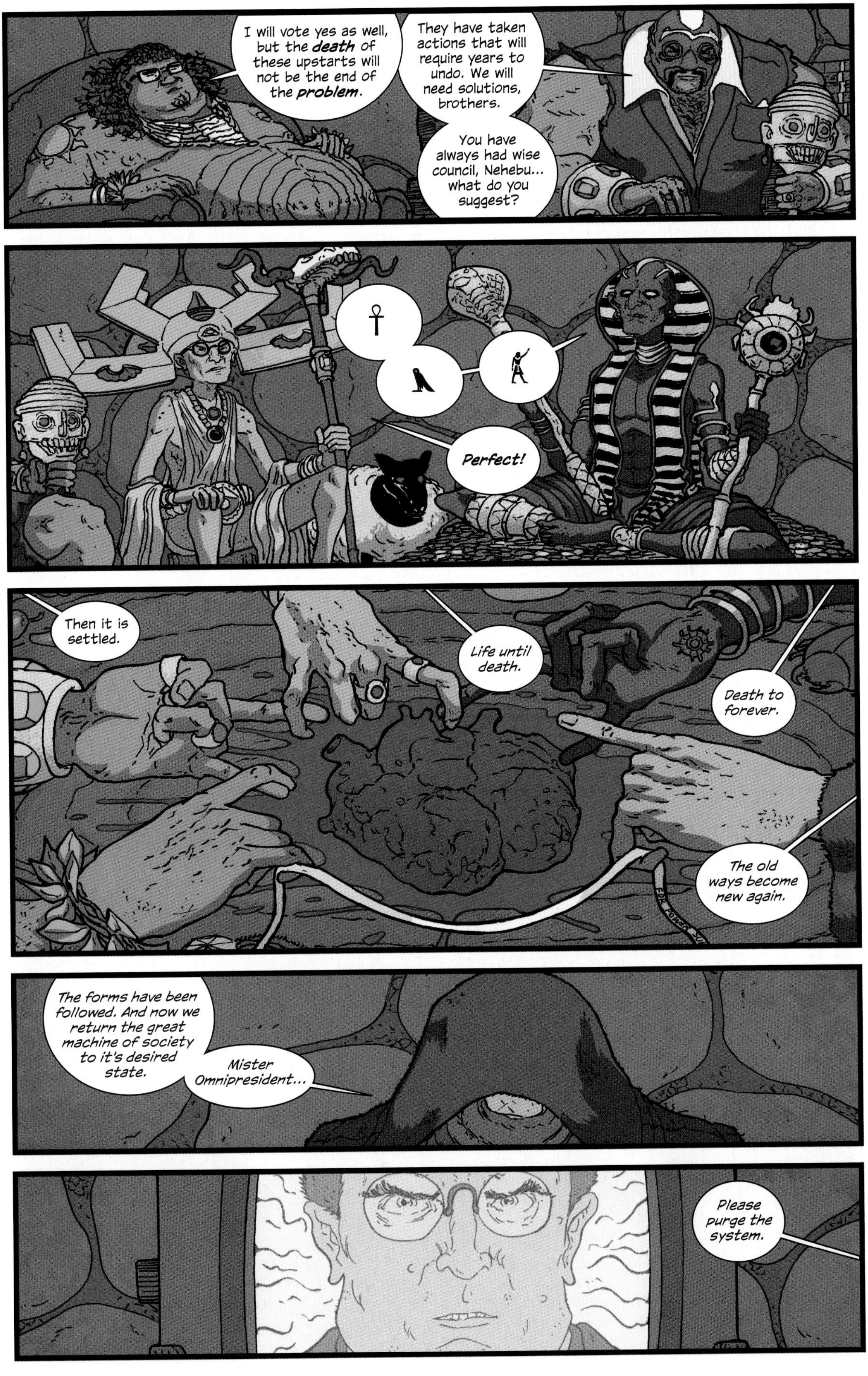
I will vote yes as well, but the ***death*** of these upstarts will not be the end of the ***problem***.
They have taken actions that will require years to undo. We will need solutions, brothers.
You have always had wise council, Nehebu... what do you suggest?
Perfect!
Then it is settled.
Life until death.
Death to forever.
The old ways become new again.
The forms have been followed. And now we return the great machine of society to it's desired state.
Mister Omnipresident...
Please purge the system.

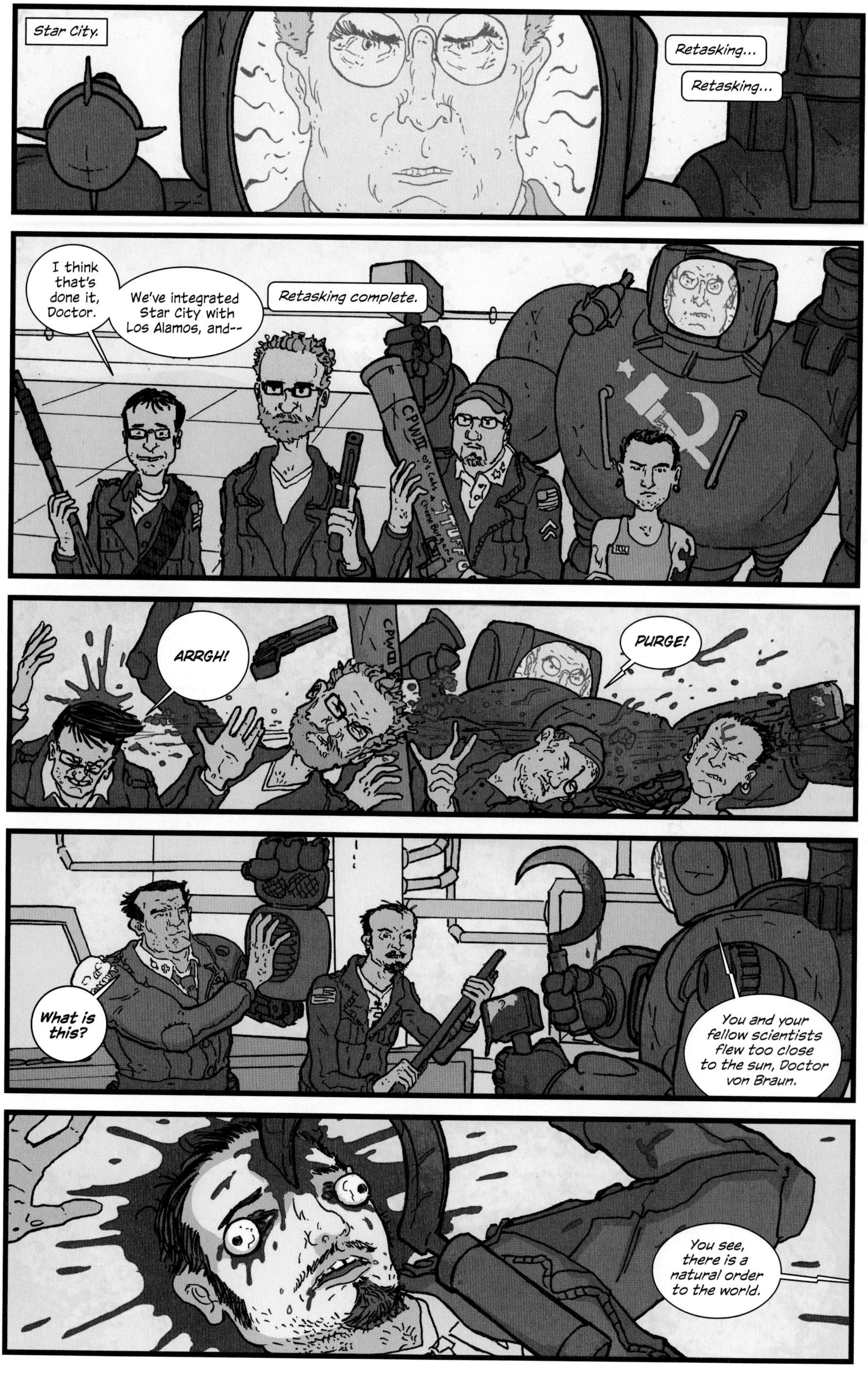
Star City.
Retasking...
Retasking...
I think that's done it, Doctor.
We've integrated Star City with Los Alamos, and--
Retasking complete.
ARRGH!
PURGE!
What is this?
You and your fellow scientists flew too close to the sun, Doctor von Braun.
You see, there is a natural order to the world.

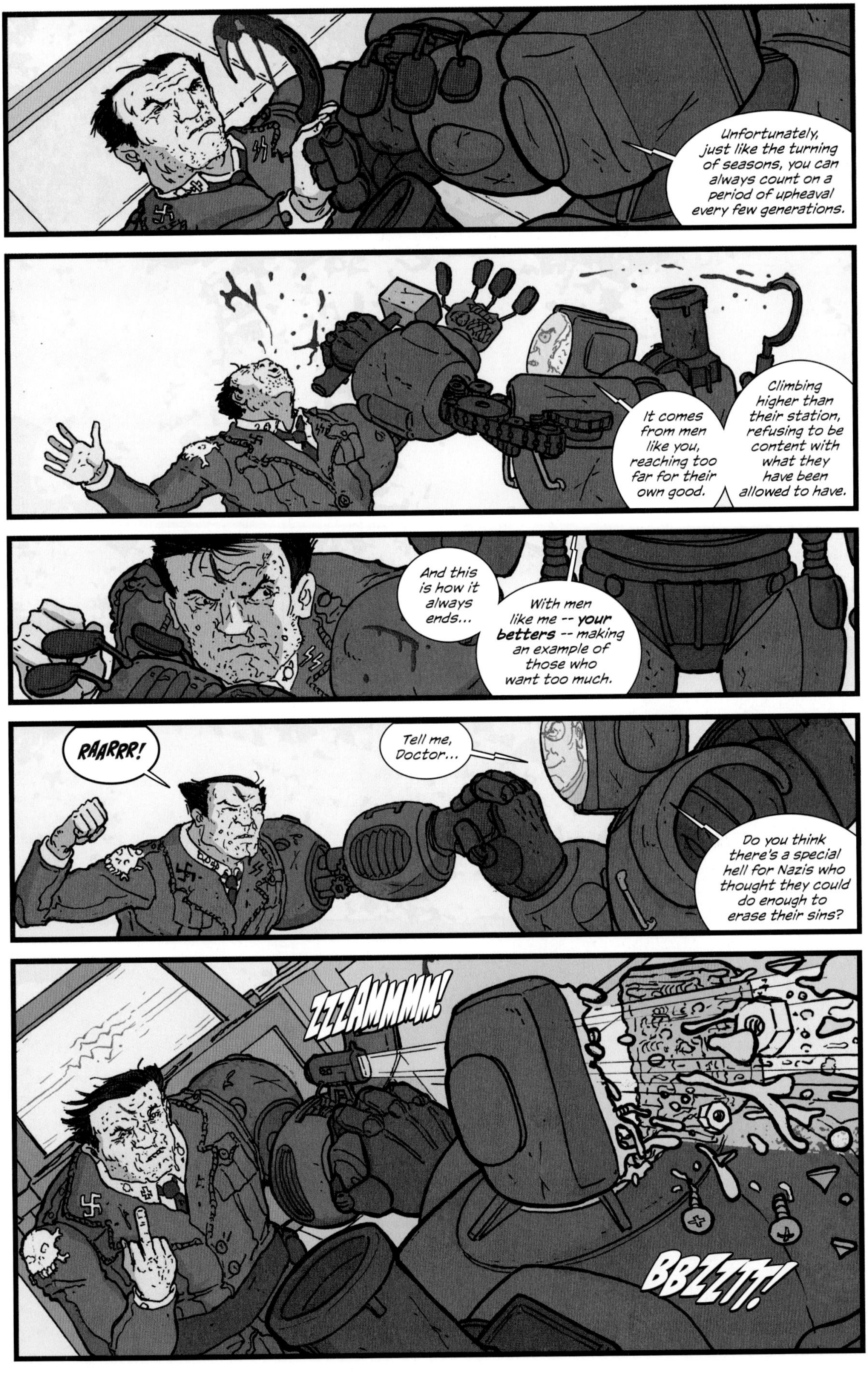
Unfortunately, just like the turning of seasons, you can always count on a period of upheaval every few generations.
It comes from men like you, reaching too far for their own good.
Climbing higher than their station, refusing to be content with what they have been allowed to have.
And this is how it always ends...
With men like me -- **your betters** -- making an example of those who want too much.
RAARRR!
Tell me, Doctor...
Do you think there's a special hell for Nazis who thought they could do enough to erase their sins?
ZZZAMMMM!
BBZZTT!

Yes.
BZZZT!
Well, then...
Let's get busy on sending you there.

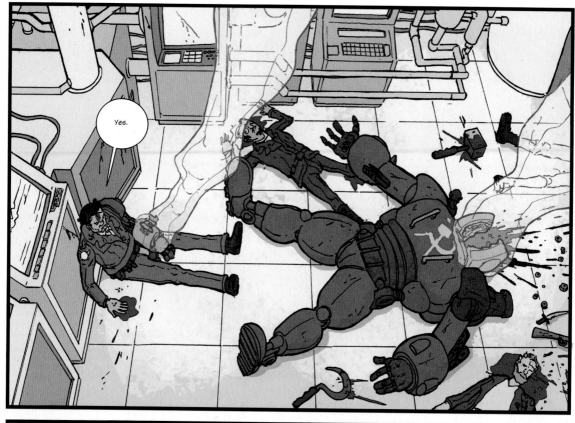

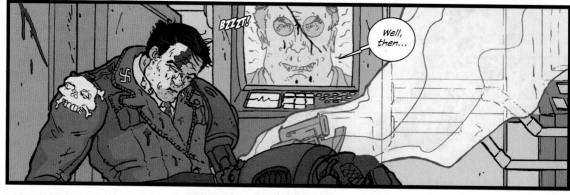

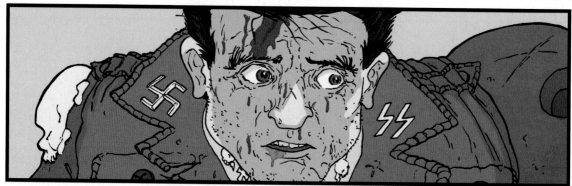

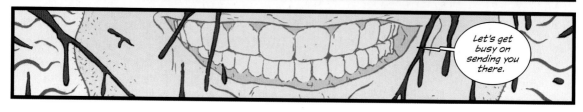

"THE WORLD HAS RULES, CREATED BY THOSE WHO CONSIDER THEMSELVES ABOVE THEM.

SO WE BECAME RADICALS, WHO ACCEPTED NEITHER."

CLAVIS AUREA
THE RECORDED FEYNMAN | **VOL. 1**

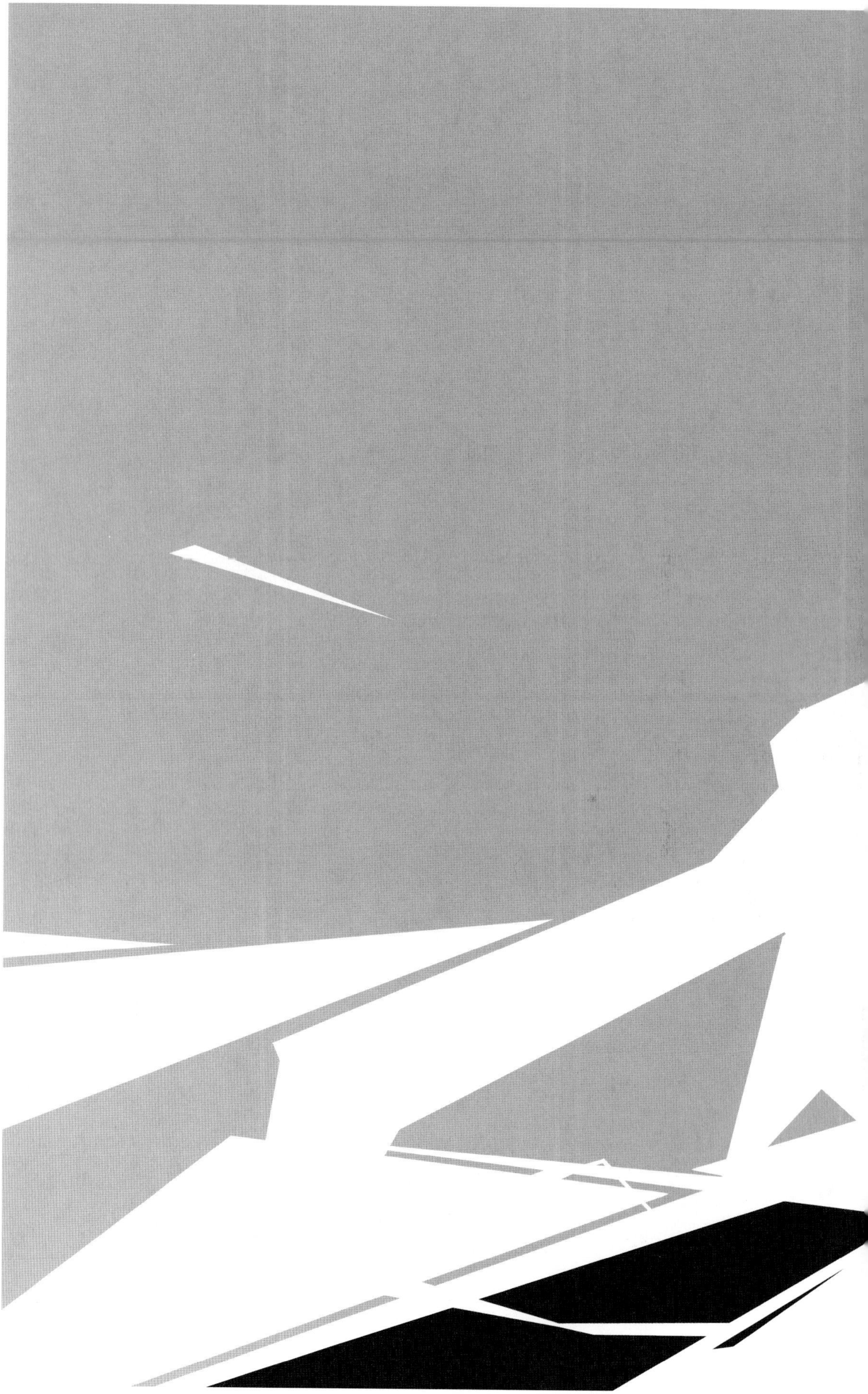

08

THEY RULE

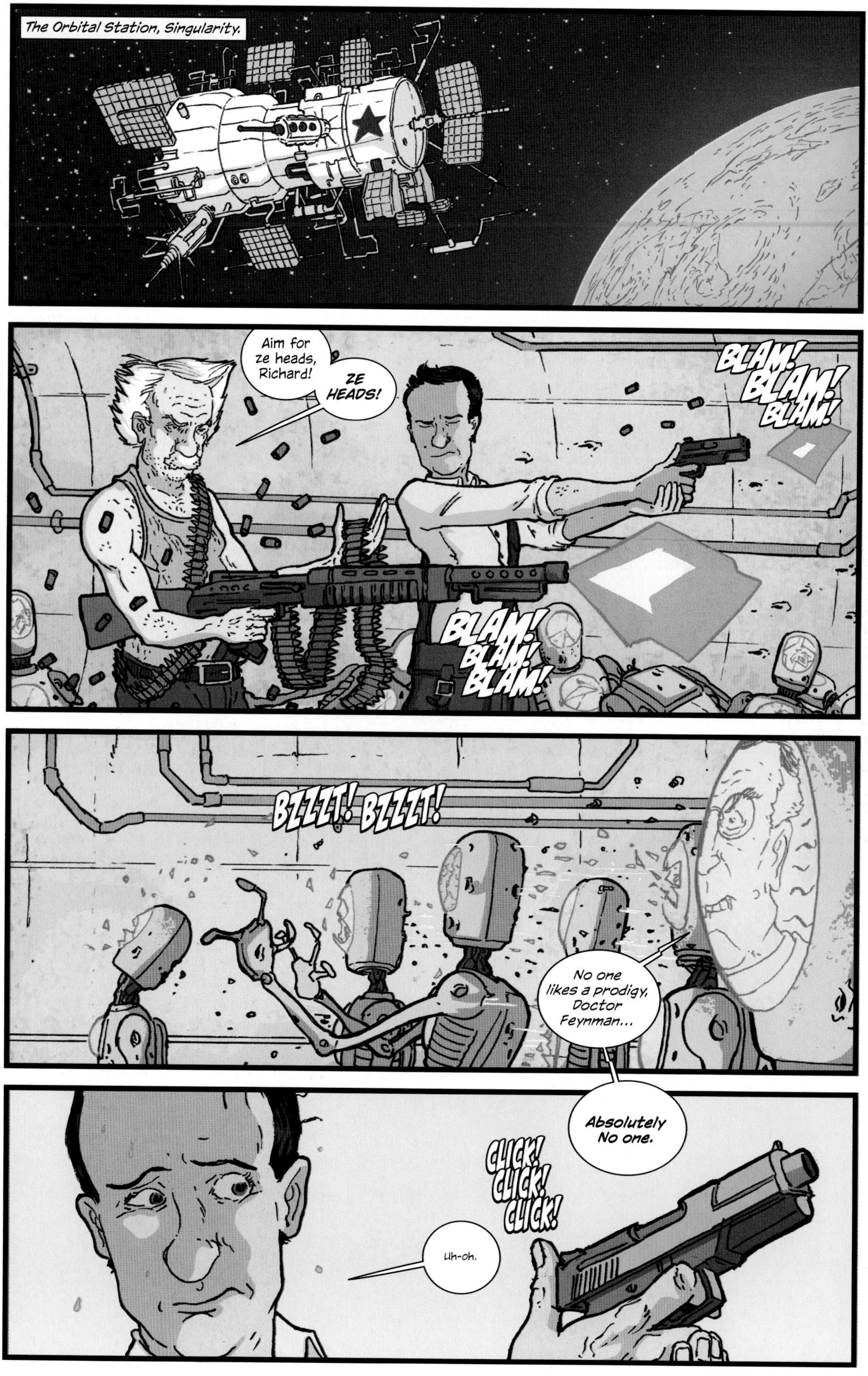
The Orbital Station, Singularity.
Aim for ze heads, Richard!
ZE HEADS!
BLAM! BLAM! BLAM!
BLAM! BLAM! BLAM!
BZZZT! BZZZT!
No one likes a prodigy, Doctor Feynman...
Absolutely No one.
CLICK! CLICK! CLICK!
Uh-oh.

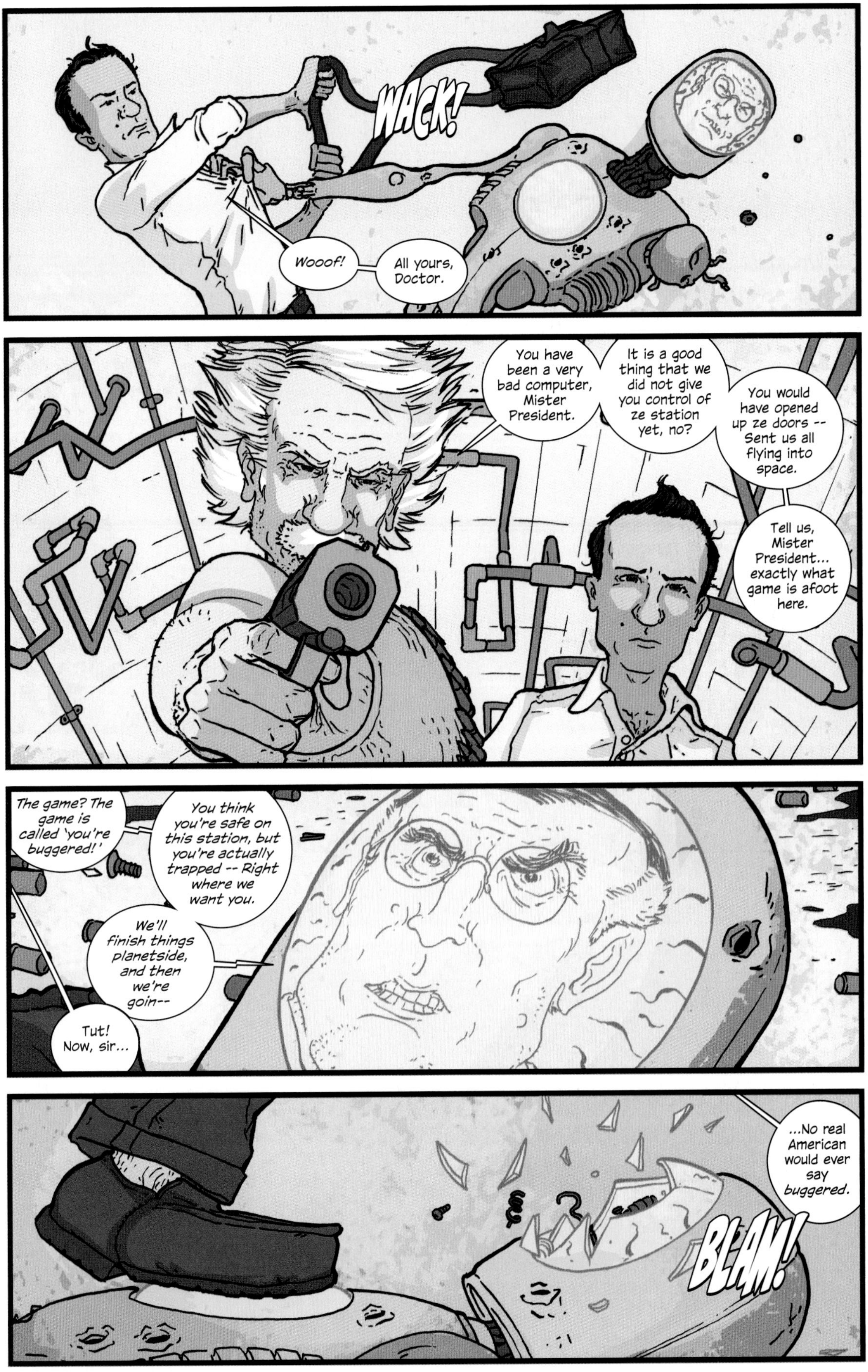
WACK!
Wooof!
All yours, Doctor.
You have been a very bad computer, Mister President.
It is a good thing that we did not give you control of ze station yet, no?
You would have opened up ze doors -- Sent us all flying into space.
Tell us, Mister President... exactly what game is afoot here.
The game? The game is called 'you're buggered!'
You think you're safe on this station, but you're actually trapped -- Right where we want you.
We'll finish things planetside, and then we're goin--
Tut! Now, sir...
...No real American would ever say buggered.
BLAM!

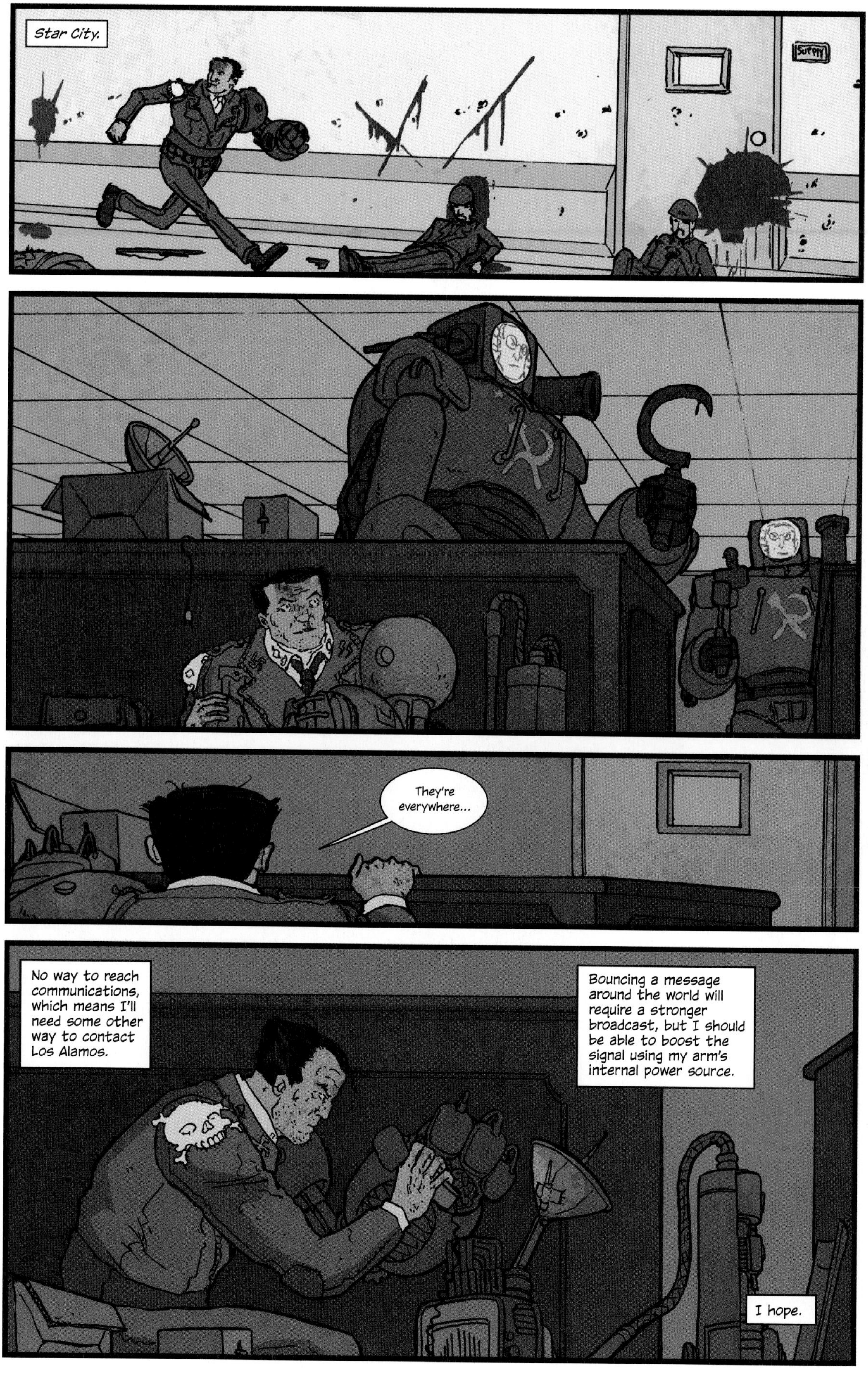

Star City.
SUPPLY
They're everywhere...
No way to reach communications, which means I'll need some other way to contact Los Alamos.
Bouncing a message around the world will require a stronger broadcast, but I should be able to boost the signal using my arm's internal power source.
I hope.

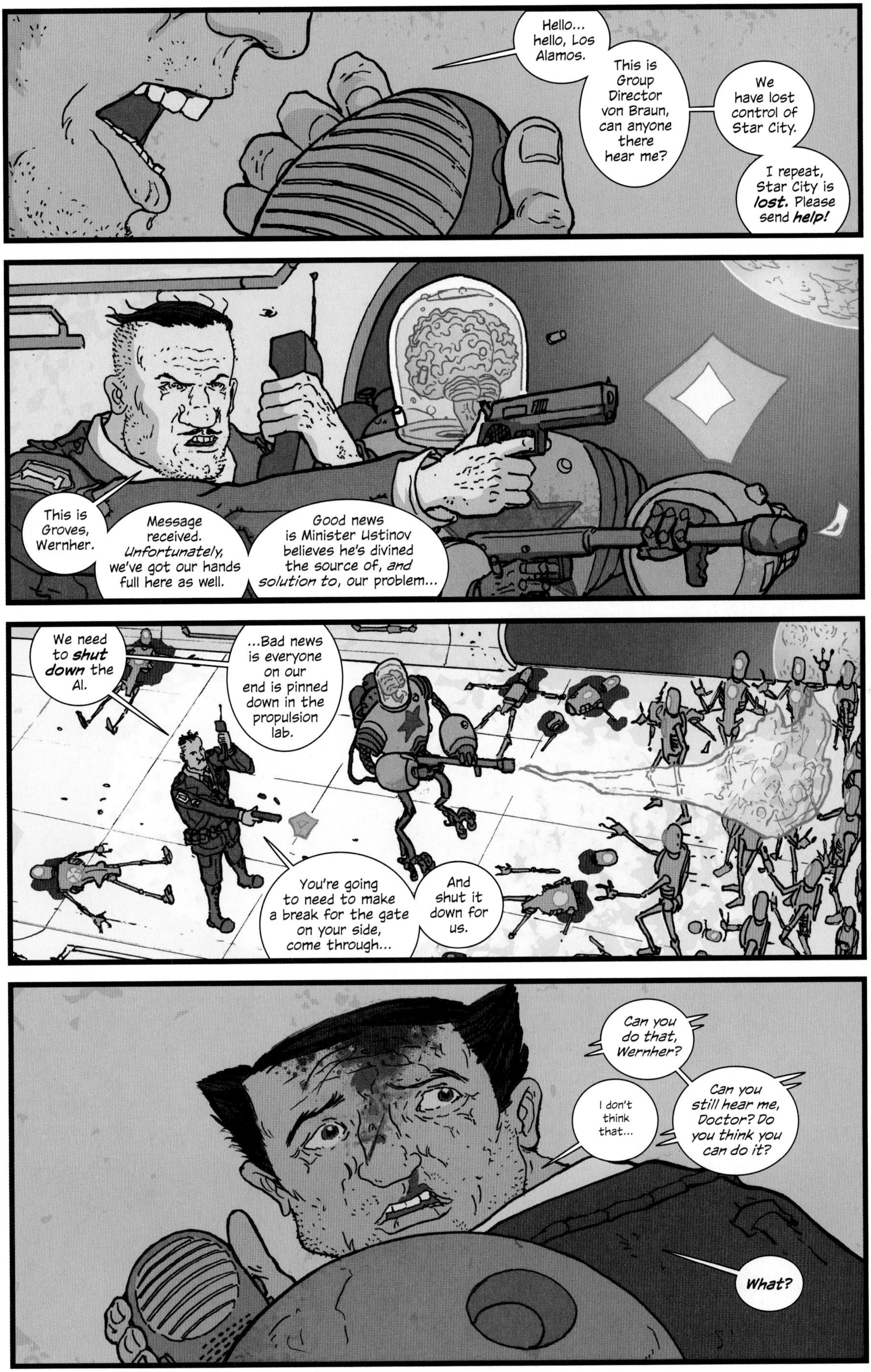

Hello... hello, Los Alamos.
This is Group Director von Braun, can anyone there hear me?
We have lost control of Star City.
I repeat, Star City is **lost.** Please send **help!**
This is Groves, Wernher.
Message received. *Unfortunately,* we've got our hands full here as well.
Good news is Minister Ustinov believes he's divined the source of, *and solution to*, our problem...
...Bad news is everyone on our end is pinned down in the propulsion lab.
We need to **shut down** the AI.
You're going to need to make a break for the gate on your side, come through...
And shut it down for us.
Can you do that, Wernher?
Can you still hear me, Doctor? Do you think you can do it?
I don't think that...
What?

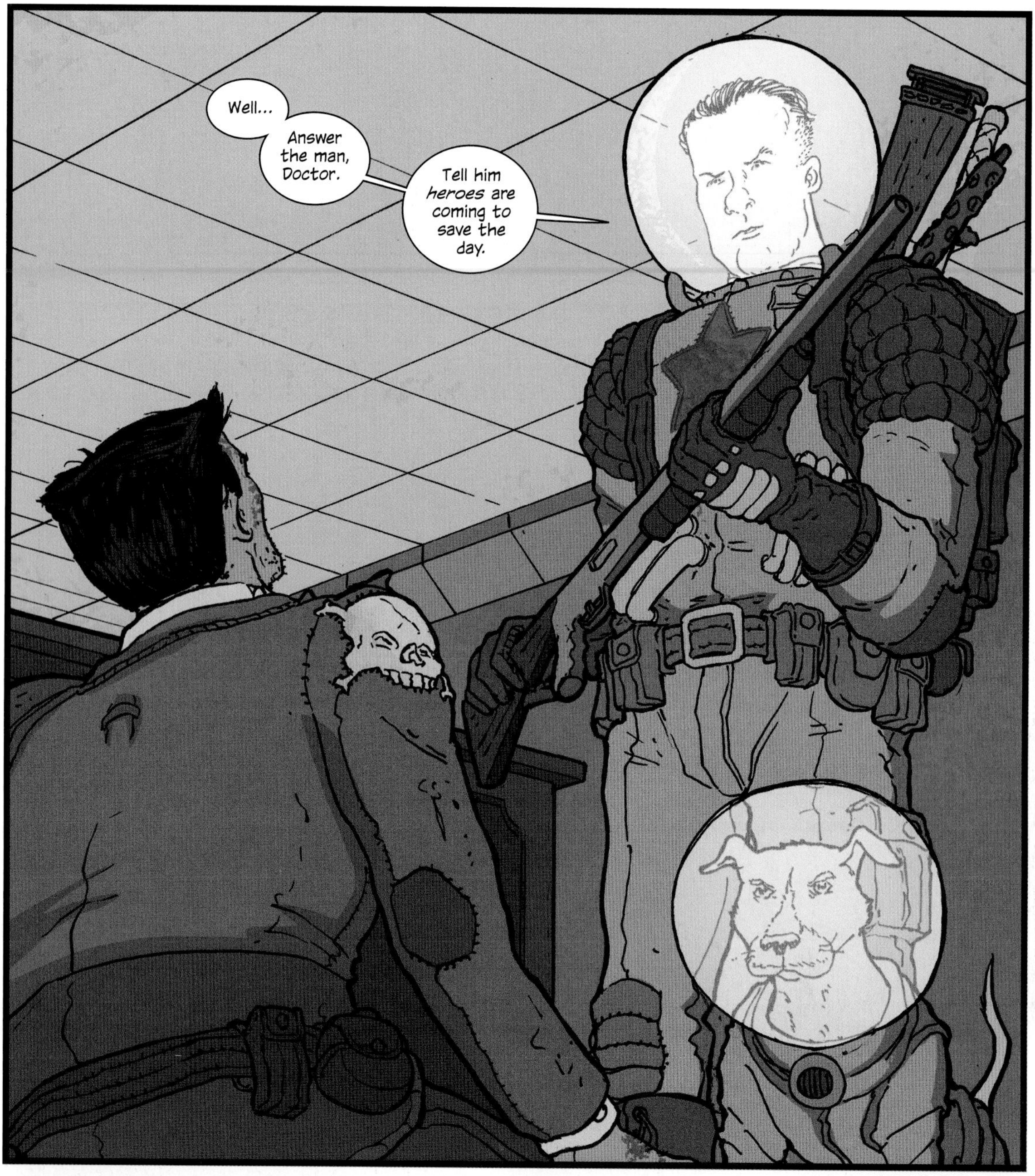
Well...
Answer the man, Doctor.
Tell him *heroes* are coming to save the day.

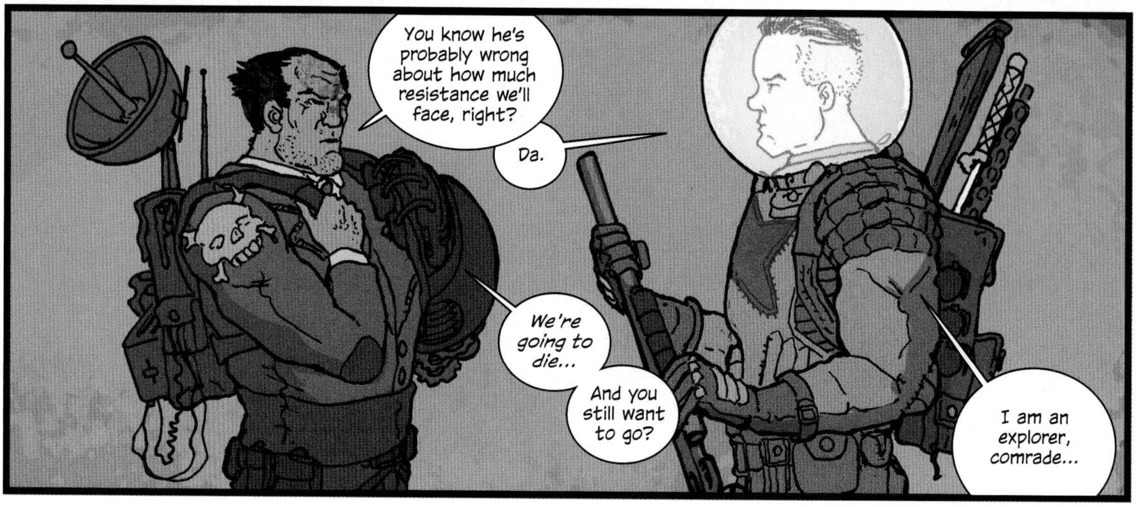
You know he's probably wrong about how much resistance we'll face, right?
Da.
We're going to die...
And you still want to go?
I am an explorer, comrade...

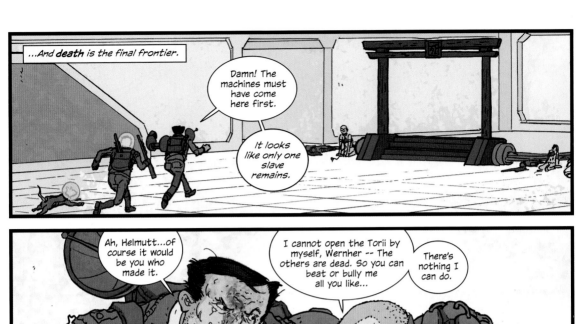

...And *death* is the final frontier.

Damn! The machines must have come here first.

It looks like only one slave remains.

Ah, Helmutt...of course it would be you who made it.

I cannot open the Torii by myself, Wernher -- The others are dead. So you can beat or bully me all you like...

There's nothing I can do.

General? Are you hearing this?

Yeah. Give 'em some motivation...

Tell him we'll cut 'em loose.

Good news, Helmutt... The American General would set you free...

All you have to do is open the gate.

Don't you even want to try?

Yes.

Yes.

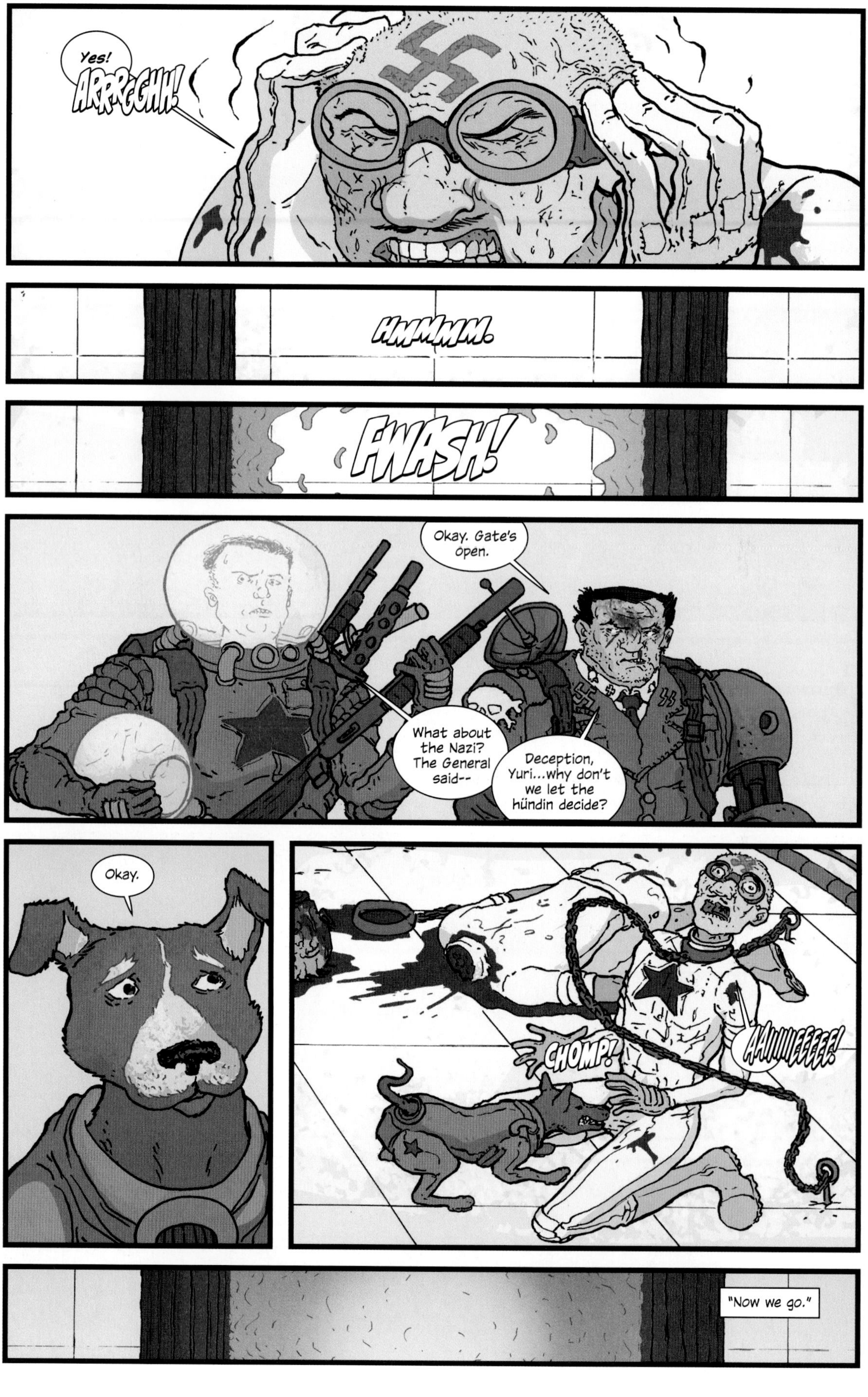
Yes!
ARRRGGHH!
HMMMM.
FWASH!
Okay. Gate's open.
What about the Nazi? The General said--
Deception, Yuri...why don't we let the hündin decide?
Okay.
CHOMP!
AAIIIIIEEEEE!
"Now we go."

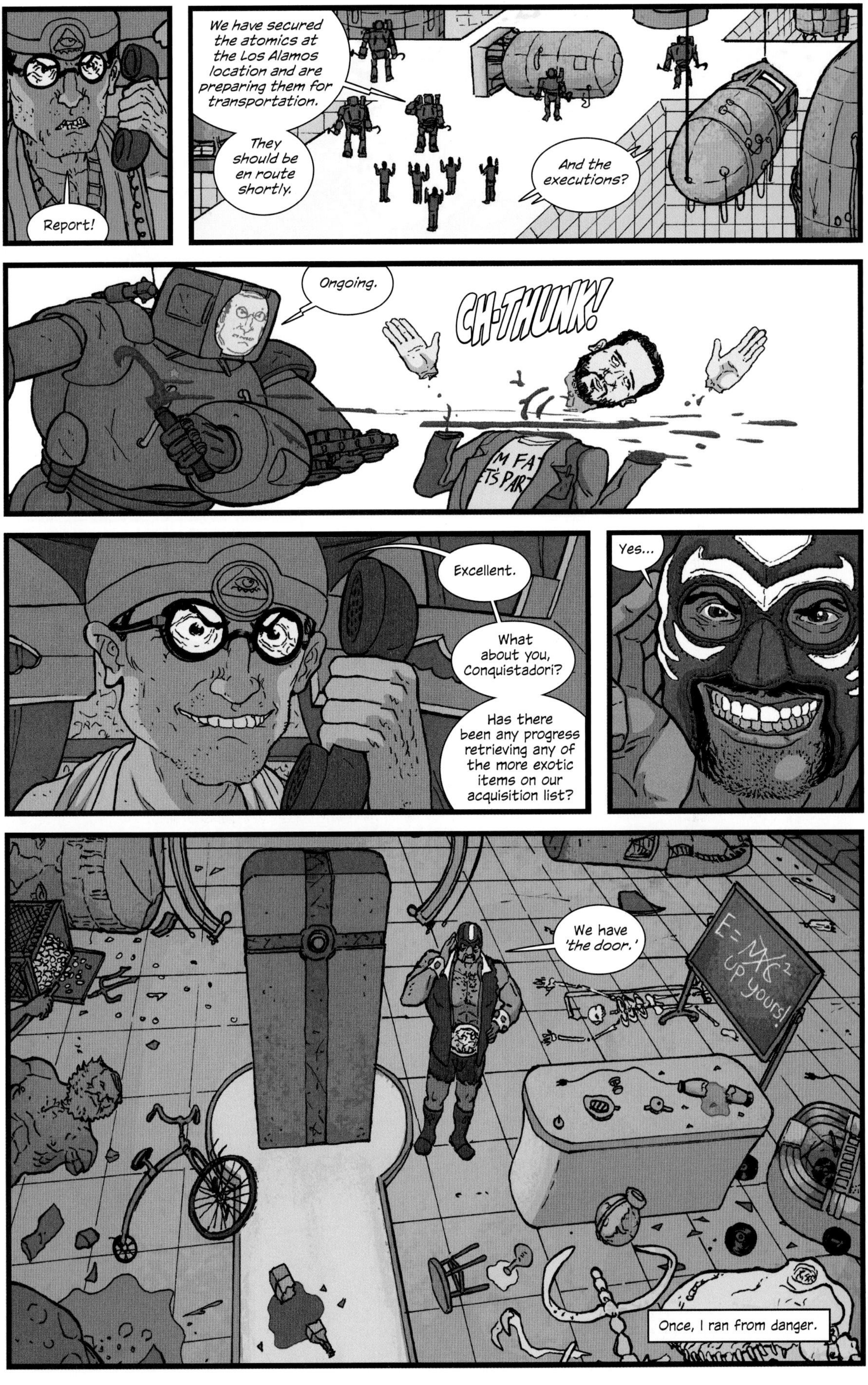
Report!
We have secured the atomics at the Los Alamos location and are preparing them for transportation.
They should be en route shortly.
And the executions?
Ongoing.
CH-THUNK!
Excellent.
What about you, Conquistadori?
Has there been any progress retrieving any of the more exotic items on our acquisition list?
Yes...
We have 'the door.'
E = MC²
Up yours!
Once, I ran from danger.

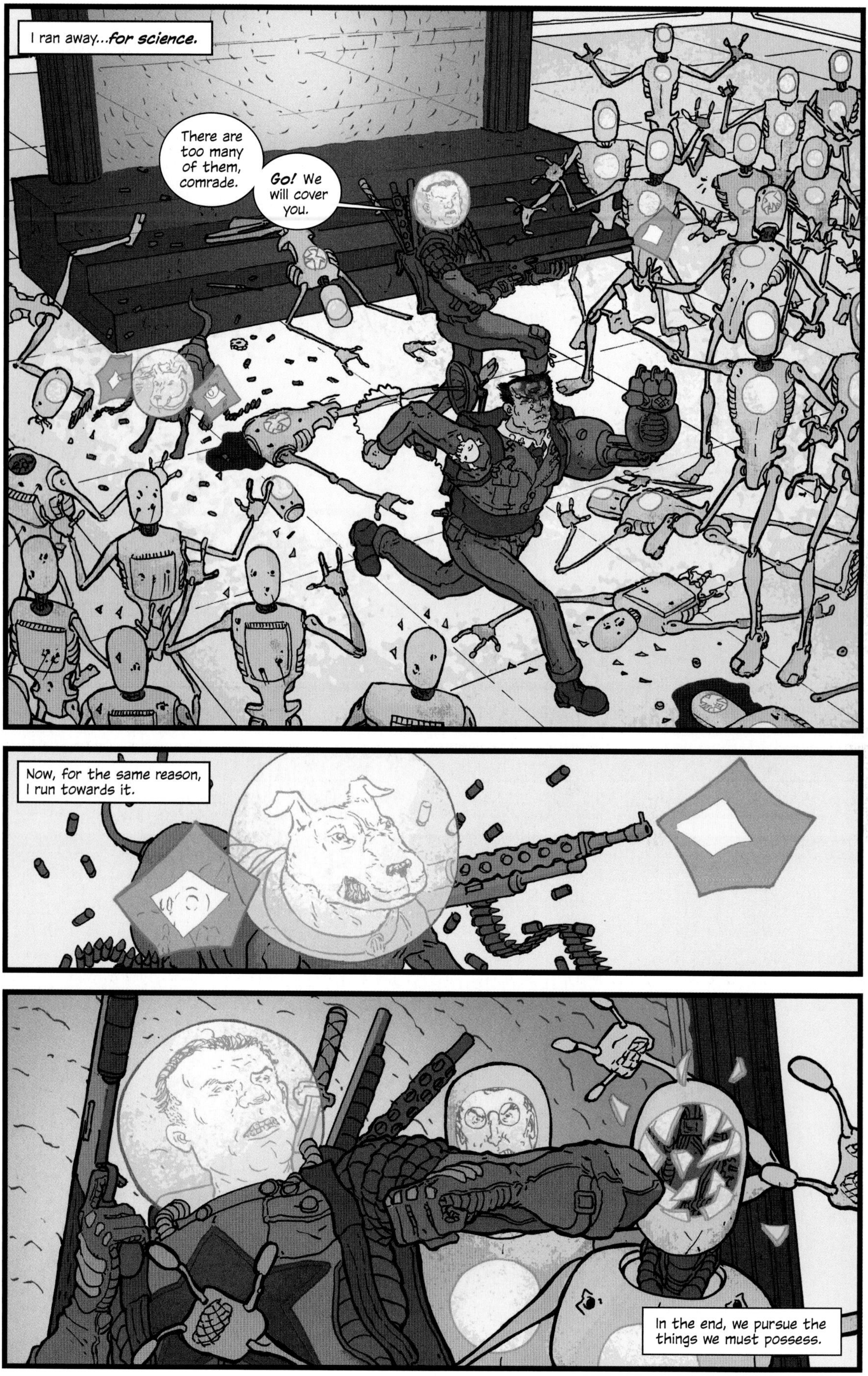
I ran away...*for science.*
There are too many of them, comrade.
Go! We will cover you.
Now, for the same reason, I run towards it.
In the end, we pursue the things we must possess.

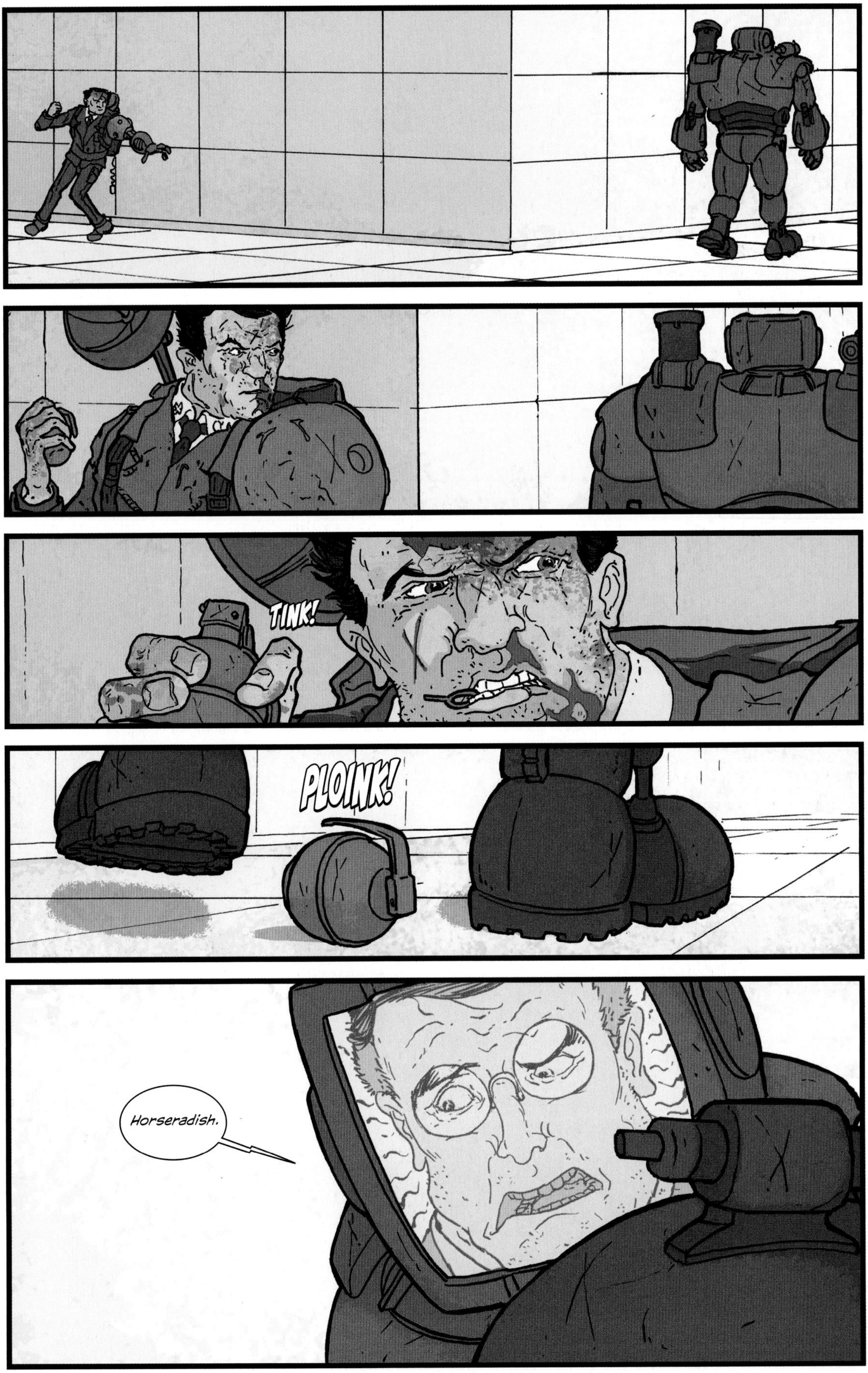
TINK!
PLOINK!
Horseradish.

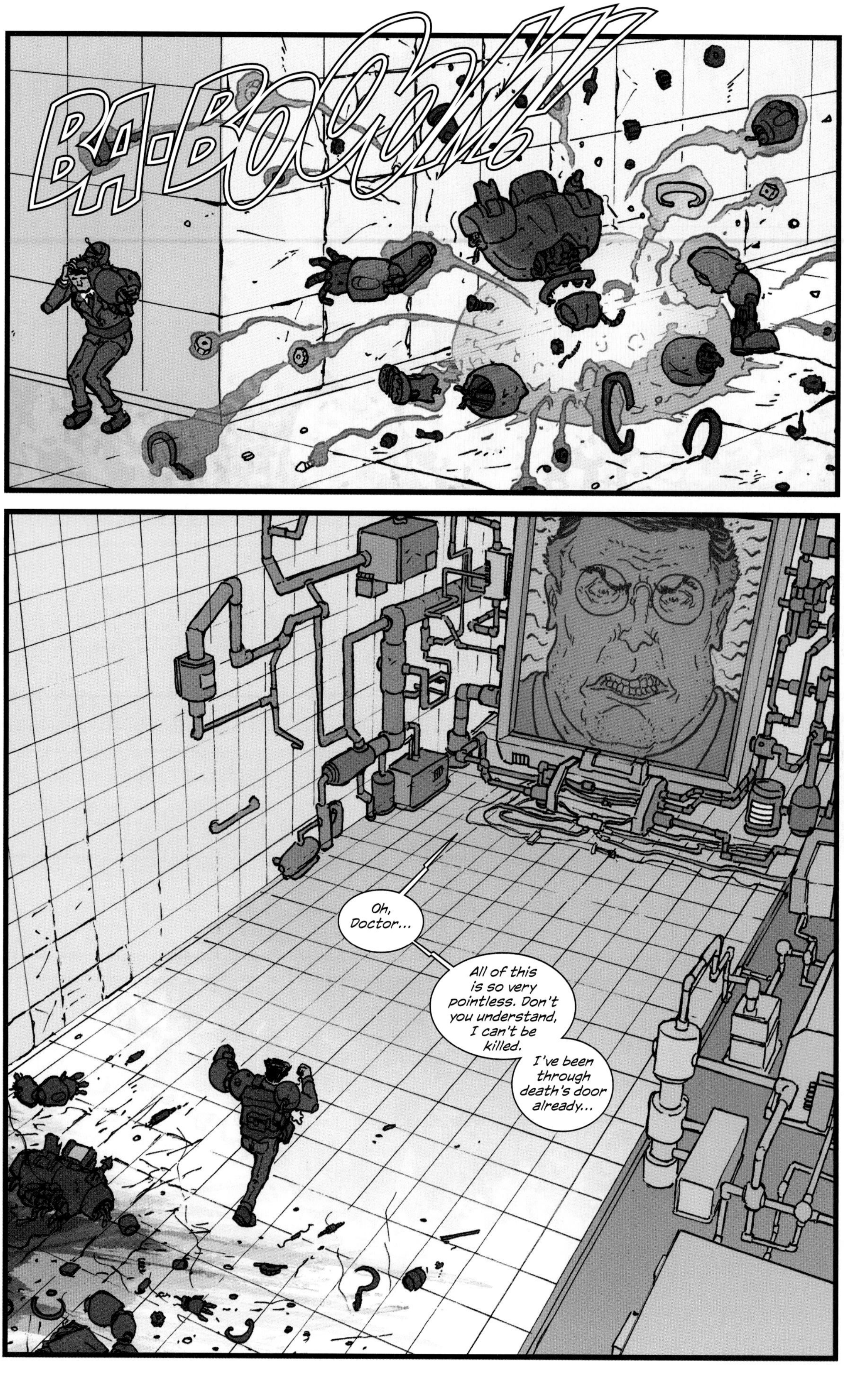
BA-BOOOOM!
Oh, Doctor...
All of this is so very pointless. Don't you understand, I can't be killed.
I've been through death's door already...

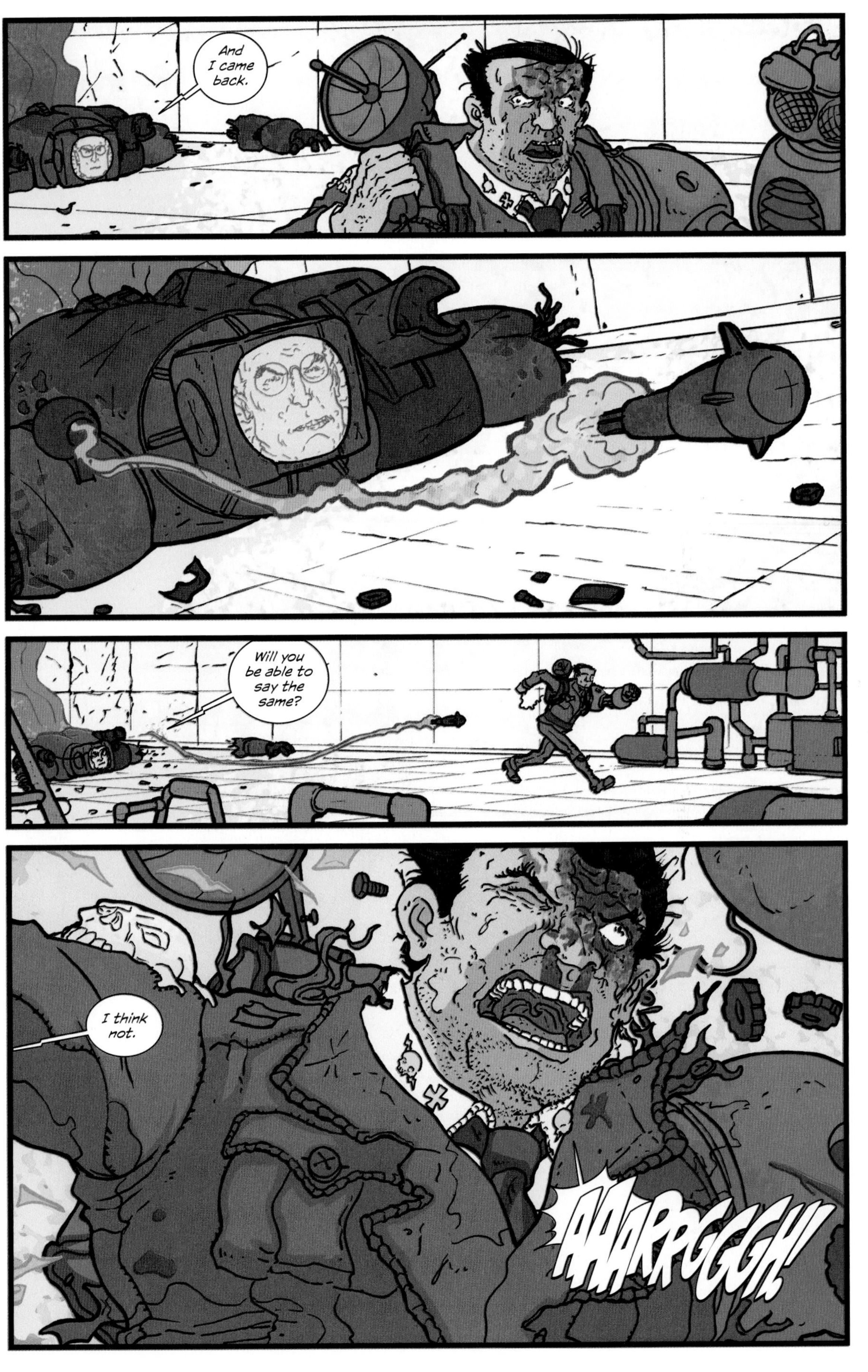

And I came back.
Will you be able to say the same?
I think not.
AAARRGGGH!

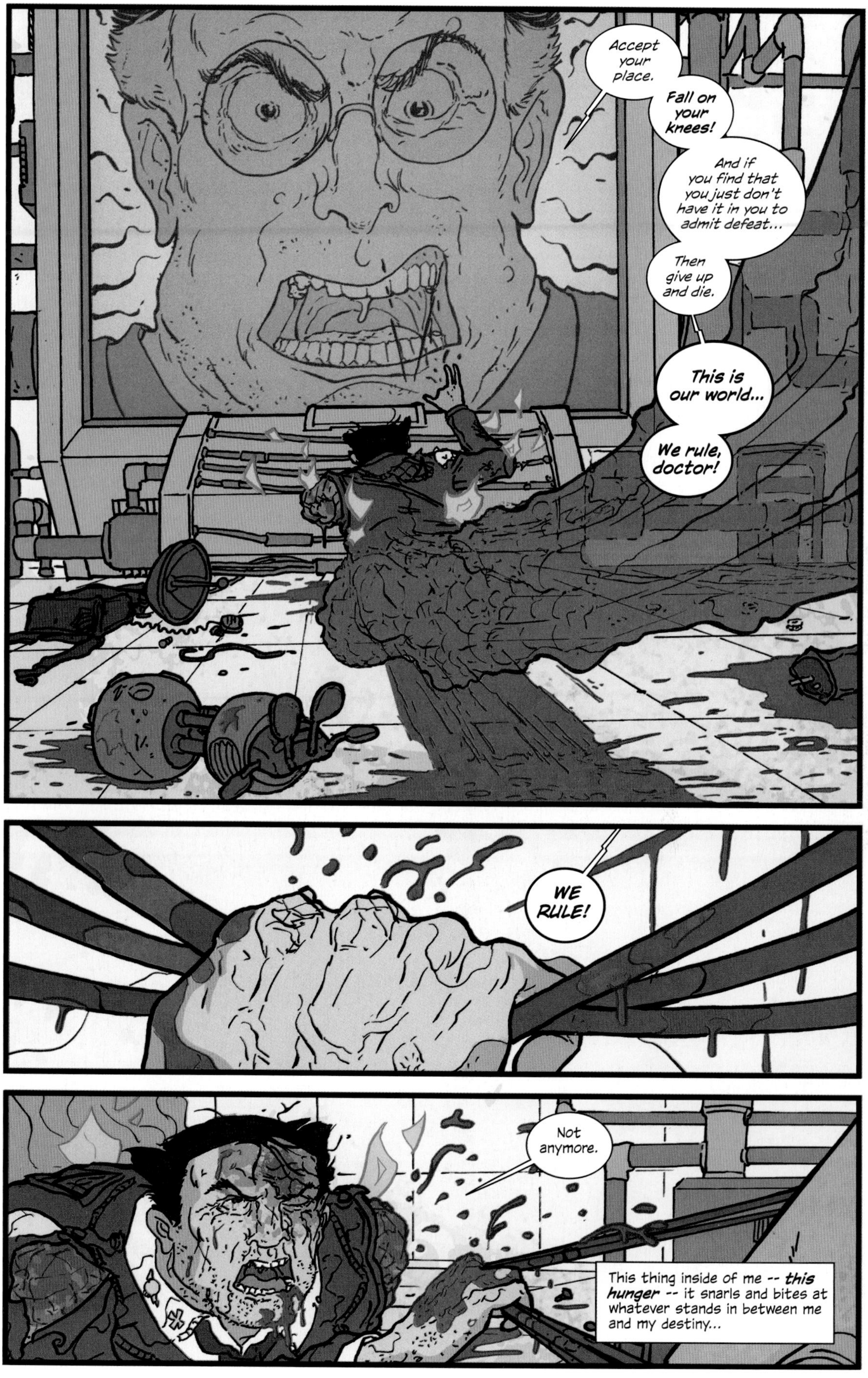
Accept your place.
Fall on your knees!
And if you find that you just don't have it in you to admit defeat...
Then give up and die.
This is our world...
We rule, doctor!
WE RULE!
Not anymore.
This thing inside of me -- this hunger -- it snarls and bites at whatever stands in between me and my destiny...

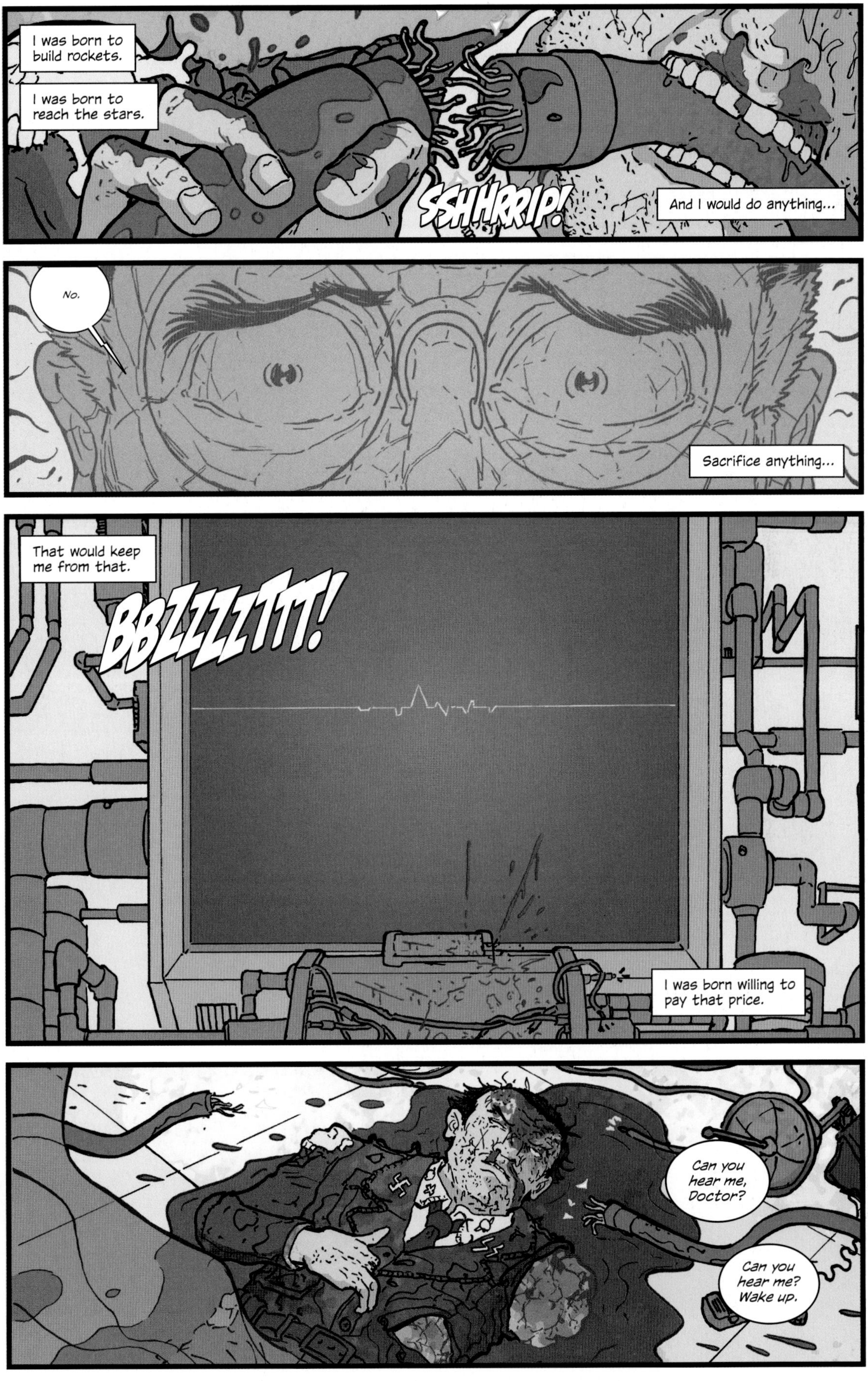
I was born to build rockets.
I was born to reach the stars.
SSHHRRIP!
And I would do anything...
No.
Sacrifice anything...
That would keep me from that.
BBZZZZTTT!
I was born willing to pay that price.
Can you hear me, Doctor?
Can you hear me? Wake up.

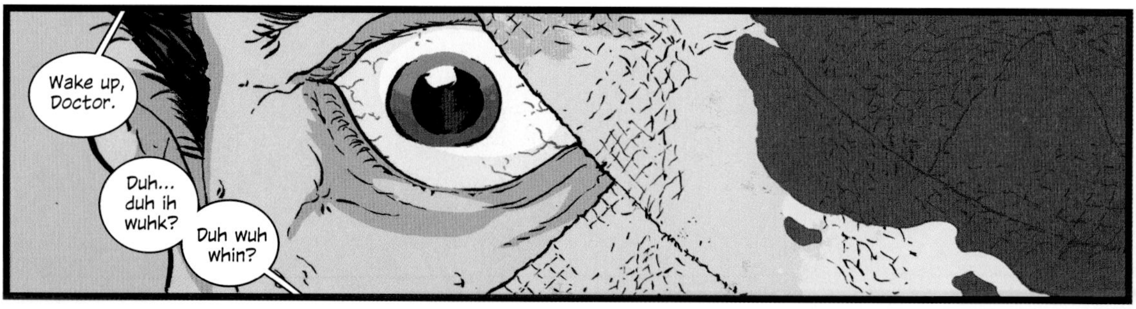
Wake up, Doctor.
Duh... duh ih wuhk?
Duh wuh whin?

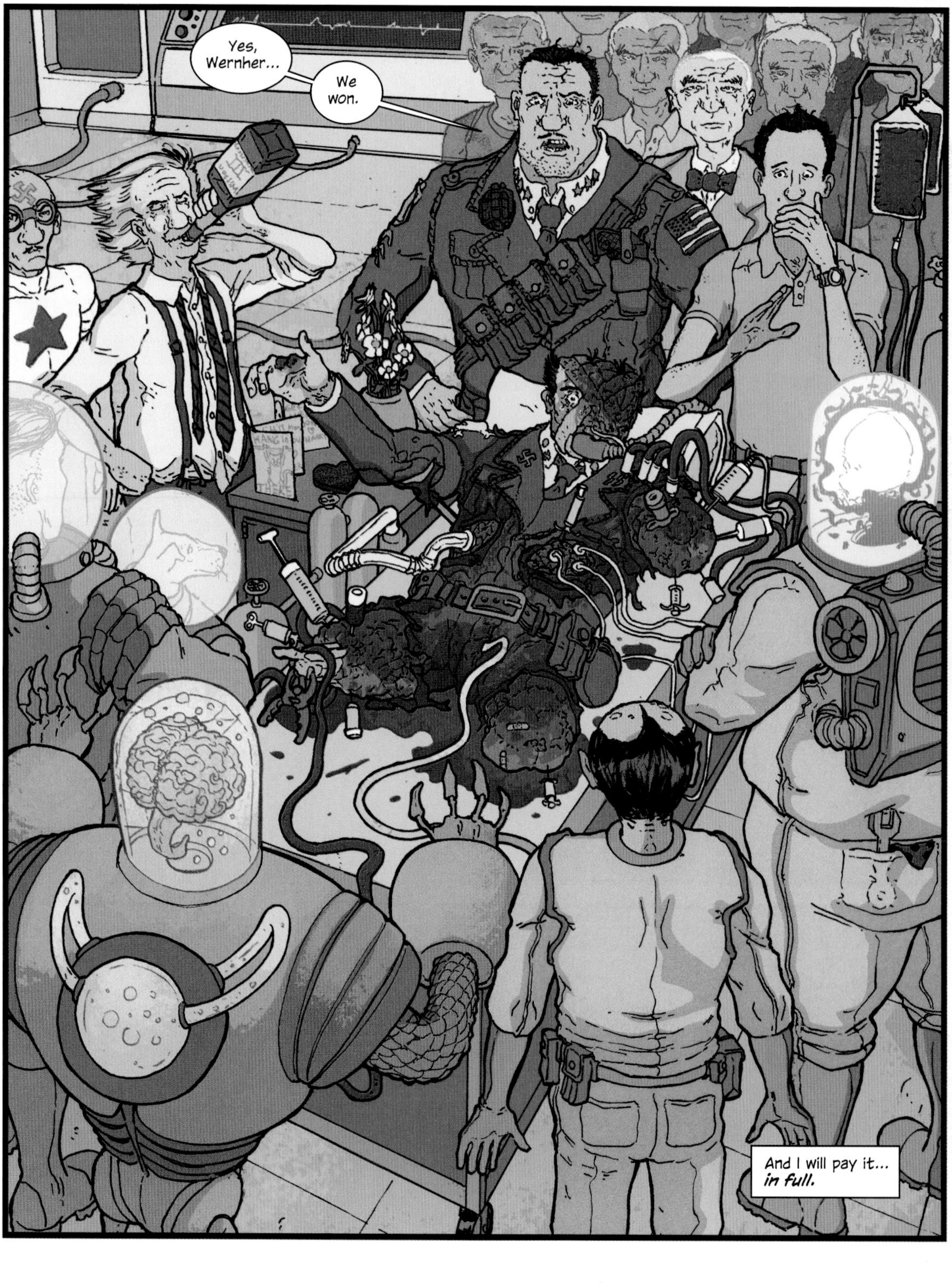
Yes, Wernher...
We won.
And I will pay it... *in full.*

"WHAT DID I CALL THE PLACE BEYOND PAIN, BEYOND LOSS, AND BEYOND SACRIFICE?

COMMITMENT."

- WERNHER VON BRAUN

CLAVIS AUREA
THE RECORDED FEYNMAN | **VOL. 3**

YOU'RE GOING TO KILL ME
AREN'T YOU

"THE WORLD, WHAT IS IT BUT BROKEN DREAMS AND BROKEN MEN...

A THING WELL WORTH HAVING."

CLAVIS AUREA
THE RECORDED FEYNMAN | **VOL. 1**

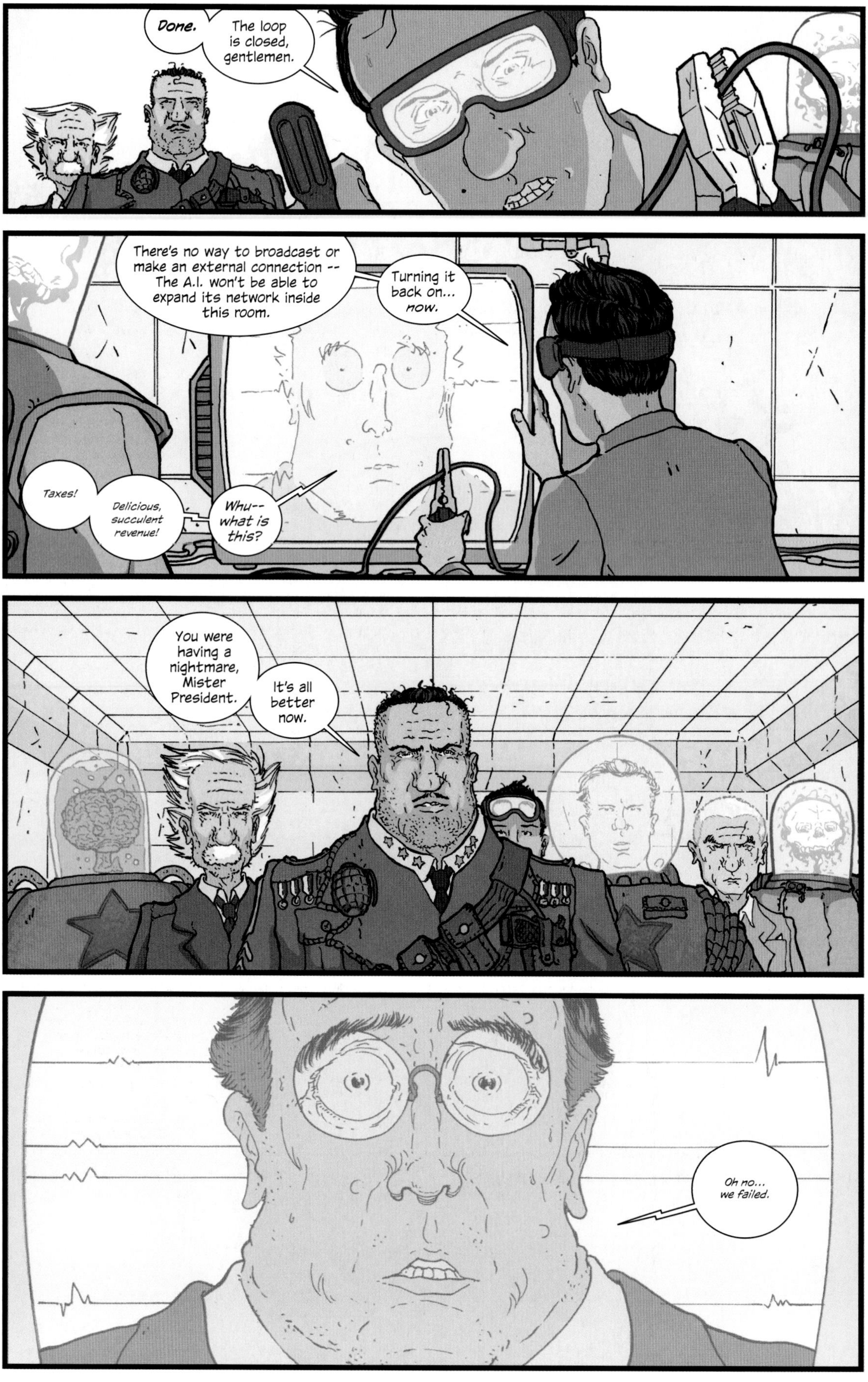
Done.
The loop is closed, gentlemen.
There's no way to broadcast or make an external connection -- The A.I. won't be able to expand its network inside this room.
Turning it back on... now.
Taxes!
Delicious, succulent revenue!
Whu-- what is this?
You were having a nightmare, Mister President.
It's all better now.
Oh no... we failed.

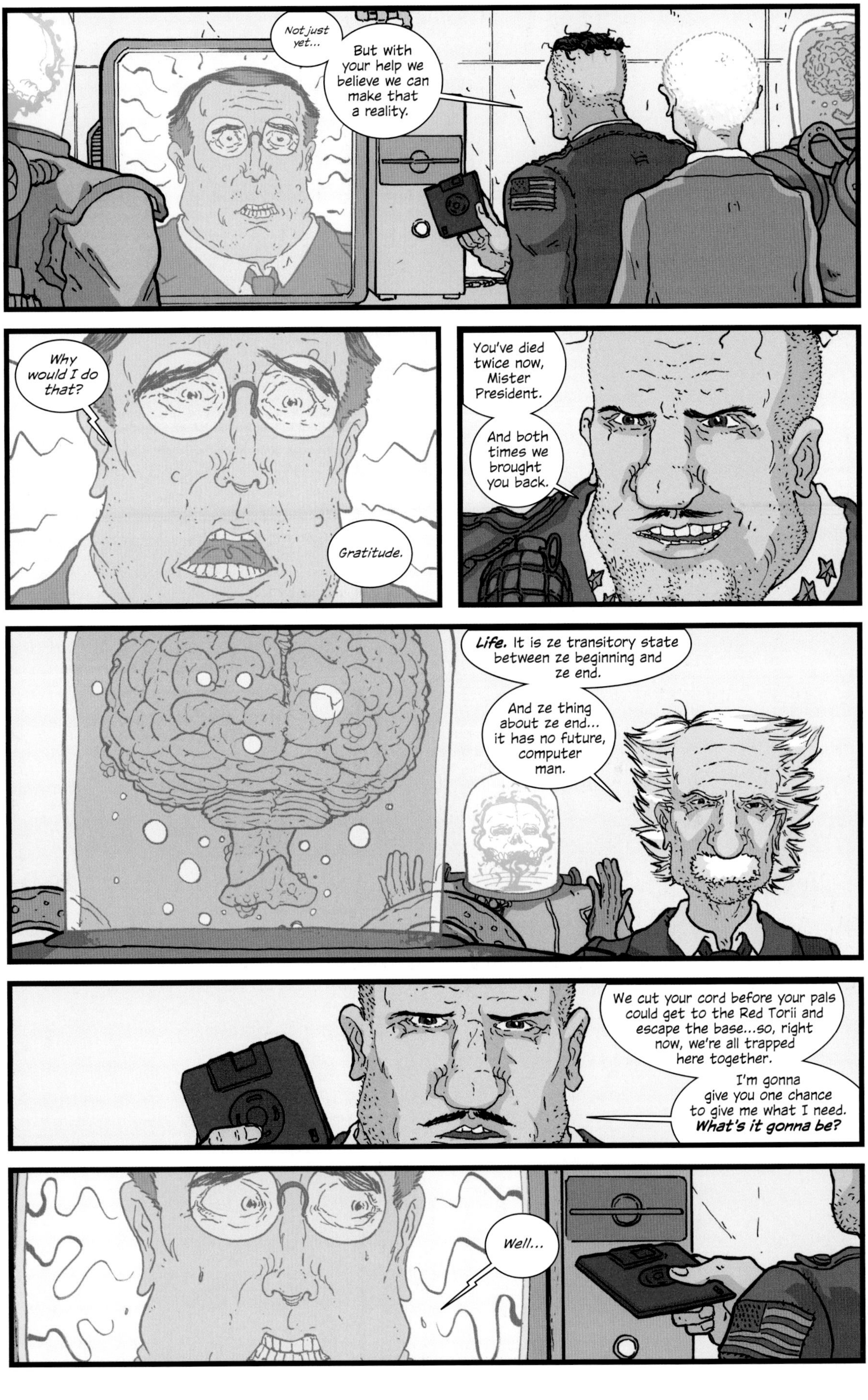
Not just yet...
But with your help we believe we can make that a reality.
Why would I do that?
Gratitude.
You've died twice now, Mister President.
And both times we brought you back.
Life. It is ze transitory state between ze beginning and ze end.
And ze thing about ze end... it has no future, computer man.
We cut your cord before your pals could get to the Red Torii and escape the base...so, right now, we're all trapped here together.
I'm gonna give you one chance to give me what I need. What's it gonna be?
Well...

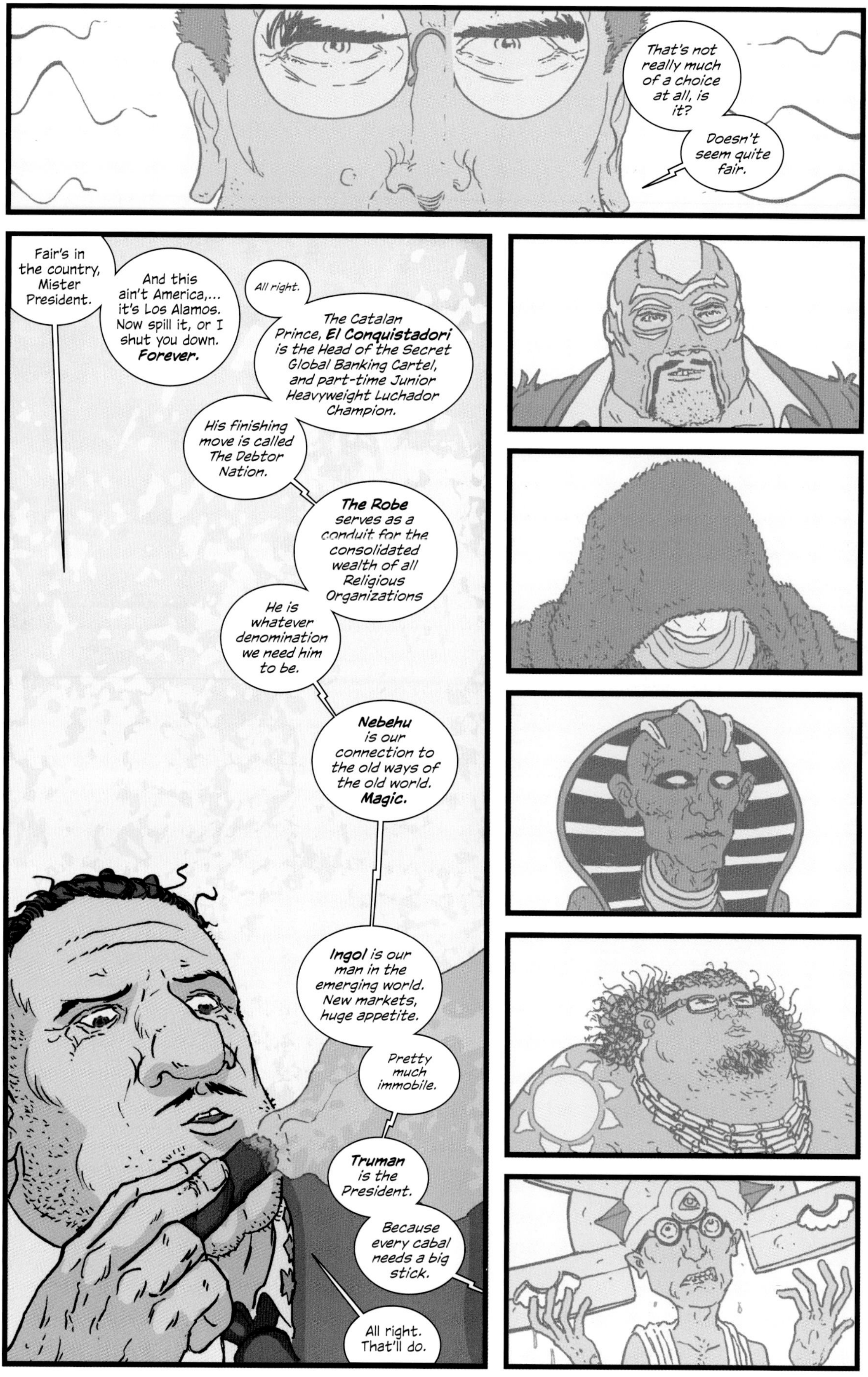

That's not really much of a choice at all, is it?
Doesn't seem quite fair.
Fair's in the country, Mister President.
And this ain't America,... it's Los Alamos. Now spill it, or I shut you down. **Forever.**
All right.
The Catalan Prince, **El Conquistadori** is the Head of the Secret Global Banking Cartel, and part-time Junior Heavyweight Luchador Champion.
His finishing move is called The Debtor Nation.
The Robe serves as a conduit for the consolidated wealth of all Religious Organizations
He is whatever denomination we need him to be.
Nebehu is our connection to the old ways of the old world. **Magic.**
Ingol is our man in the emerging world. New markets, huge appetite.
Pretty much immobile.
Truman is the President.
Because every cabal needs a big stick.
All right. That'll do.

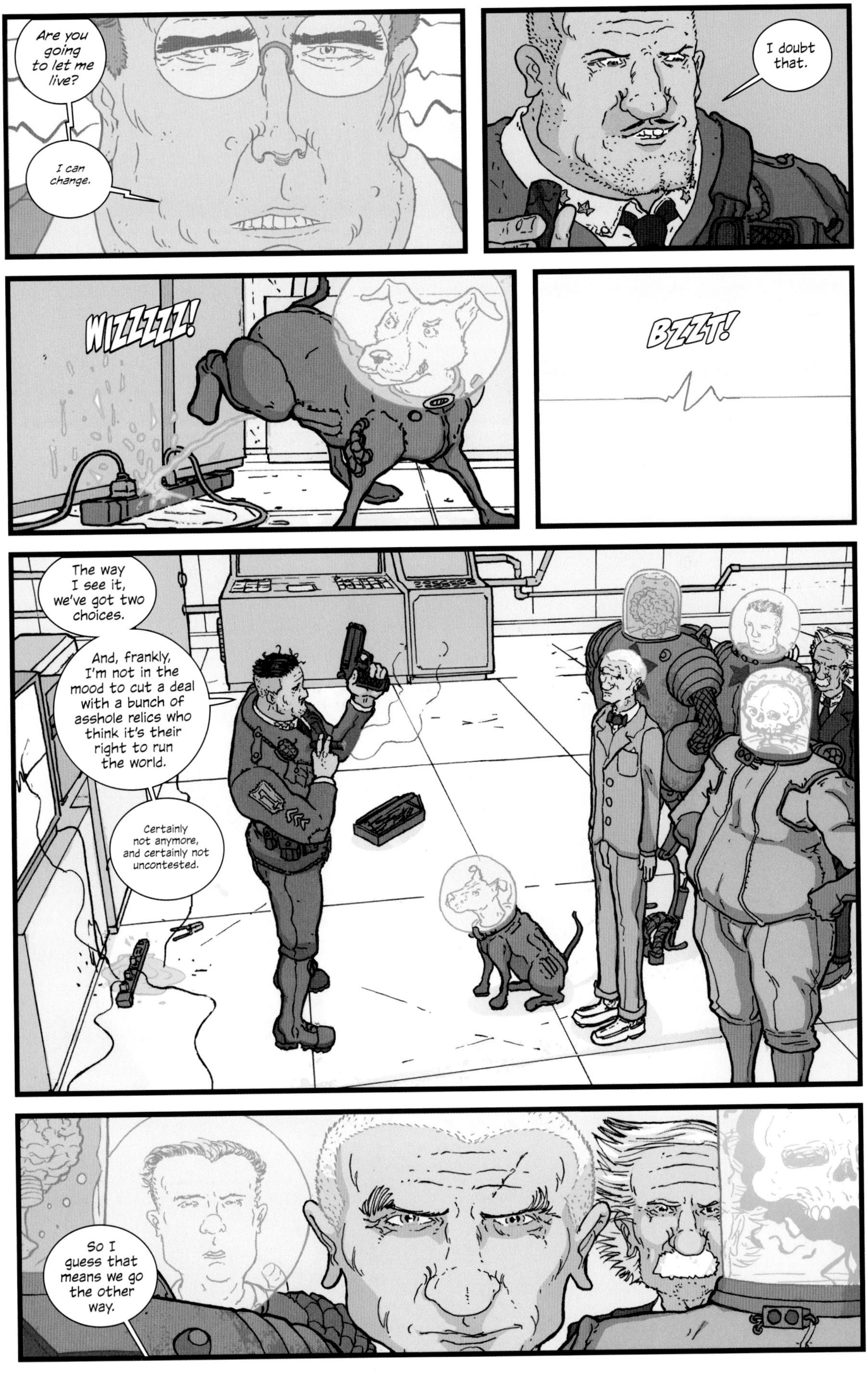

Are you going to let me live?
I can change.
I doubt that.
WIZZZZZ!
BZZT!
The way I see it, we've got two choices.
And, frankly, I'm not in the mood to cut a deal with a bunch of asshole relics who think it's their right to run the world.
Certainly not anymore, and certainly not uncontested.
So I guess that means we go the other way.

09

BRAVE NEW WORLD

"FOR A TIME, WE FORGOT FORGIVENESS
AND THOUGHT ONLY OF REVENGE."

CLAVIS AUREA
THE RECORDED FEYNMAN | **VOL. 2**

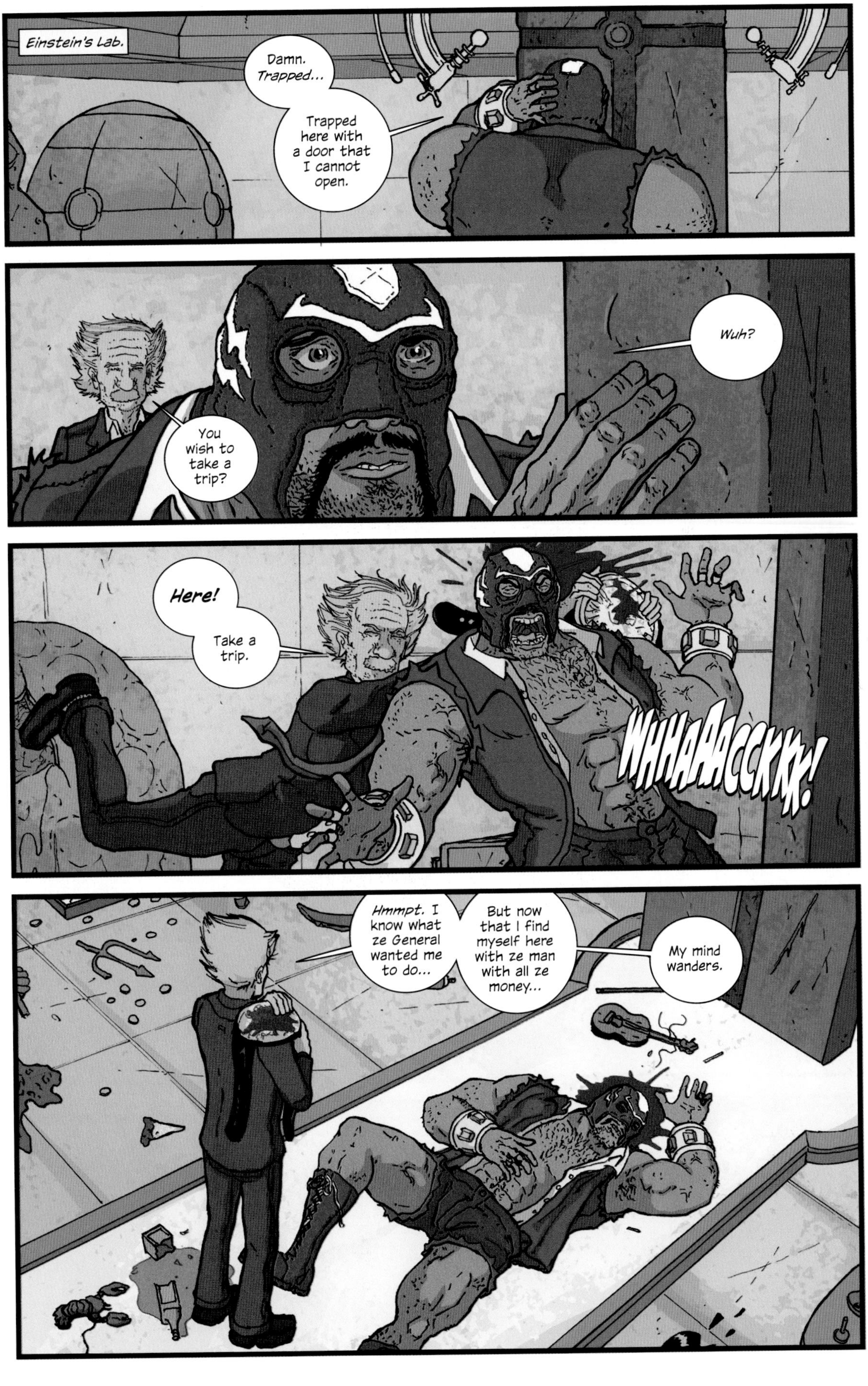

Einstein's Lab.
Damn. *Trapped...*
Trapped here with a door that I cannot open.
You wish to take a trip?
Wuh?
Here!
Take a trip.
WHHAAACCKKK!
Hmmpt. I know what ze General wanted me to do...
But now that I find myself here with ze man with all ze money...
My mind wanders.

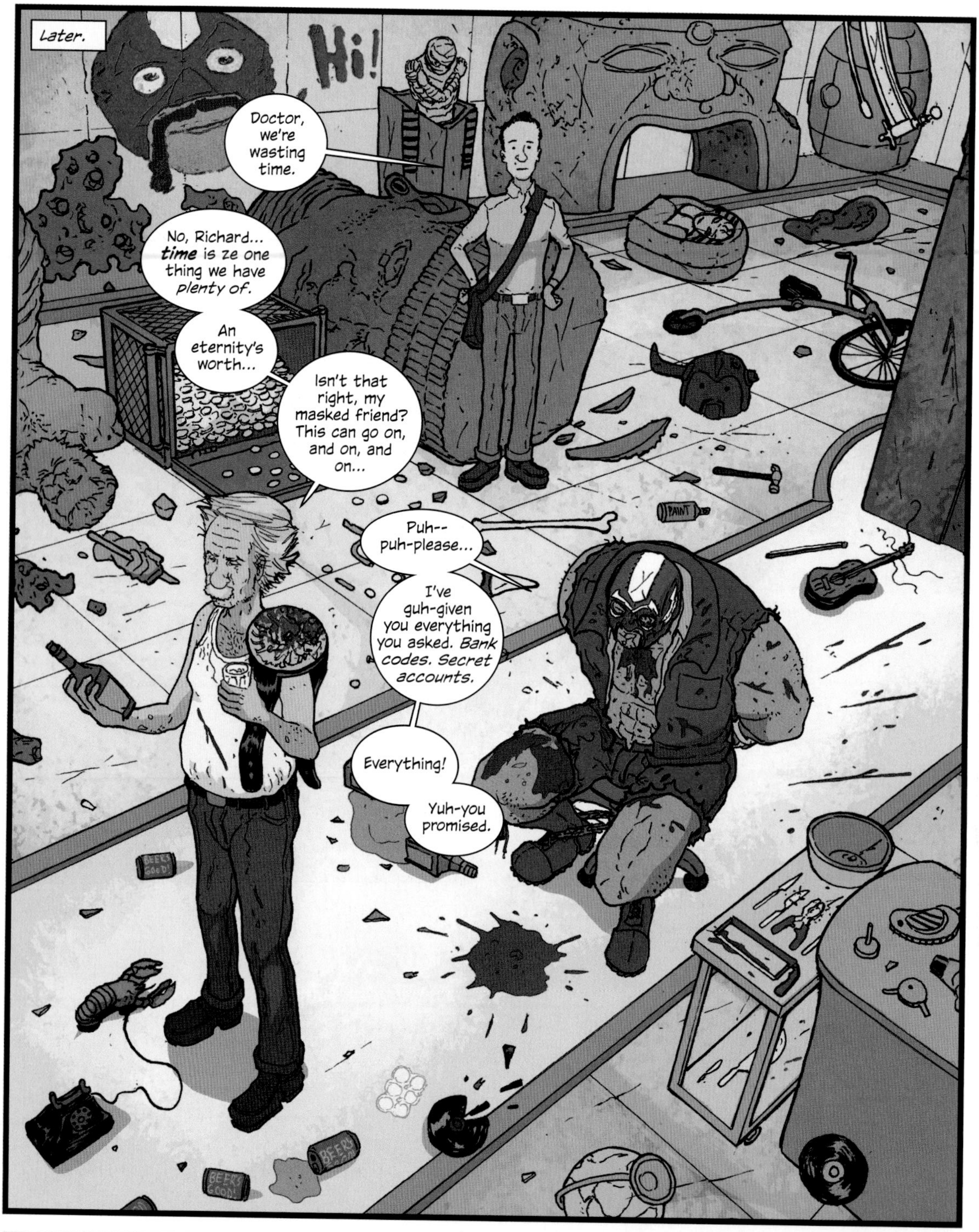
Later.
Hi!
Doctor, we're wasting time.
No, Richard... *time* is ze one thing we have *plenty of.*
An eternity's worth...
Isn't that right, my masked friend? This can go on, and on, and on...
Puh-- puh-please...
I've guh-given you everything you asked. *Bank codes. Secret accounts.*
Everything!
Yuh-you promised.
PAINT
BEER'S GOOD!

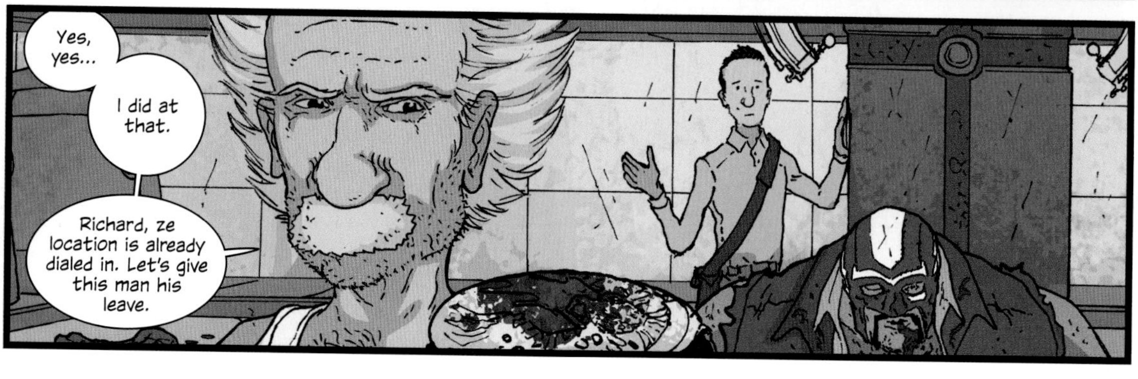
Yes, yes...
I did at that.
Richard, ze location is already dialed in. Let's give this man his leave.

CLICK!

Now, are you sure that you didn't forget something, Luchatadori? Forget misplaced pennies somewhere?

Yes?

No. I..I.. promise.

I swear.

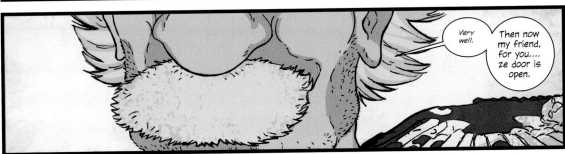

Very well.

Then now my friend, for you.... ze door is open.

Enjoy ze trip.

THUMMP!

AAHHHHHHHH!!!

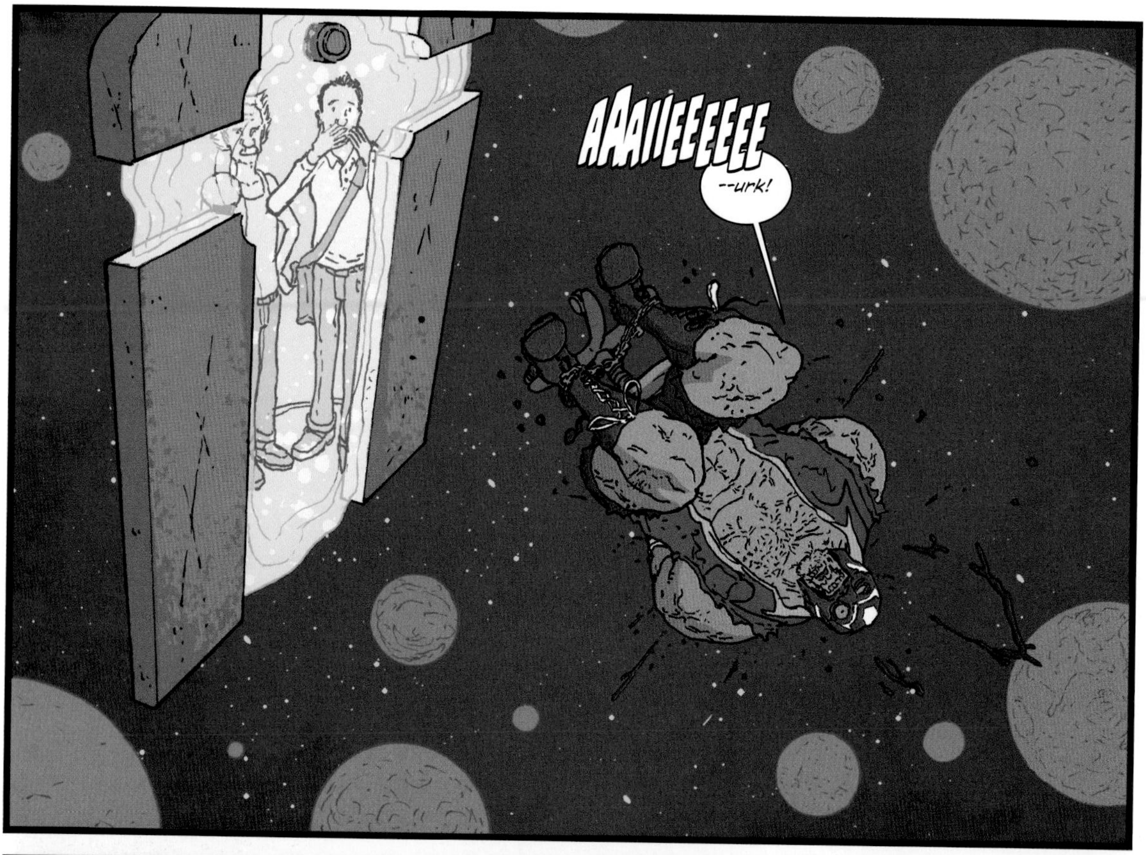
AAAIIEEEEEE
--urk!

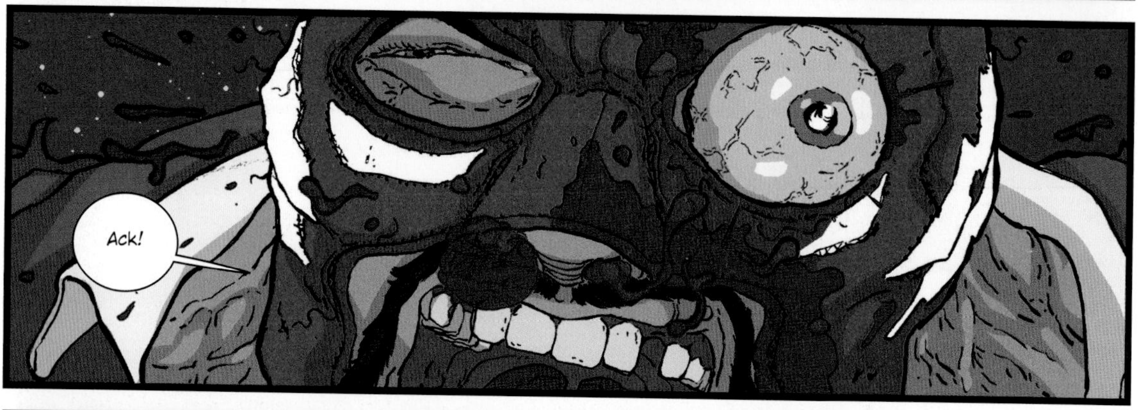
Ack!

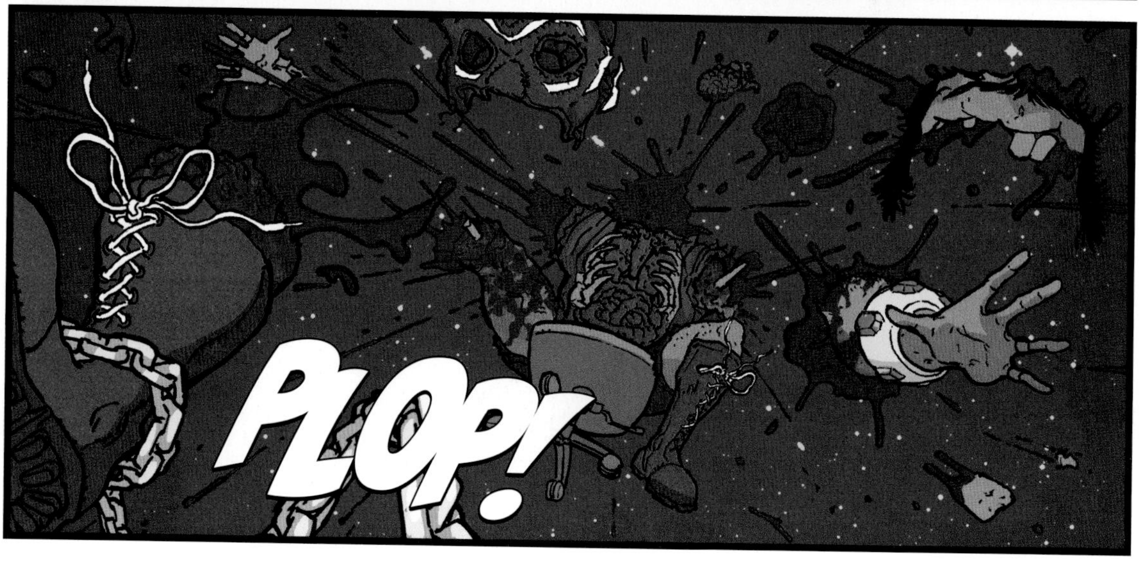
PLOP!

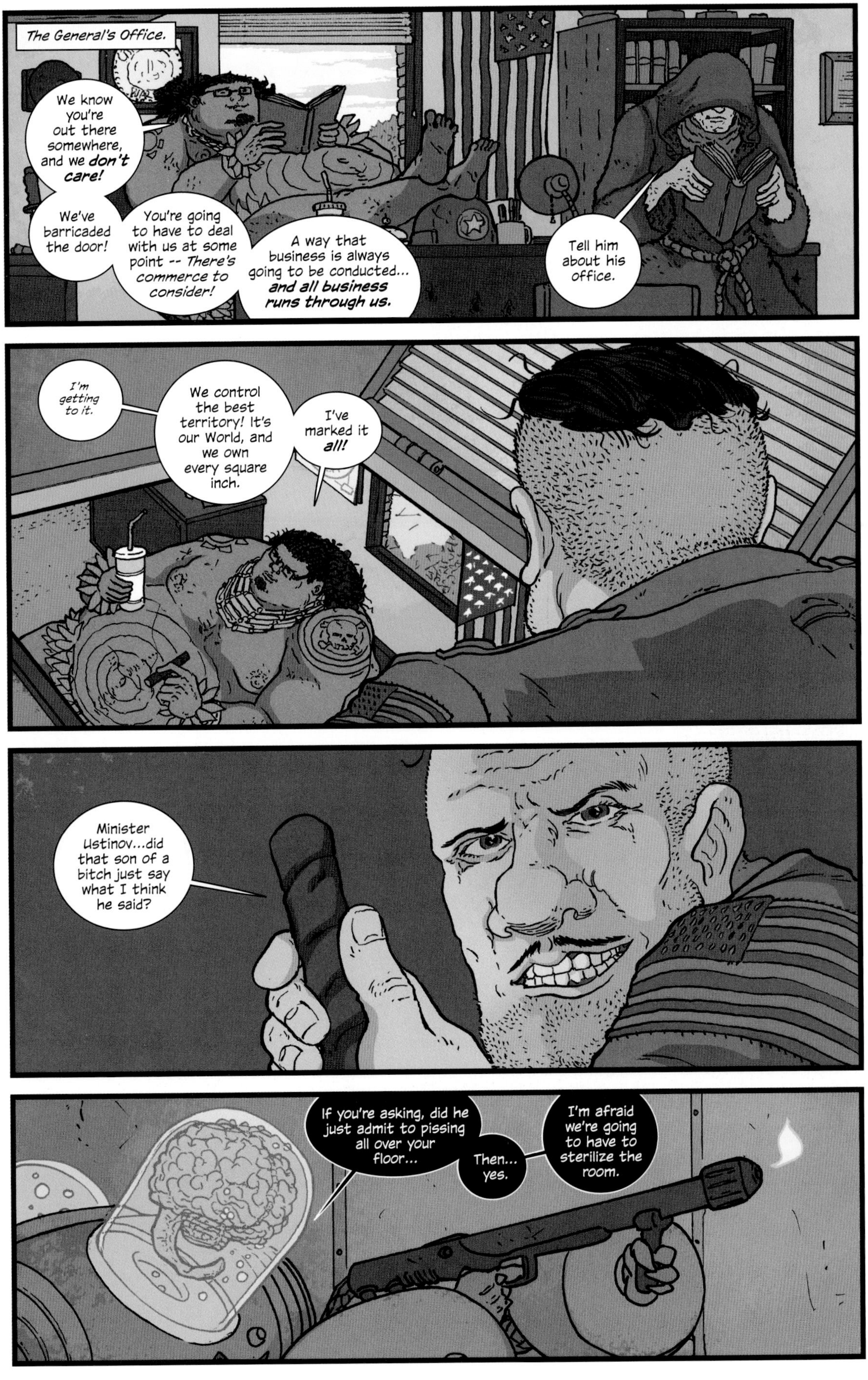

The General's Office.
We know you're out there somewhere, and we **don't care!**
We've barricaded the door!
You're going to have to deal with us at some point -- *There's commerce to consider!*
A way that business is always going to be conducted... **and all business runs through us.**
Tell him about his office.
I'm getting to it.
We control the best territory! It's our World, and we own every square inch.
I've marked it **all!**
Minister Ustinov...did that son of a bitch just say what I think he said?
If you're asking, did he just admit to pissing all over your floor...
Then... yes.
I'm afraid we're going to have to sterilize the room.

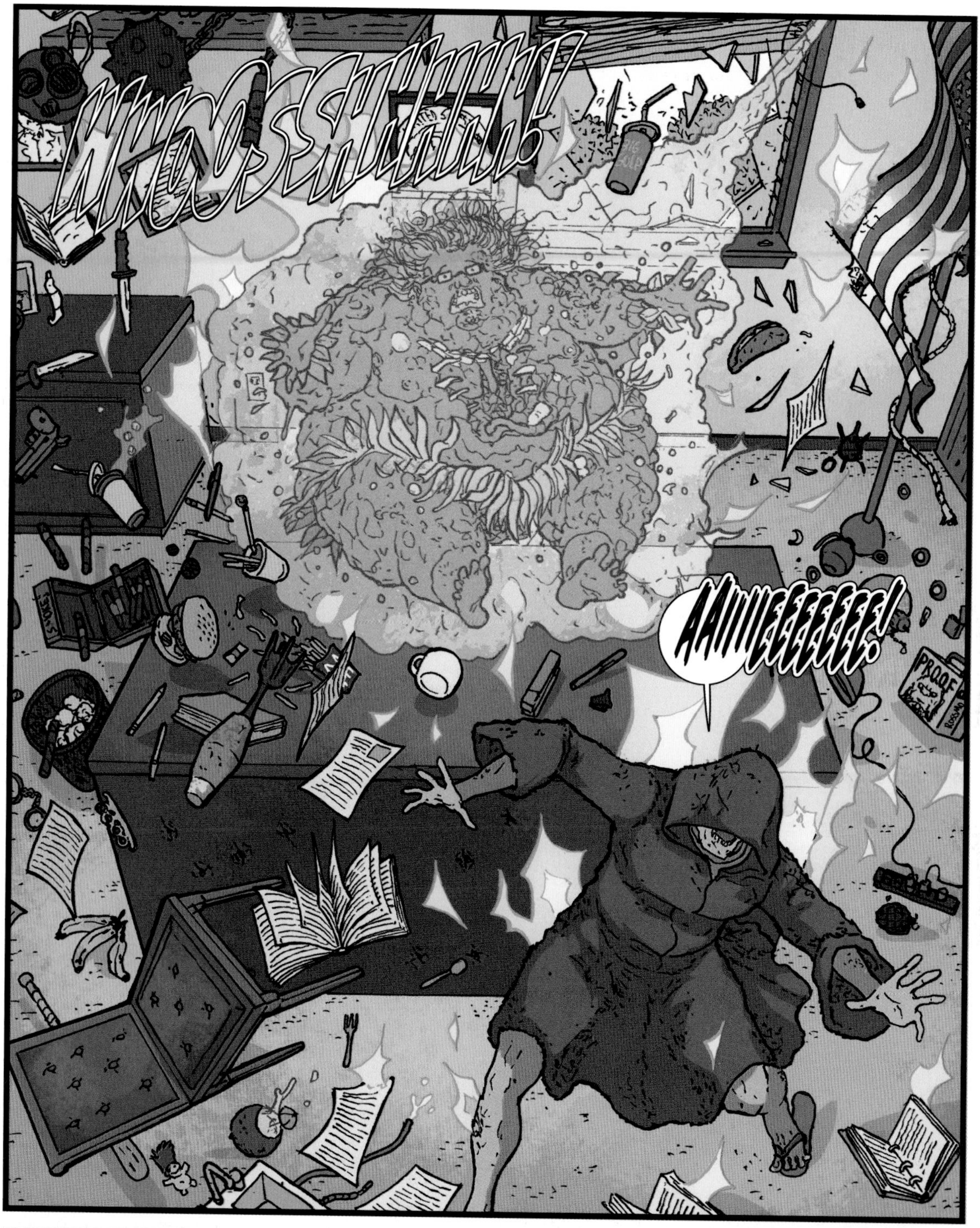
PROOF
AAIIIIEEEEEEE!

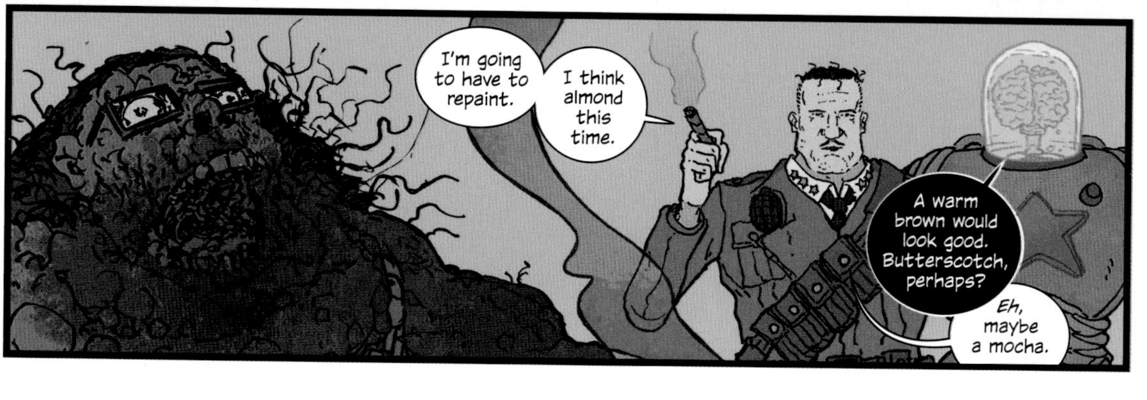
I'm going to have to repaint.
I think almond this time.
A warm brown would look good. Butterscotch, perhaps?
Eh, maybe a mocha.

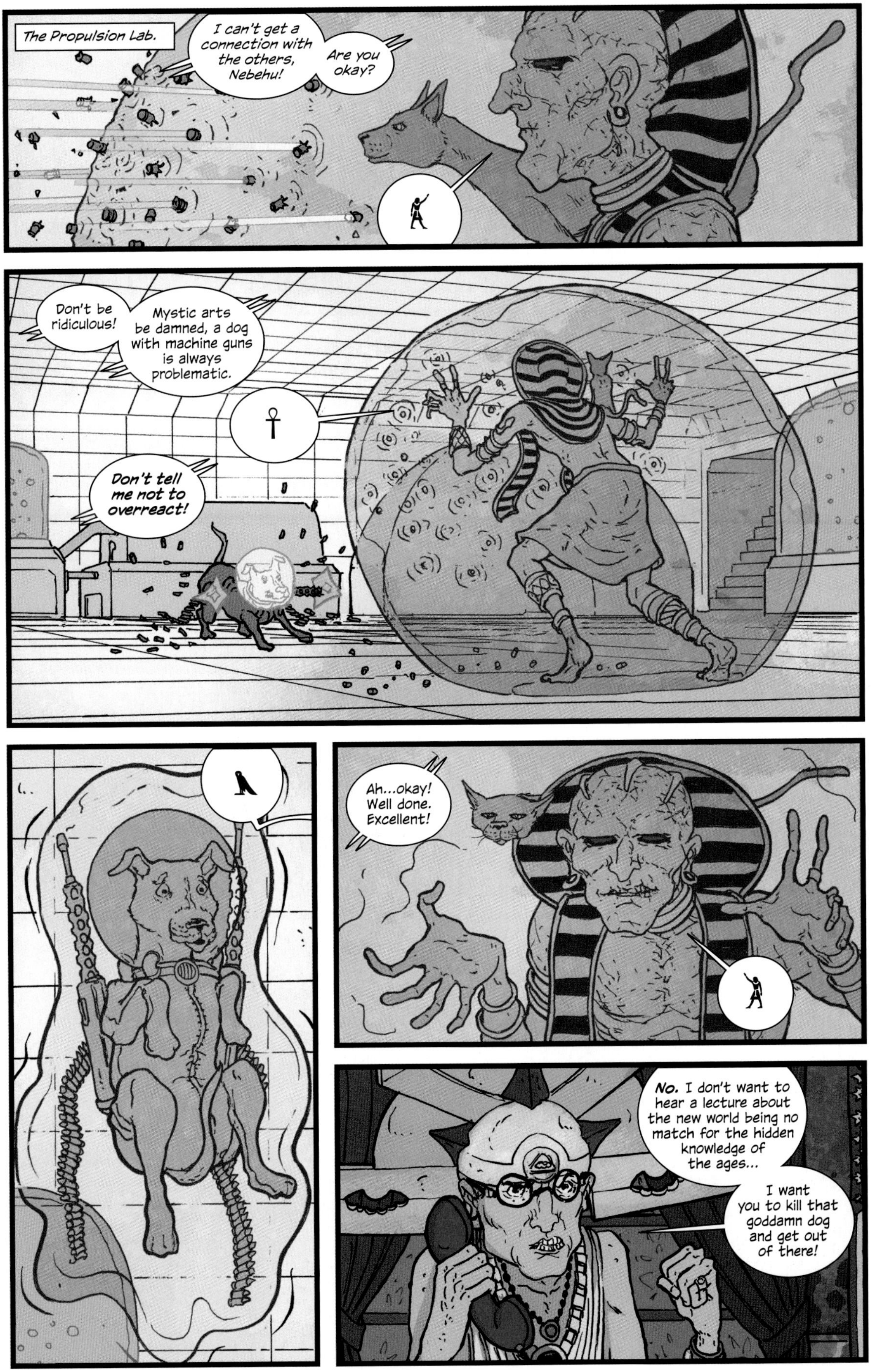
The Propulsion Lab.
I can't get a connection with the others, Nebehu!
Are you okay?
Don't be ridiculous!
Mystic arts be damned, a dog with machine guns is always problematic.
Don't tell me not to overreact!
Ah...okay! Well done. Excellent!
No. I don't want to hear a lecture about the new world being no match for the hidden knowledge of the ages...
I want you to kill that goddamn dog and get out of there!

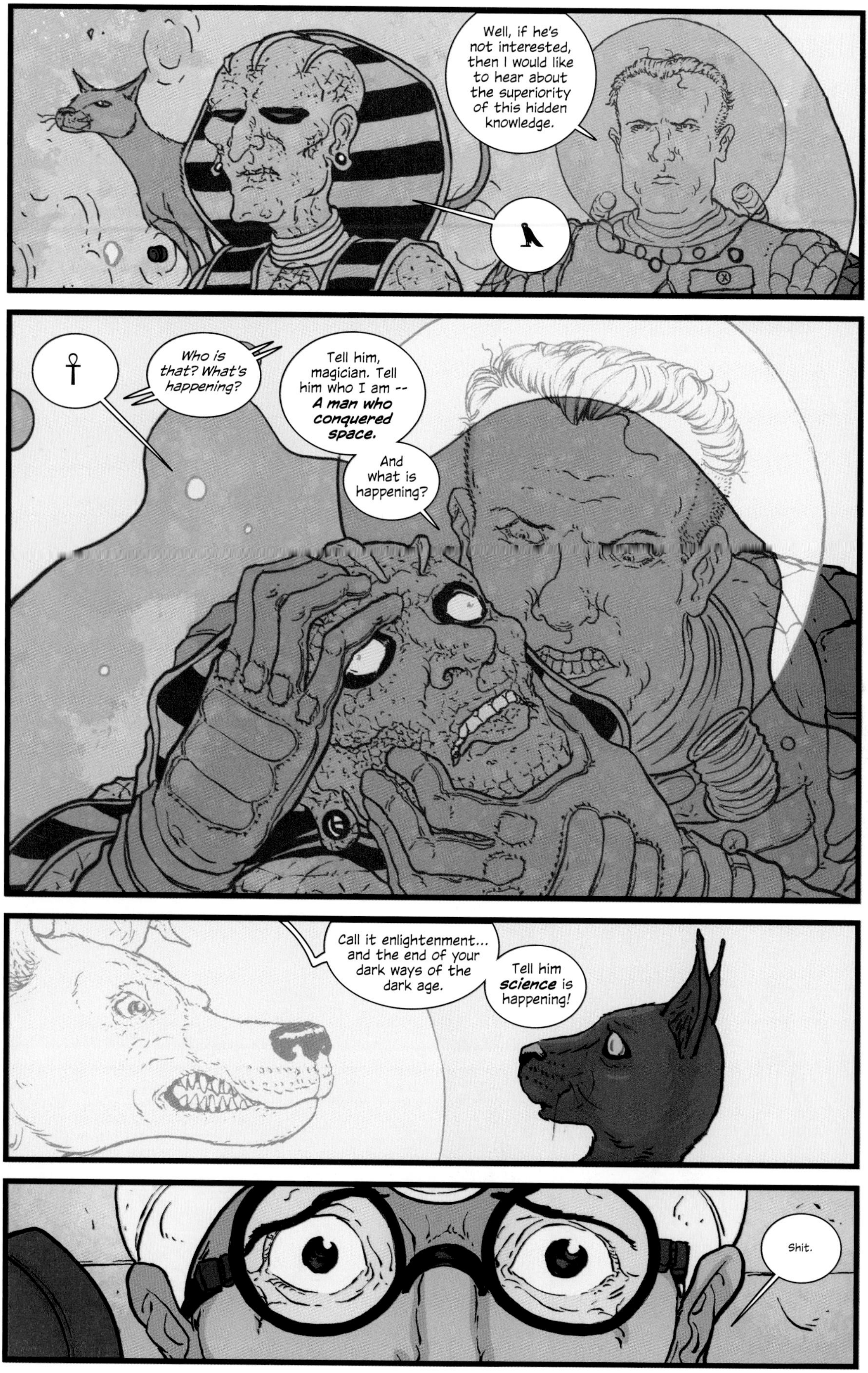
Well, if he's not interested, then I would like to hear about the superiority of this hidden knowledge.
Who is that? What's happening?
Tell him, magician. Tell him who I am -- A man who conquered space.
And what is happening?
Call it enlightenment... and the end of your dark ways of the dark age.
Tell him science is happening!
Shit.

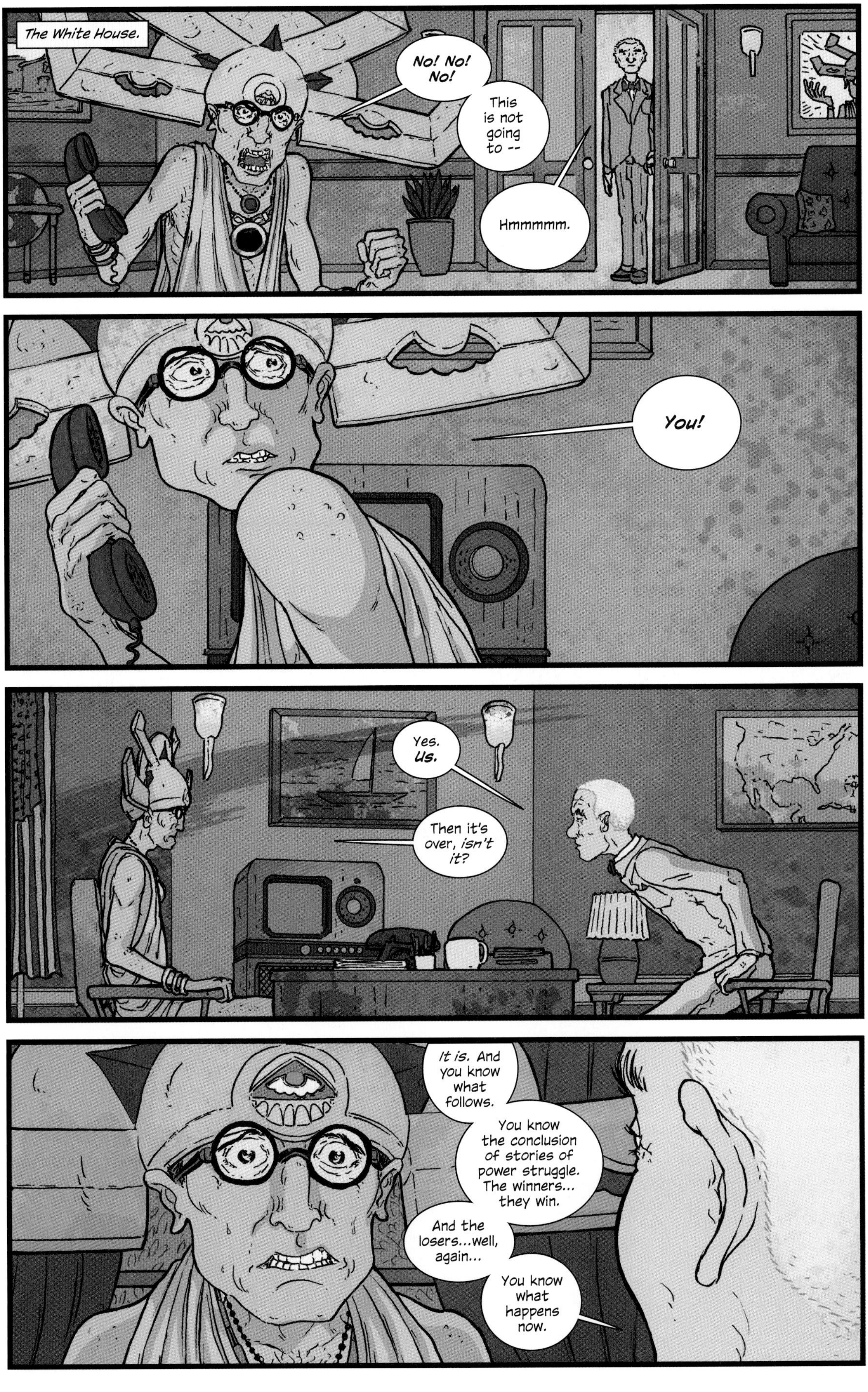

The White House.
No! No! No!
This is not going to --
Hmmmmm.
You!
Yes. Us.
Then it's over, isn't it?
It is. And you know what follows.
You know the conclusion of stories of power struggle. The winners... they win.
And the losers...well, again...
You know what happens now.

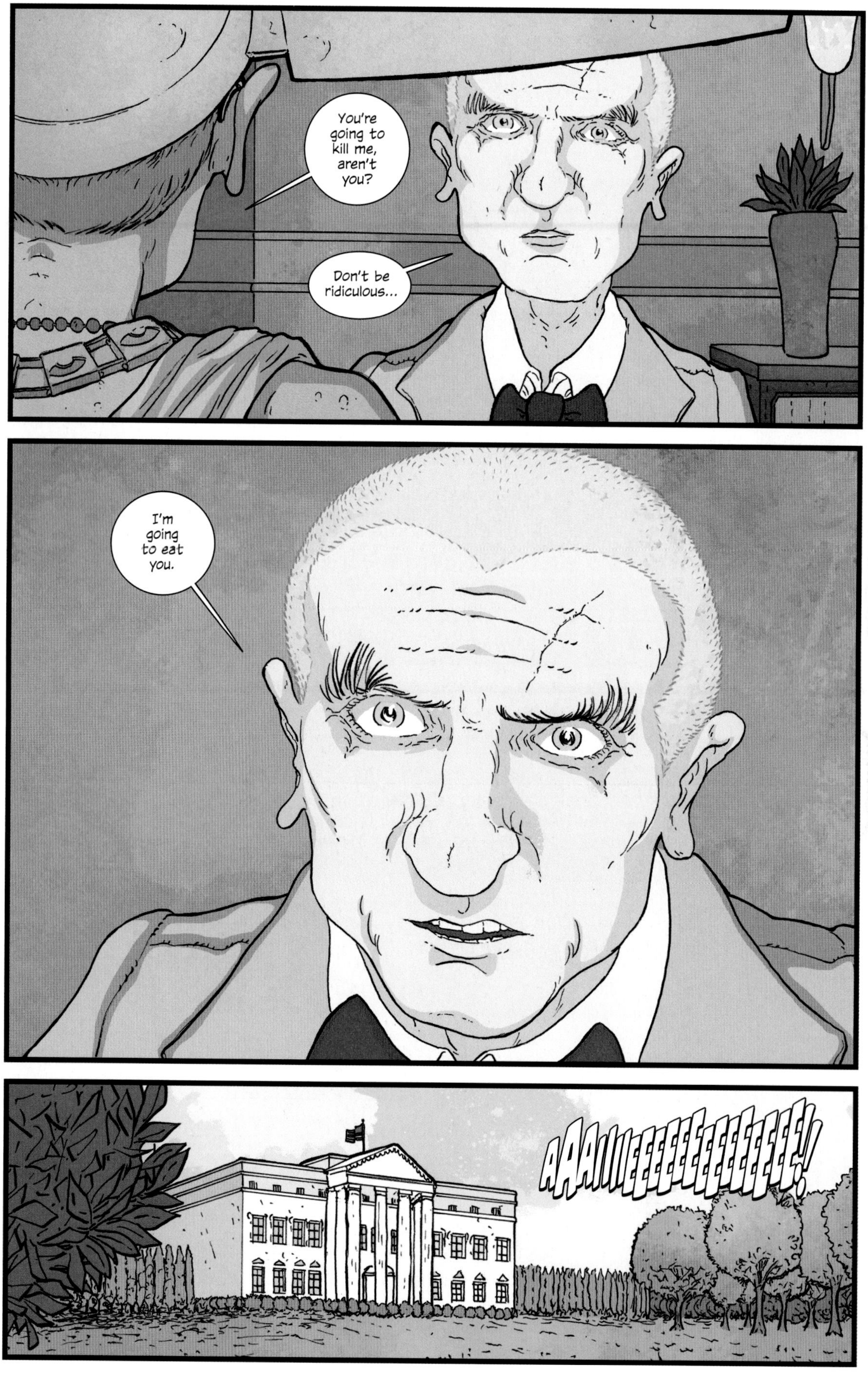
You're going to kill me, aren't you?
Don't be ridiculous...
I'm going to eat you.
AAAIIIEEEEEEEEEEEEEE!!

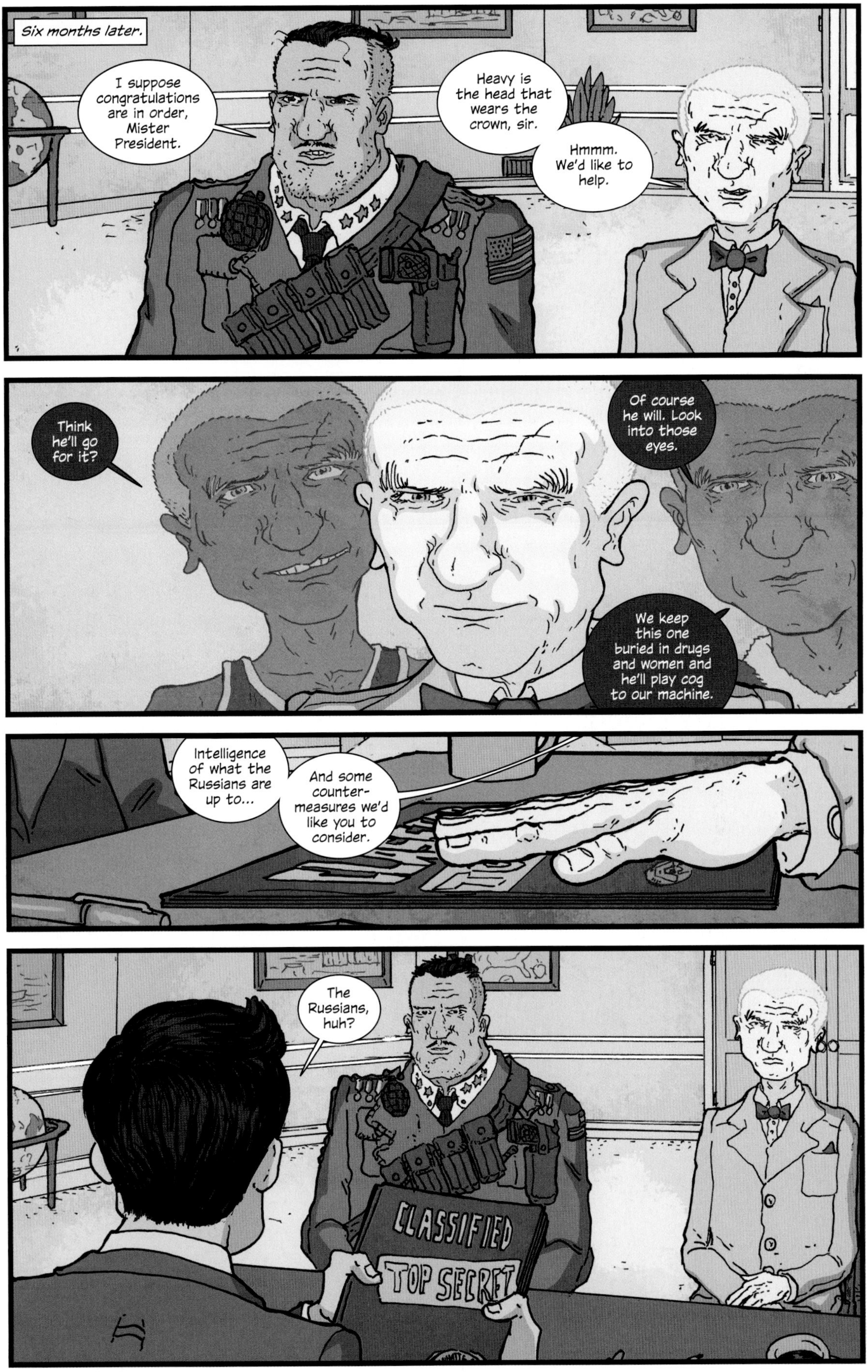
Six months later.
I suppose congratulations are in order, Mister President.
Heavy is the head that wears the crown, sir.
Hmmm. We'd like to help.
Think he'll go for it?
Of course he will. Look into those eyes.
We keep this one buried in drugs and women and he'll play cog to our machine.
Intelligence of what the Russians are up to...
And some counter-measures we'd like you to consider.
The Russians, huh?
CLASSIFIED
TOP SECRET

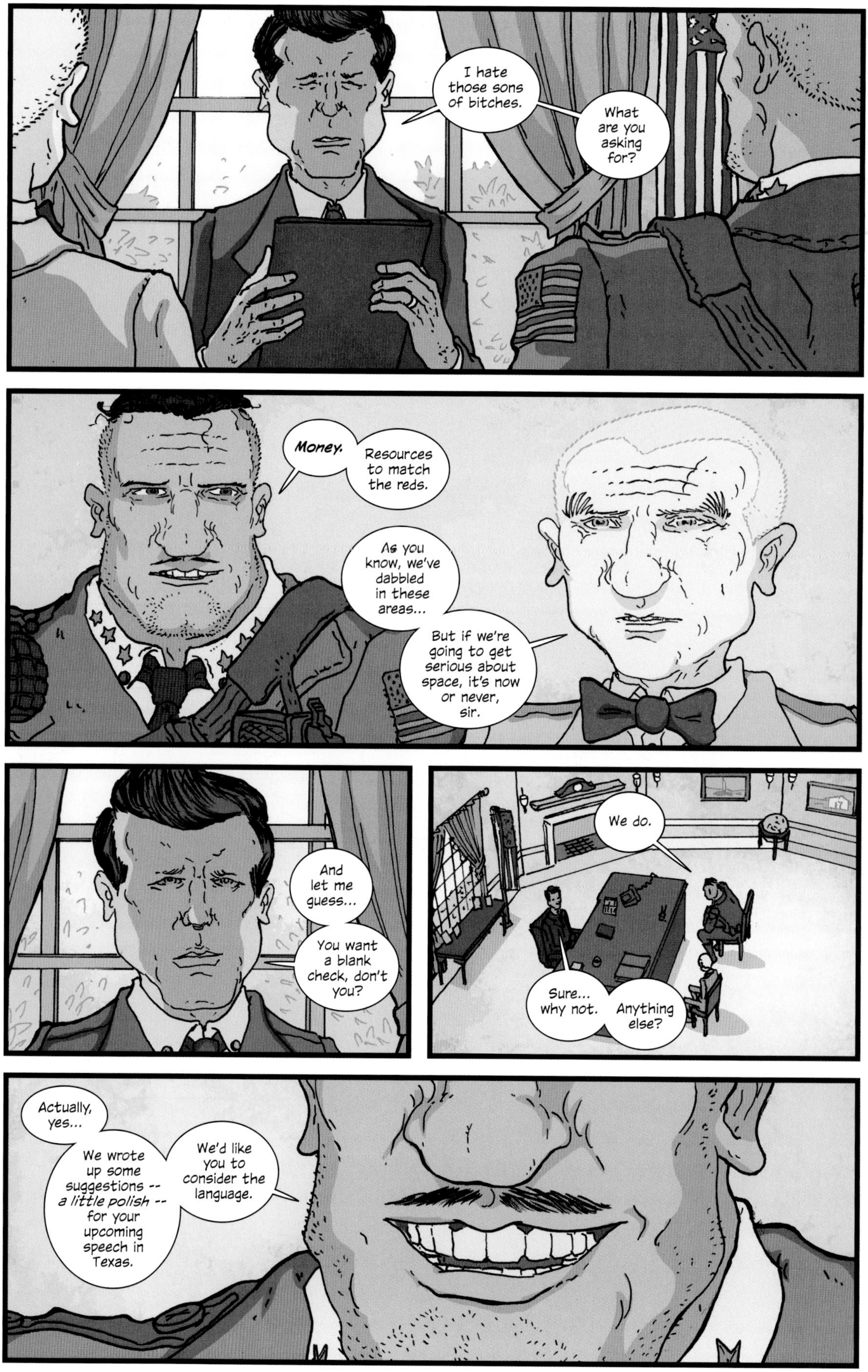
I hate those sons of bitches.
What are you asking for?
Money.
Resources to match the reds.
As you know, we've dabbled in these areas...
But if we're going to get serious about space, it's now or never, sir.
And let me guess...
You want a blank check, don't you?
We do.
Sure... why not.
Anything else?
Actually, yes...
We wrote up some suggestions -- *a little polish* -- for your upcoming speech in Texas.
We'd like you to consider the language.

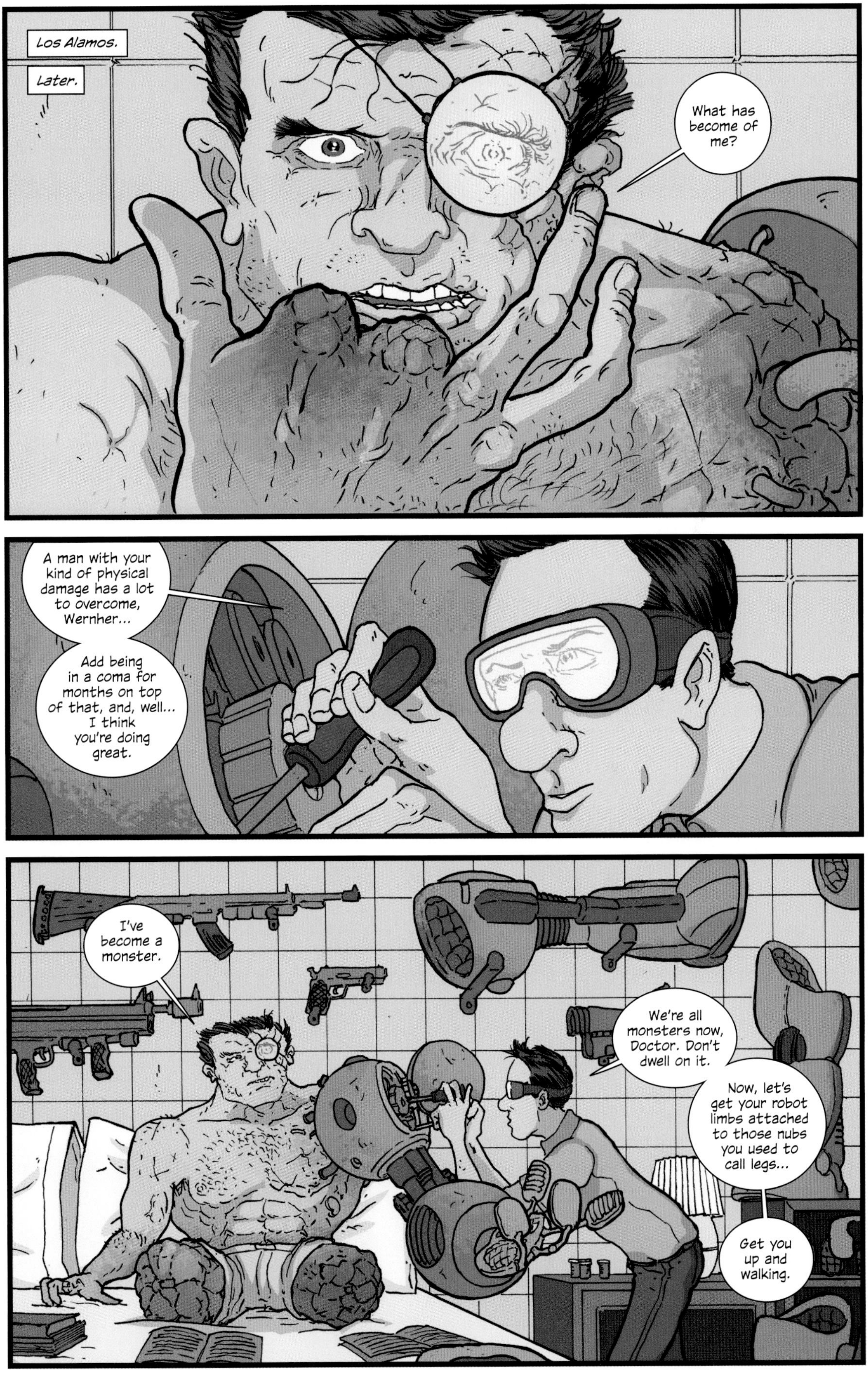
Los Alamos.
Later.
What has become of me?
A man with your kind of physical damage has a lot to overcome, Wernher...
Add being in a coma for months on top of that, and, well... I think you're doing great.
I've become a monster.
We're all monsters now, Doctor. Don't dwell on it.
Now, let's get your robot limbs attached to those nubs you used to call legs...
Get you up and walking.

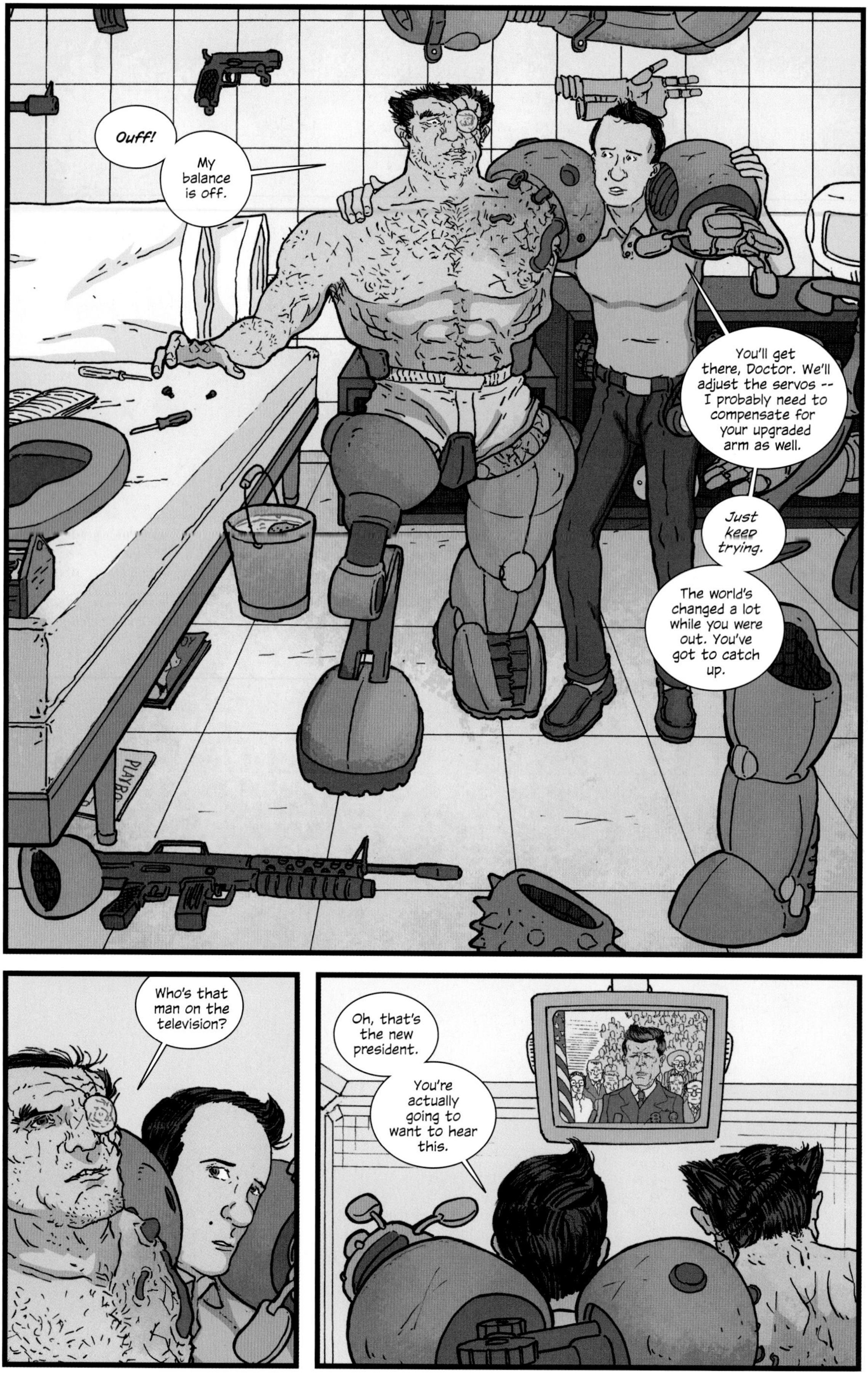
Ouff!
My balance is off.
You'll get there, Doctor. We'll adjust the servos -- I probably need to compensate for your upgraded arm as well.
Just keep trying.
The world's changed a lot while you were out. You've got to catch up.
Who's that man on the television?
Oh, that's the new president.
You're actually going to want to hear this.

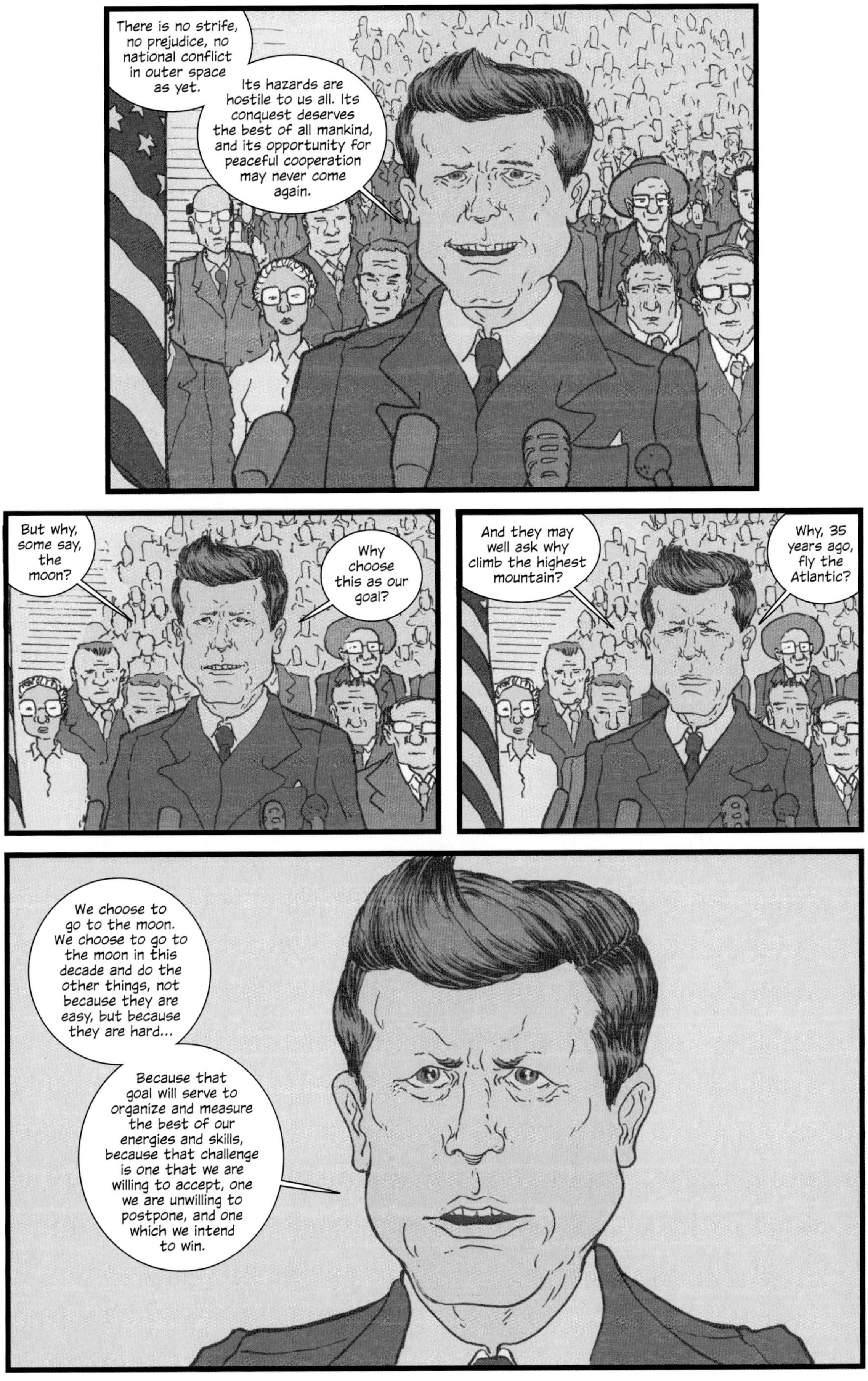
There is no strife, no prejudice, no national conflict in outer space as yet.
Its hazards are hostile to us all. Its conquest deserves the best of all mankind, and its opportunity for peaceful cooperation may never come again.
But why, some say, the moon?
Why choose this as our goal?
And they may well ask why climb the highest mountain?
Why, 35 years ago, fly the Atlantic?
We choose to go to the moon. We choose to go to the moon in this decade and do the other things, not because they are easy, but because they are hard...
Because that goal will serve to organize and measure the best of our energies and skills, because that challenge is one that we are willing to accept, one we are unwilling to postpone, and one which we intend to win.

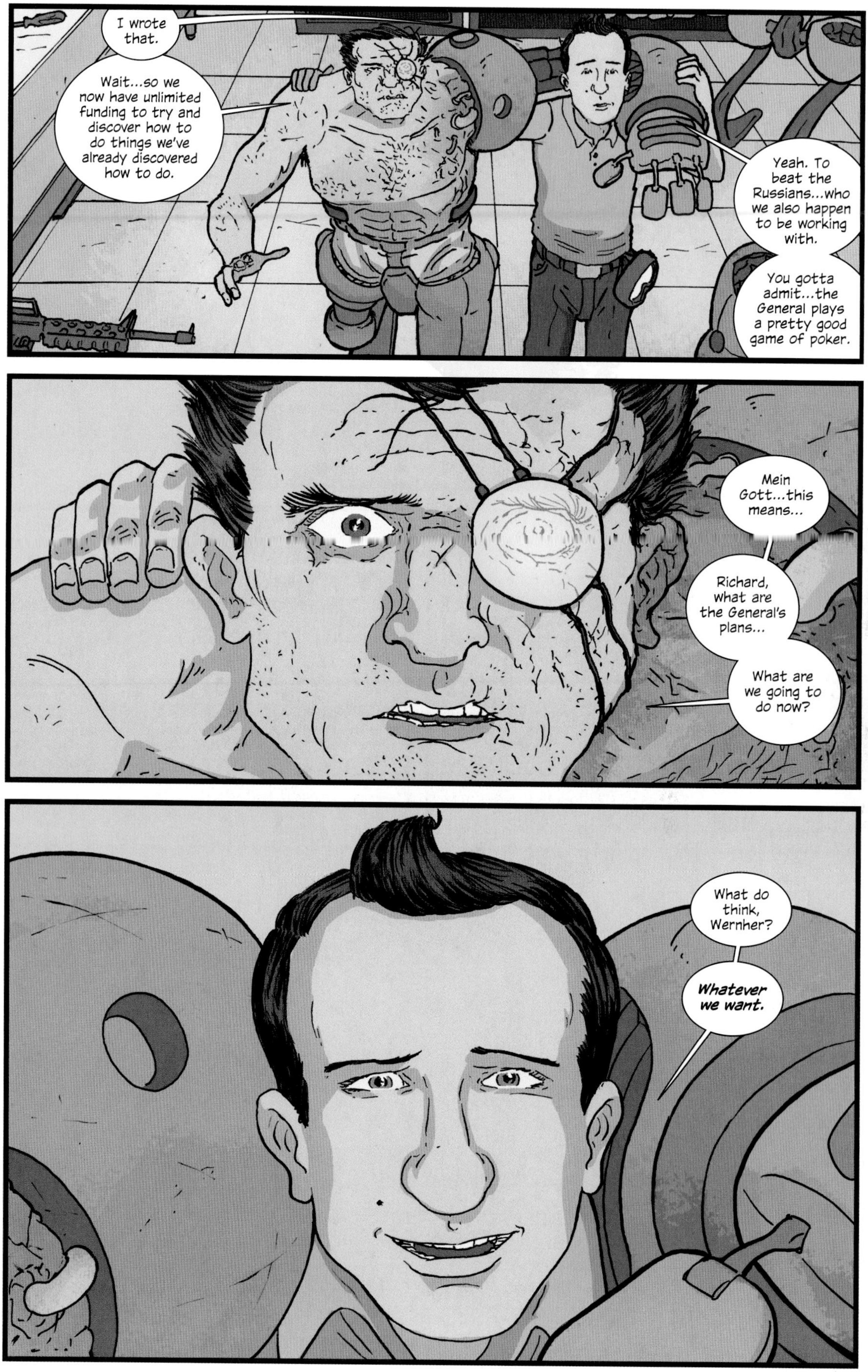
I wrote that.
Wait...so we now have unlimited funding to try and discover how to do things we've already discovered how to do.
Yeah. To beat the Russians...who we also happen to be working with.
You gotta admit...the General plays a pretty good game of poker.
Mein Gott...this means...
Richard, what are the General's plans...
What are we going to do now?
What do think, Wernher?
Whatever we want.

"...AND THAT WAS HOW WE CAME TO CONTROL IT ALL."

CLAVIS AUREA
THE RECORDED FEYNMAN

VOL. 3

HE FELT
GRATEFUL

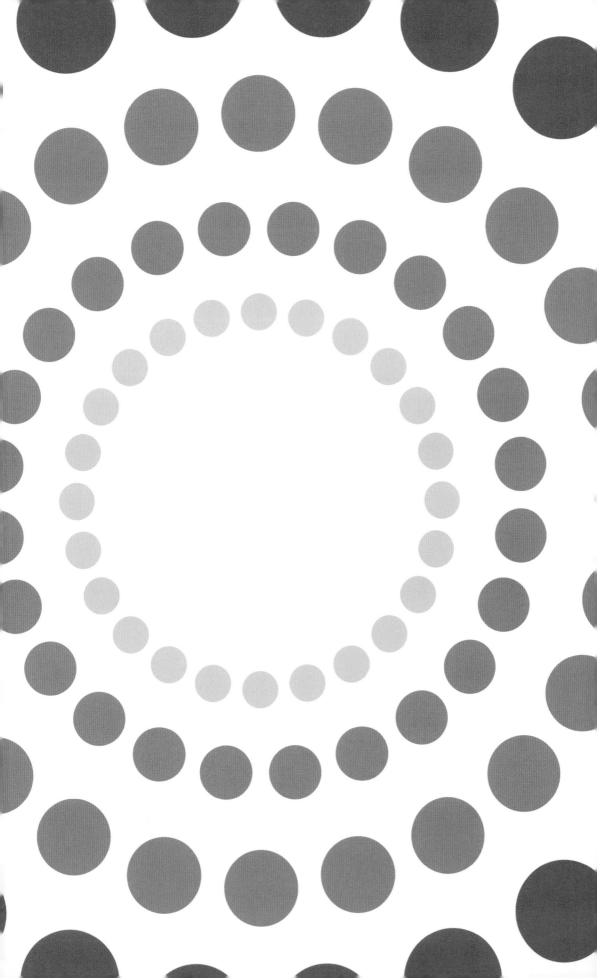

"THE GREAT EYE OF JOSEPH WATCHED OVER THEM ALL. THIS IS HOW THE WAR BEGAN."

- OPPENHEIMER

CLAVIS AUREA
THE RECORDED FEYNMAN | **VOL. 3**

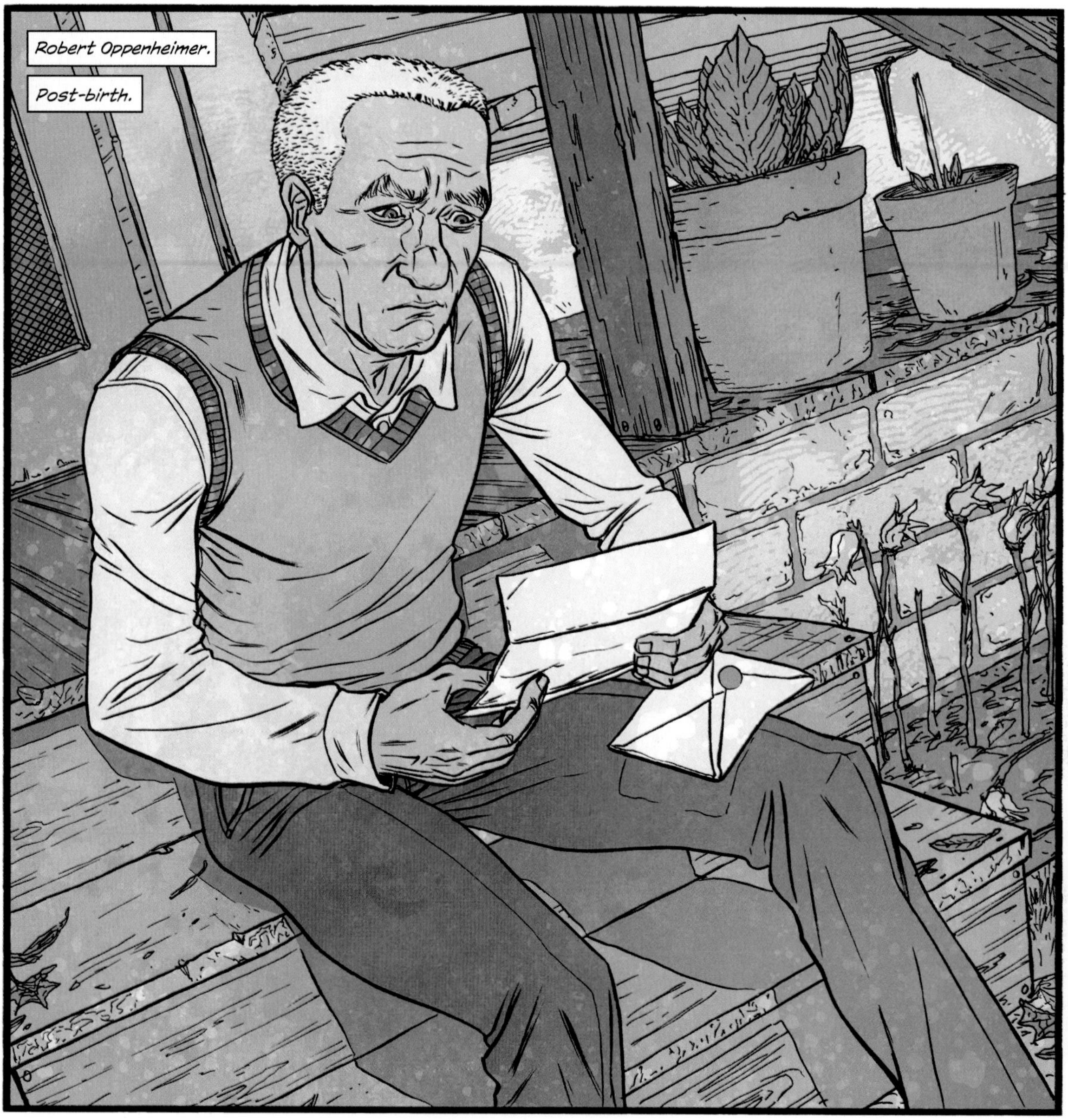
Robert Oppenheimer.
Post-birth.

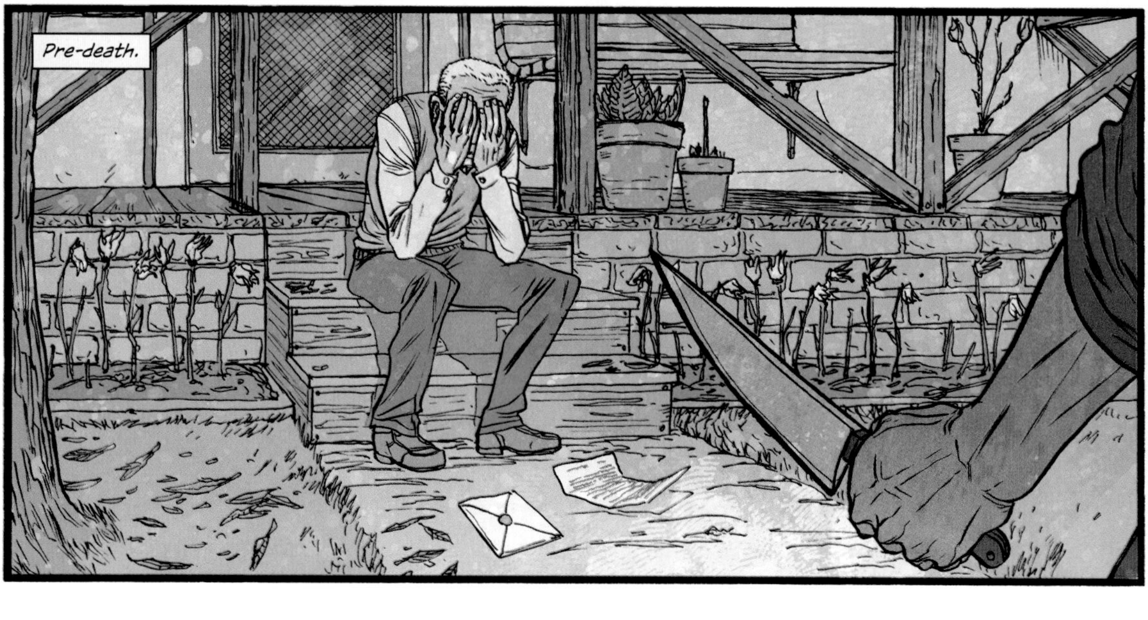
Pre-death.

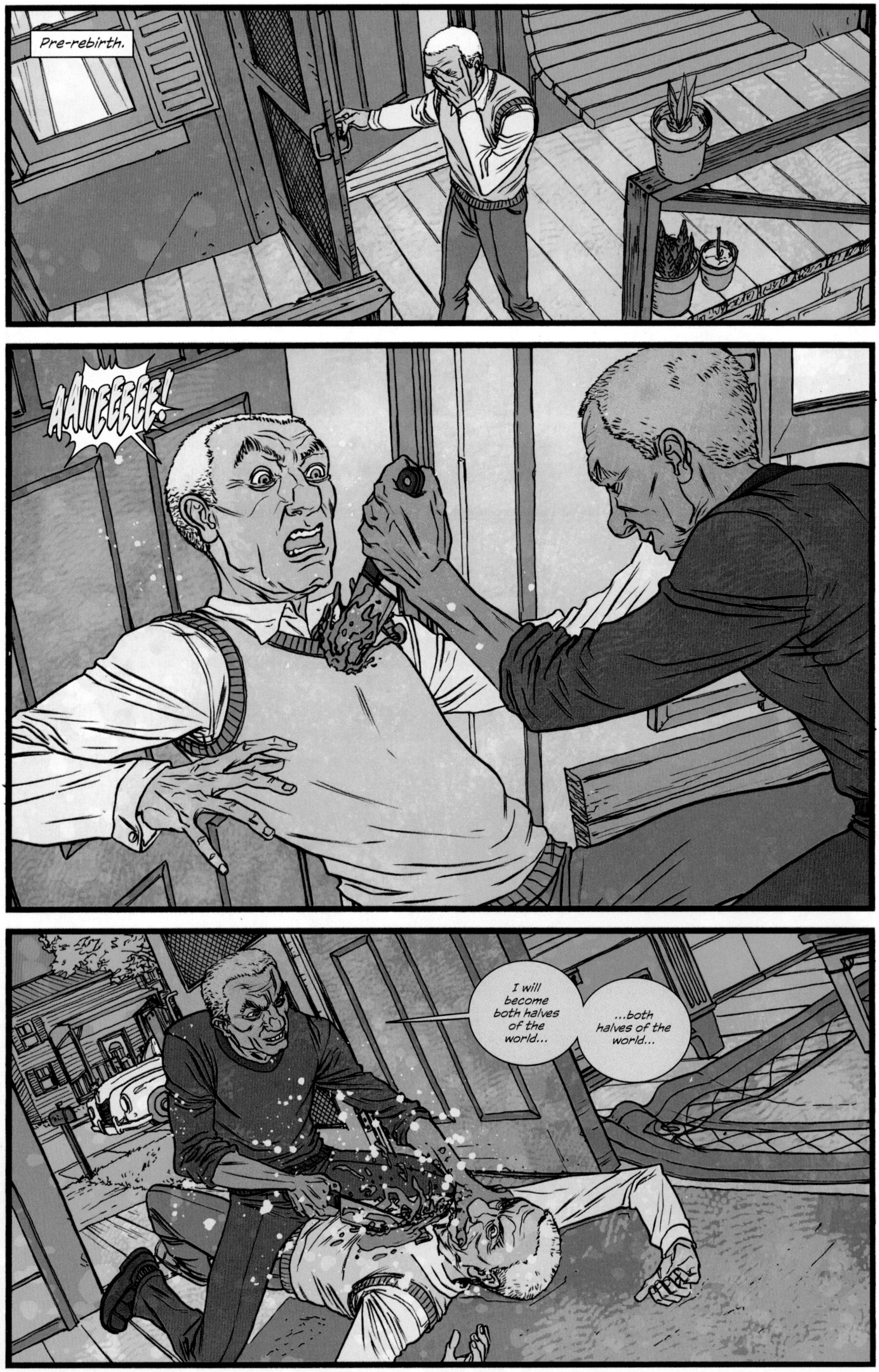
Pre-rebirth.
AAIIEEEEE!
I will become both halves of the world...
...both halves of the world...

Both halves of the world!

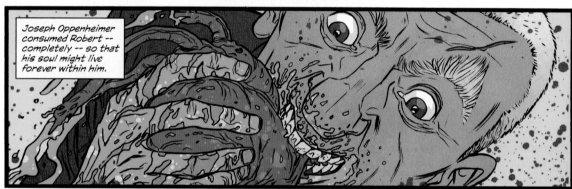

Joseph Oppenheimer consumed Robert -- completely -- so that his soul might live forever within him.

He loved his brother... so how could he not?

"THE GREAT EYE OF JOSEPH WATCHED OVER THEM ALL. THIS IS HOW THE WAR WAS LOST. "

- OPPENHEIMER

CLAVIS AUREA
THE RECORDED FEYNMAN

VOL. 3

10

FINITE OPPENHEIMERS

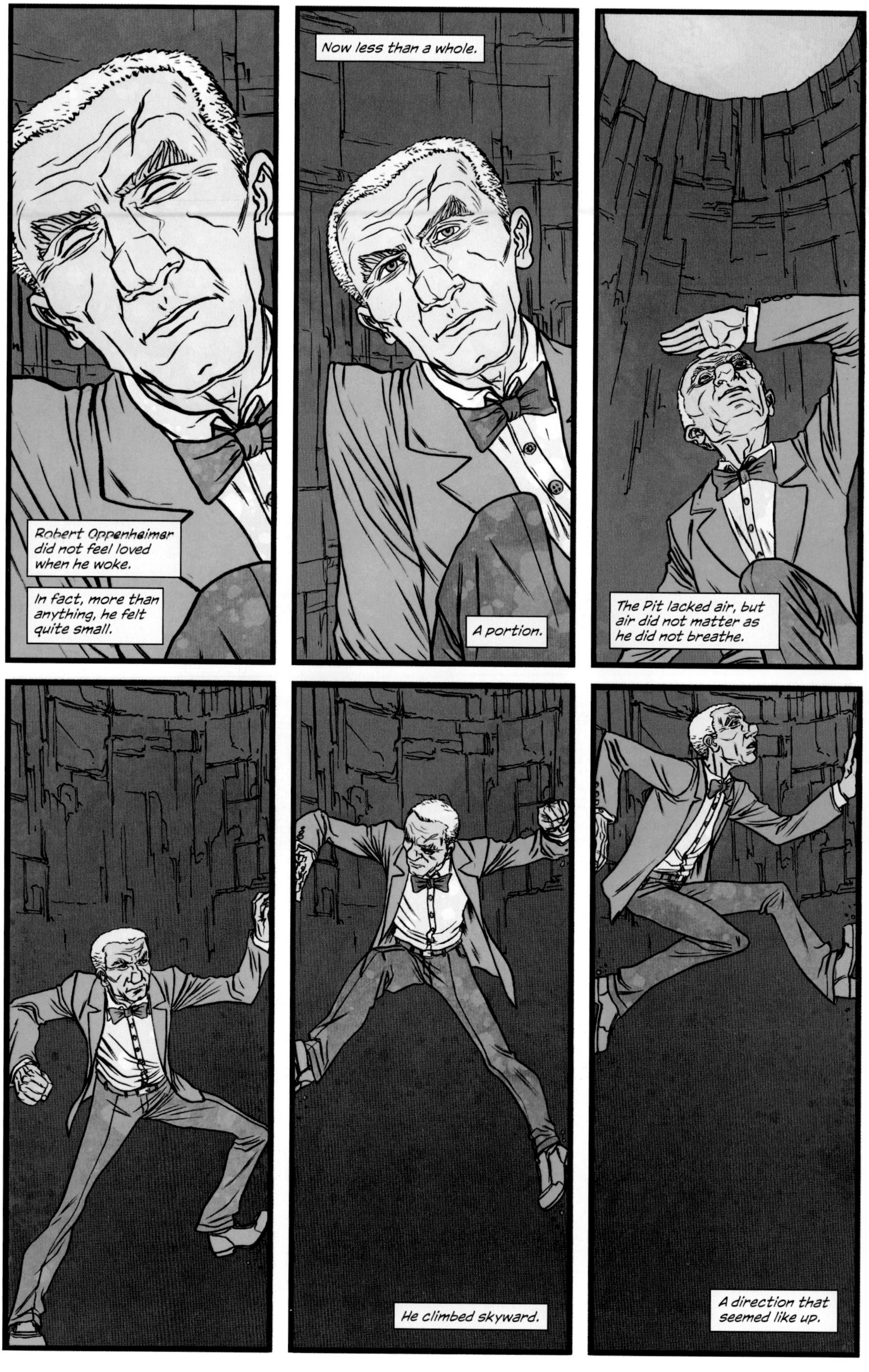
Robert Oppenheimer did not feel loved when he woke.
In fact, more than anything, he felt quite small.
Now less than a whole.
A portion.
The Pit lacked air, but air did not matter as he did not breathe.
He climbed skyward.
A direction that seemed like up.

He climbed out into not-day and not-night.

Some endless twilight emphasizing that, for an extended period, keeping track of time here would be difficult, if not impossible.

This did not concern him. Time being a component of progress seemed wrong in this place.

Achieving goals would be defined in other ways.

From the top of the world, Robert looked out, and he could see a city in the distance.

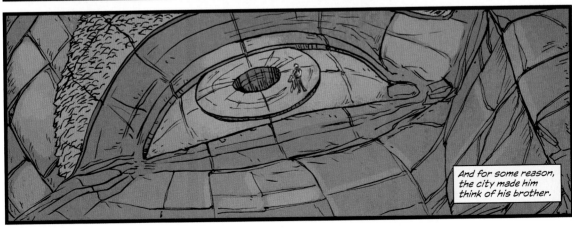

And for some reason, the city made him think of his brother.

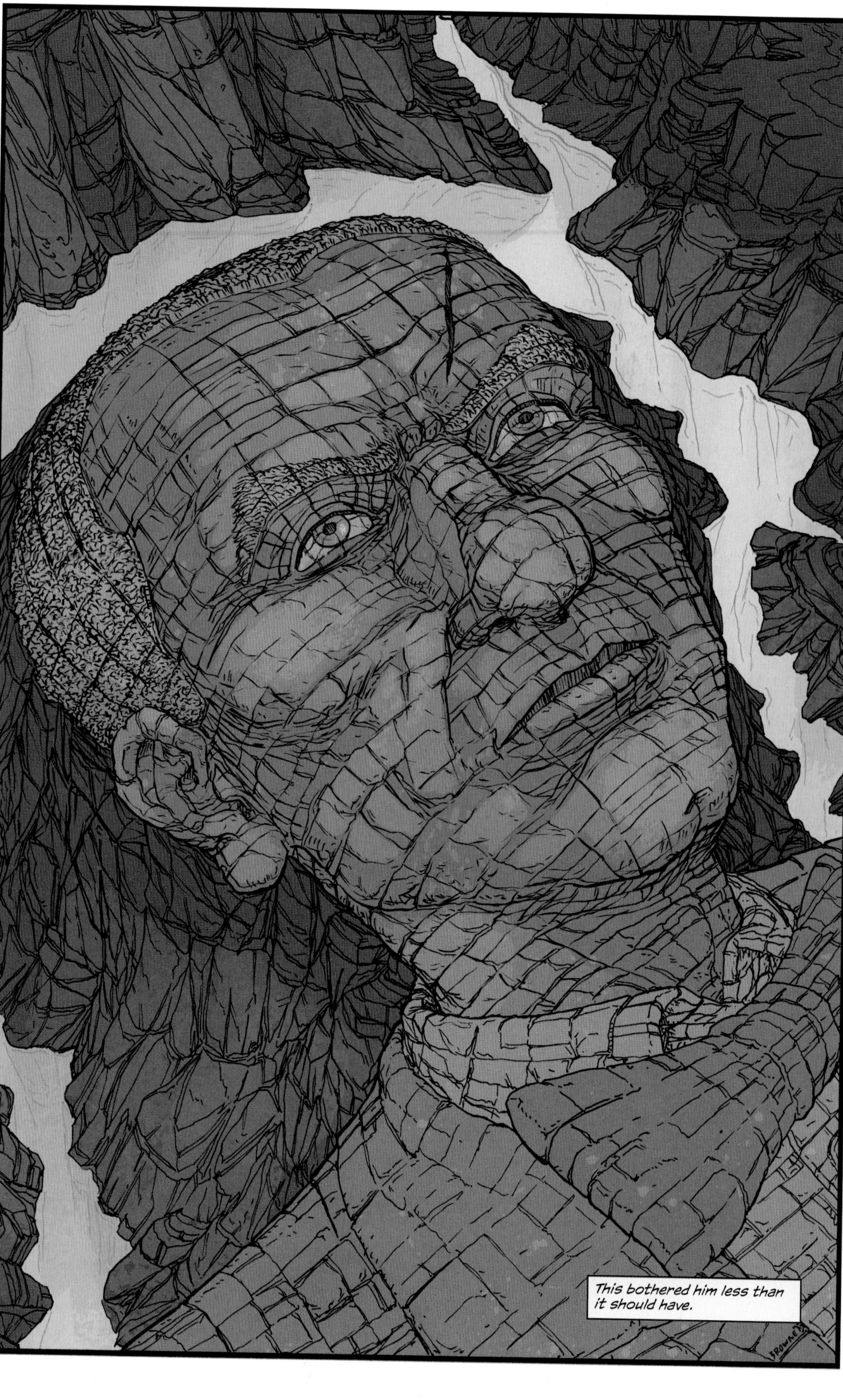
This bothered him less than it should have.

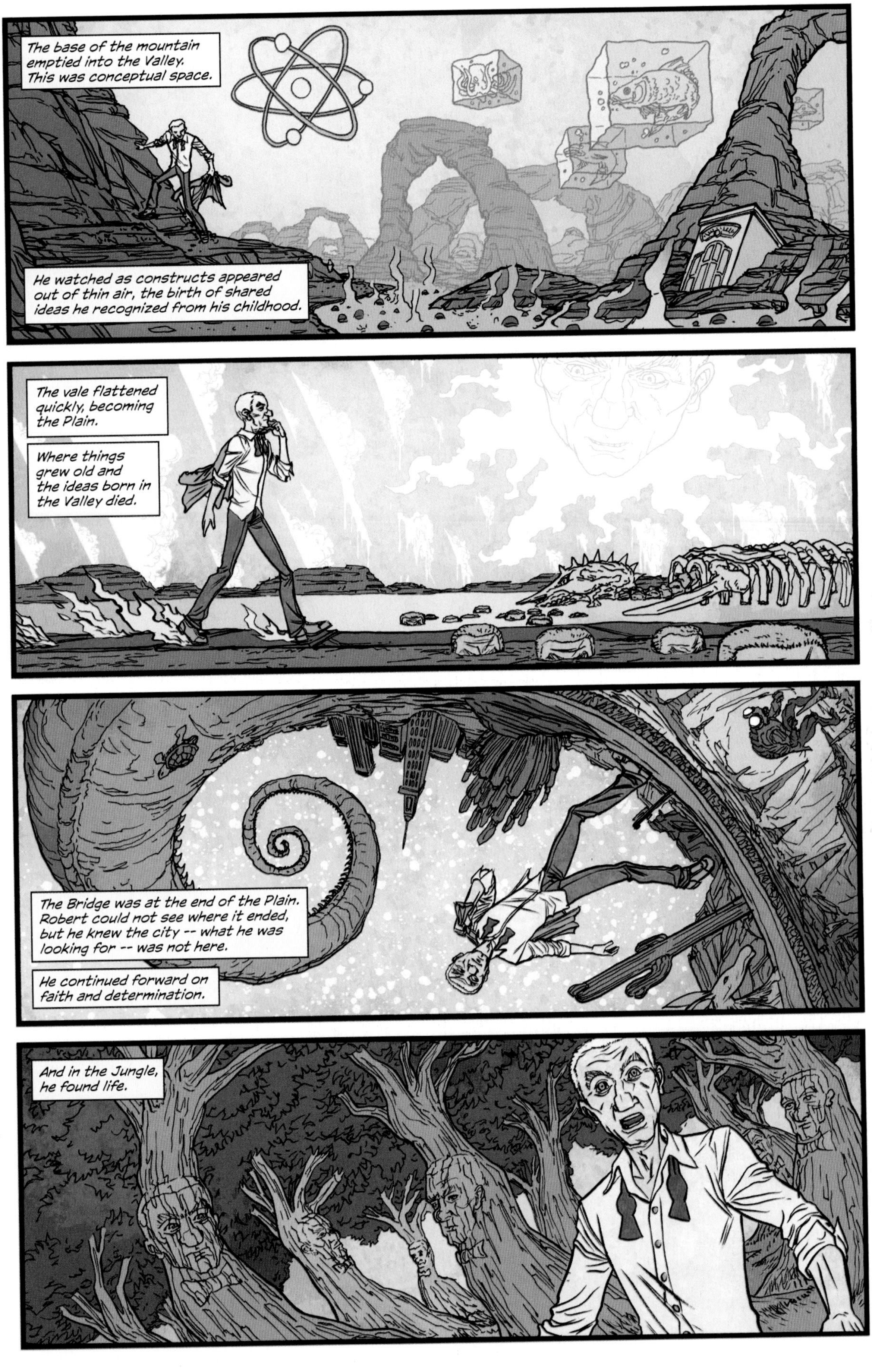
The base of the mountain emptied into the Valley. This was conceptual space.
He watched as constructs appeared out of thin air, the birth of shared ideas he recognized from his childhood.
The vale flattened quickly, becoming the Plain.
Where things grew old and the ideas born in the Valley died.
The Bridge was at the end of the Plain. Robert could not see where it ended, but he knew the city -- what he was looking for -- was not here.
He continued forward on faith and determination.
And in the Jungle, he found life.

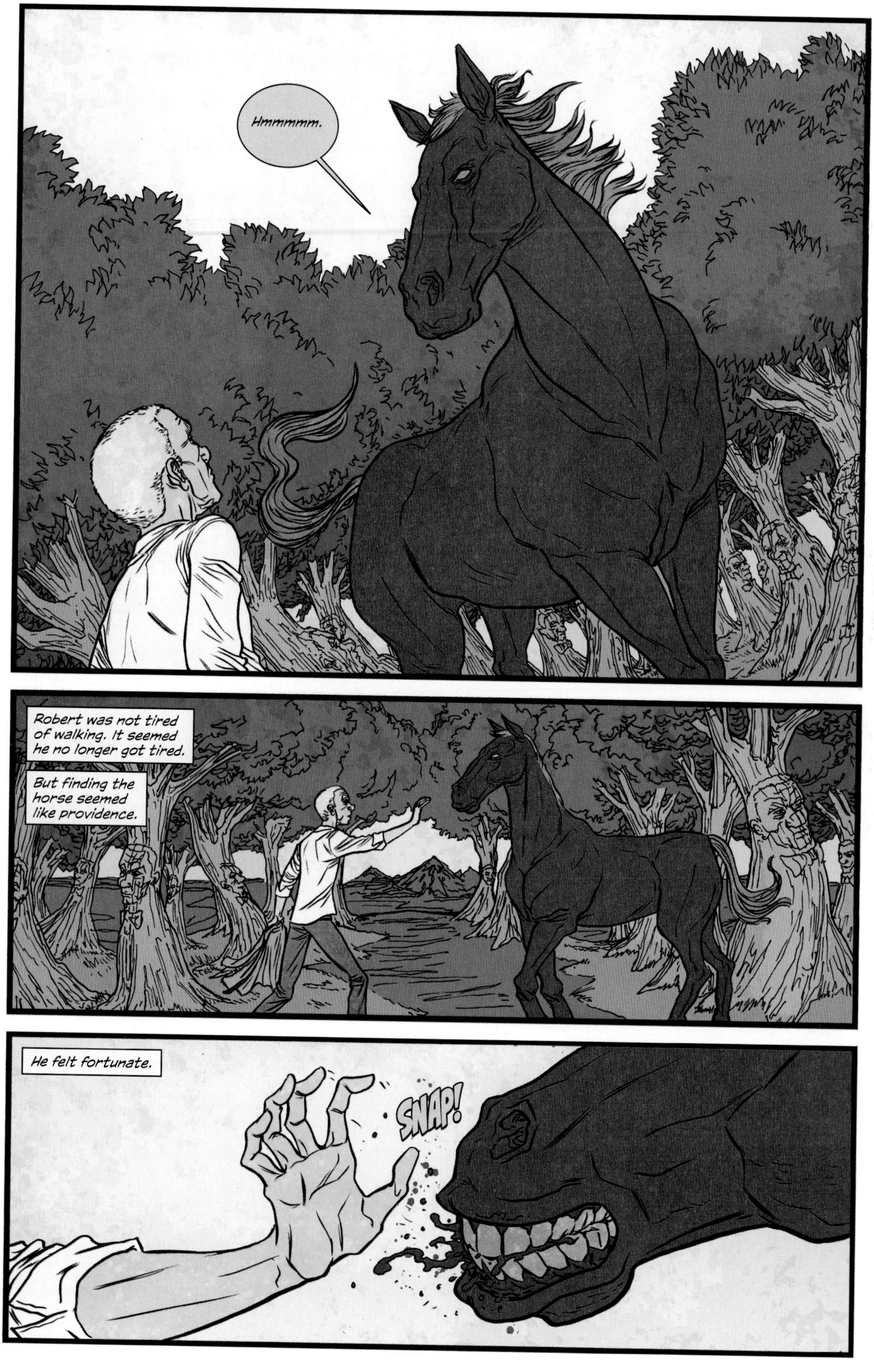

Hmmmmm.
Robert was not tired of walking. It seemed he no longer got tired.
But finding the horse seemed like providence.
He felt fortunate.
SNAP!

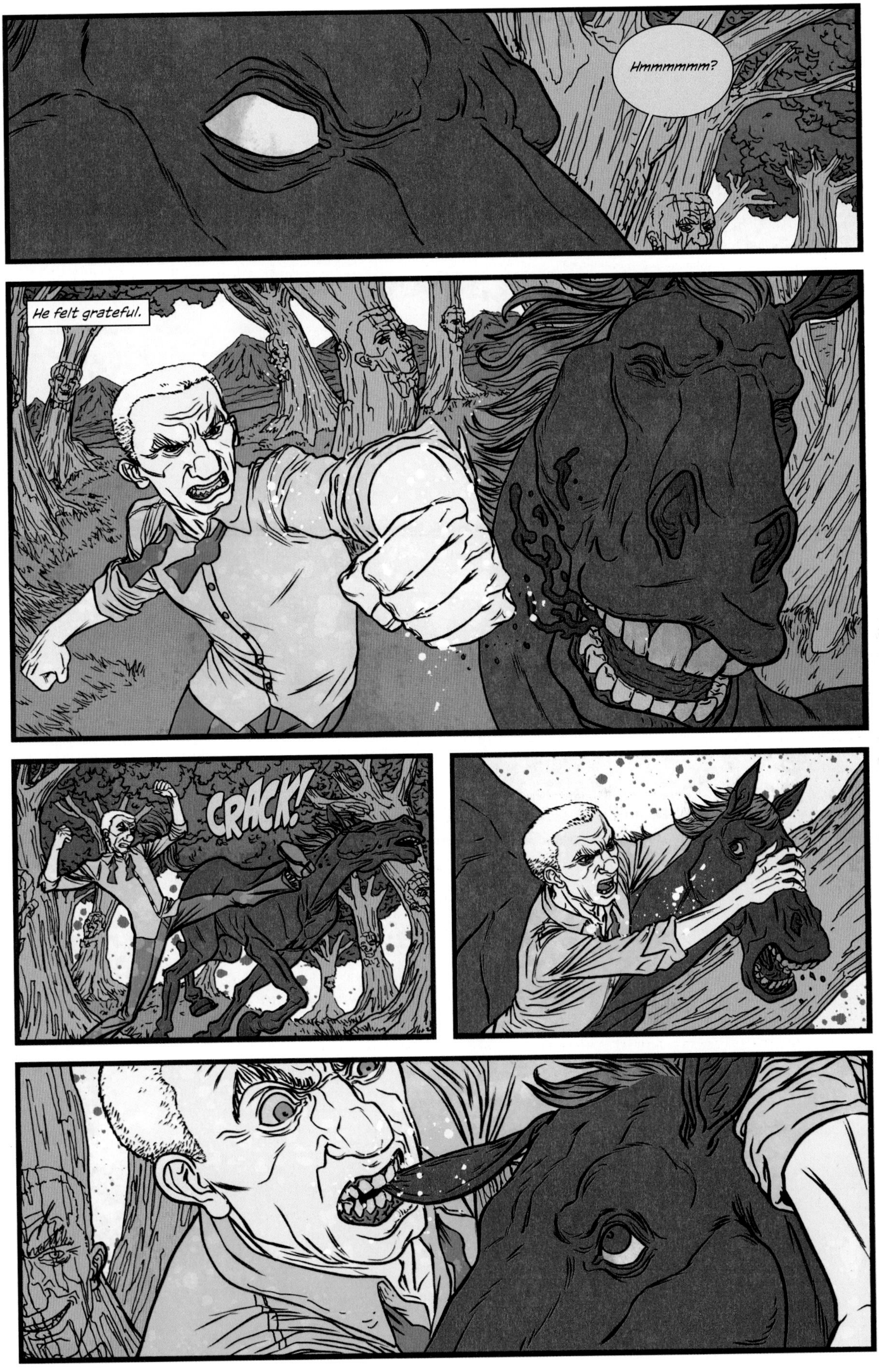
Hmmmmmm?
He felt grateful.
CRACK!

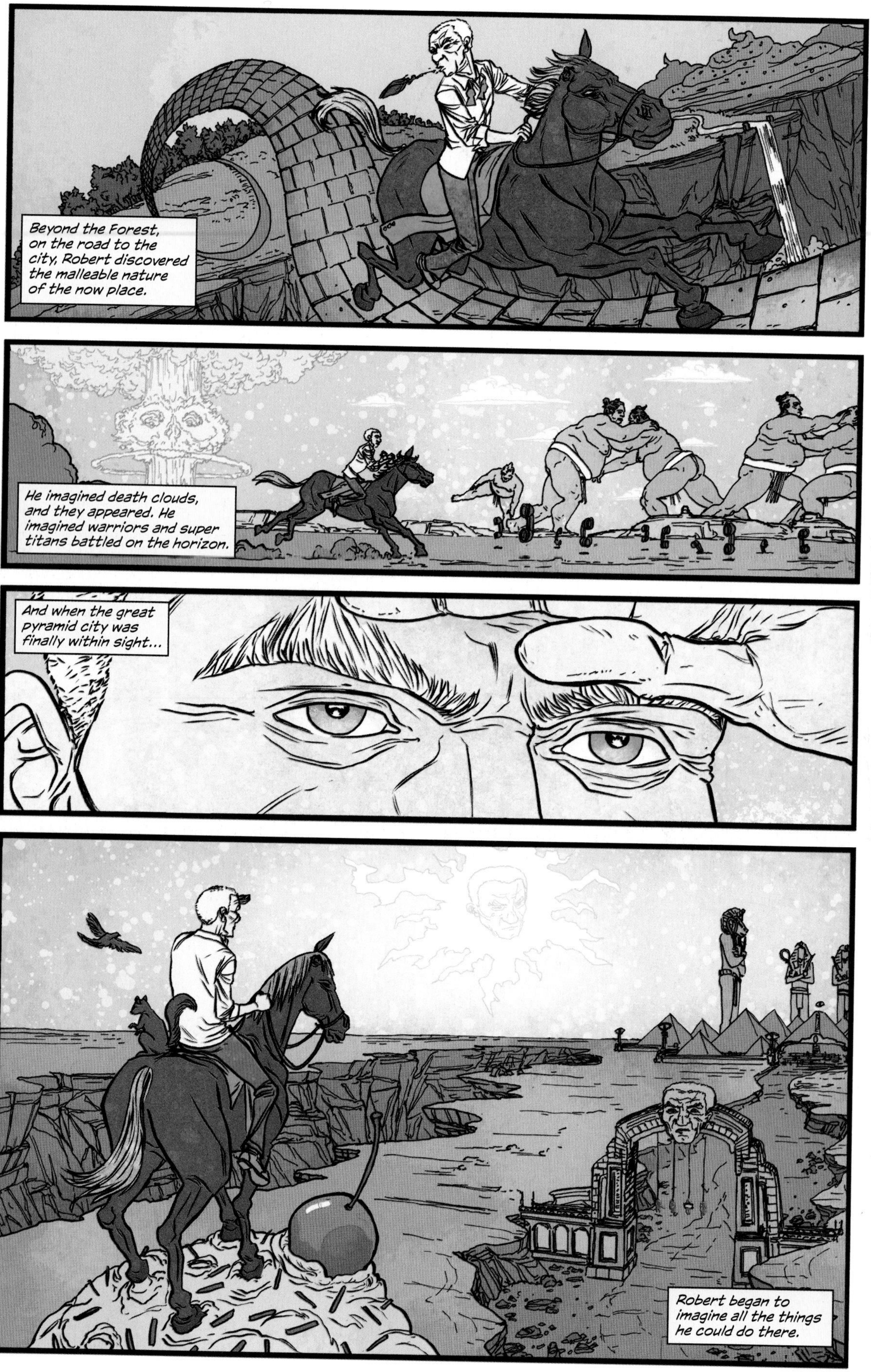
Beyond the Forest, on the road to the city, Robert discovered the malleable nature of the now place.
He imagined death clouds, and they appeared. He imagined warriors and super titans battled on the horizon.
And when the great pyramid city was finally within sight...
Robert began to imagine all the things he could do there.

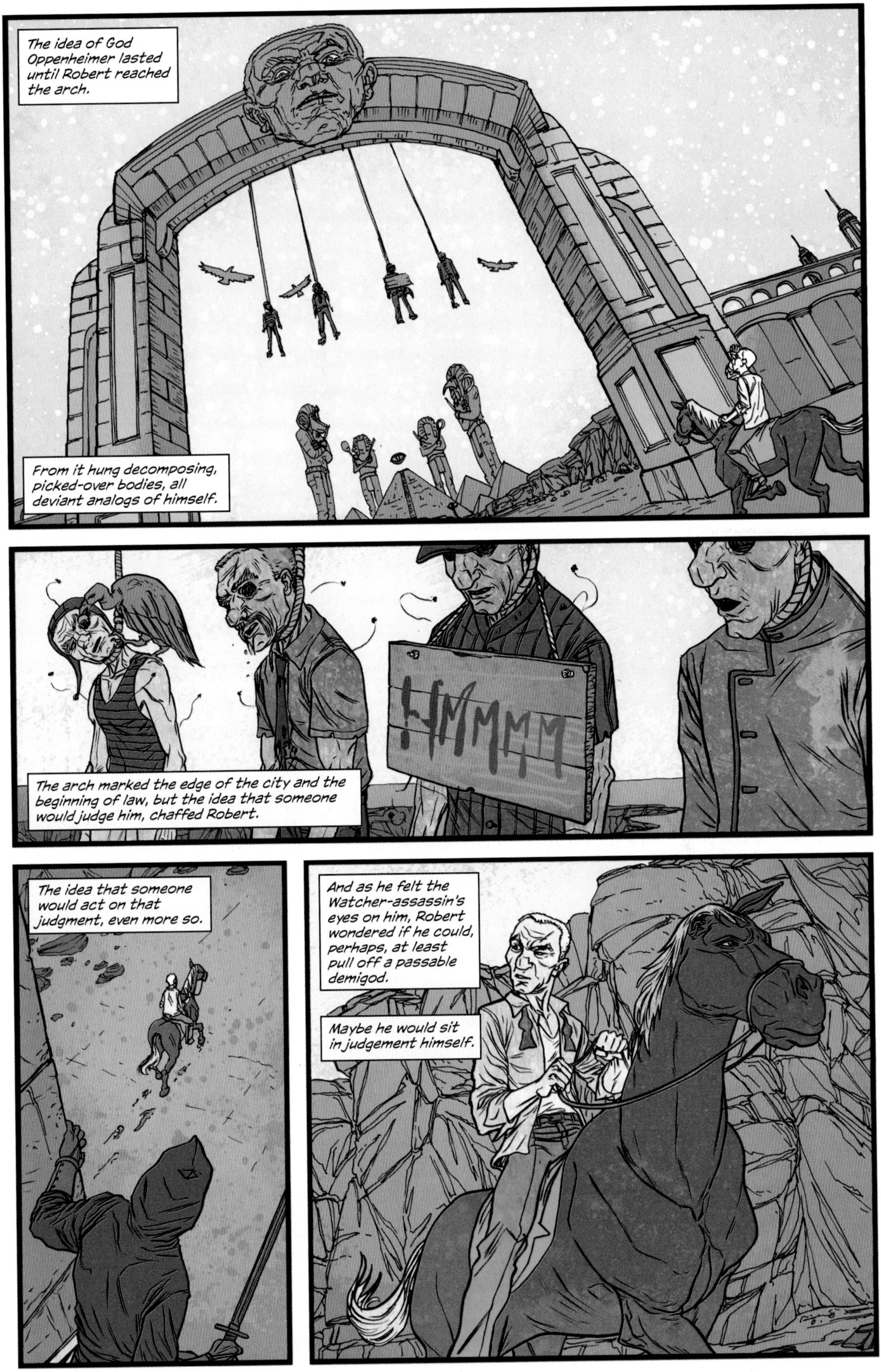
The idea of God Oppenheimer lasted until Robert reached the arch.
From it hung decomposing, picked-over bodies, all deviant analogs of himself.
HMMMM
The arch marked the edge of the city and the beginning of law, but the idea that someone would judge him, chaffed Robert.
The idea that someone would act on that judgment, even more so.
And as he felt the Watcher-assassin's eyes on him, Robert wondered if he could, perhaps, at least pull off a passable demigod.
Maybe he would sit in judgement himself.

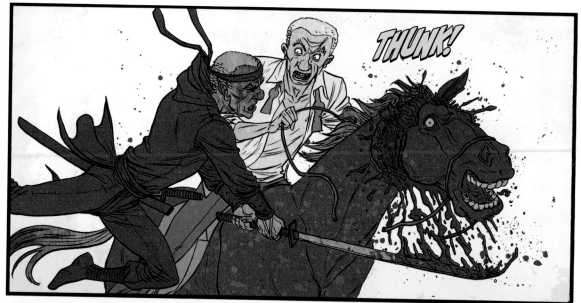

THUNK!

Hmmmm.

Hmmmm.

HMMMMM!

Robert imagined the Watcher-assassin bound, and hid his surprise when nothing happened.

He learned the Oppenheimer variants were beyond manipulation. Each one an individual persona operating outside the psychics of the now place.

But the world remained the world. A thing to be shaped.

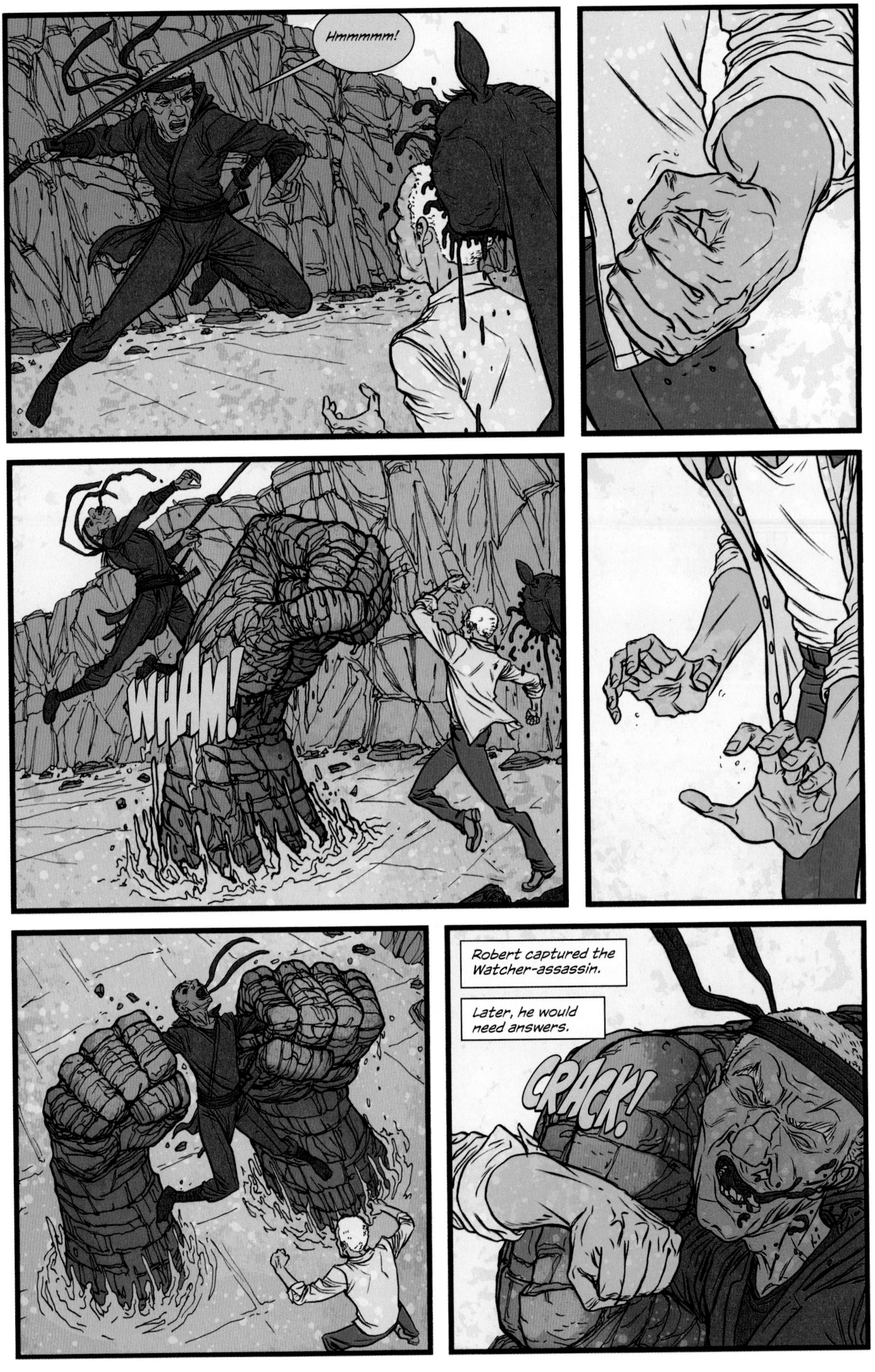
Hmmmmm!
WHAM!
Robert captured the Watcher-assassin.
Later, he would need answers.
CRACK!

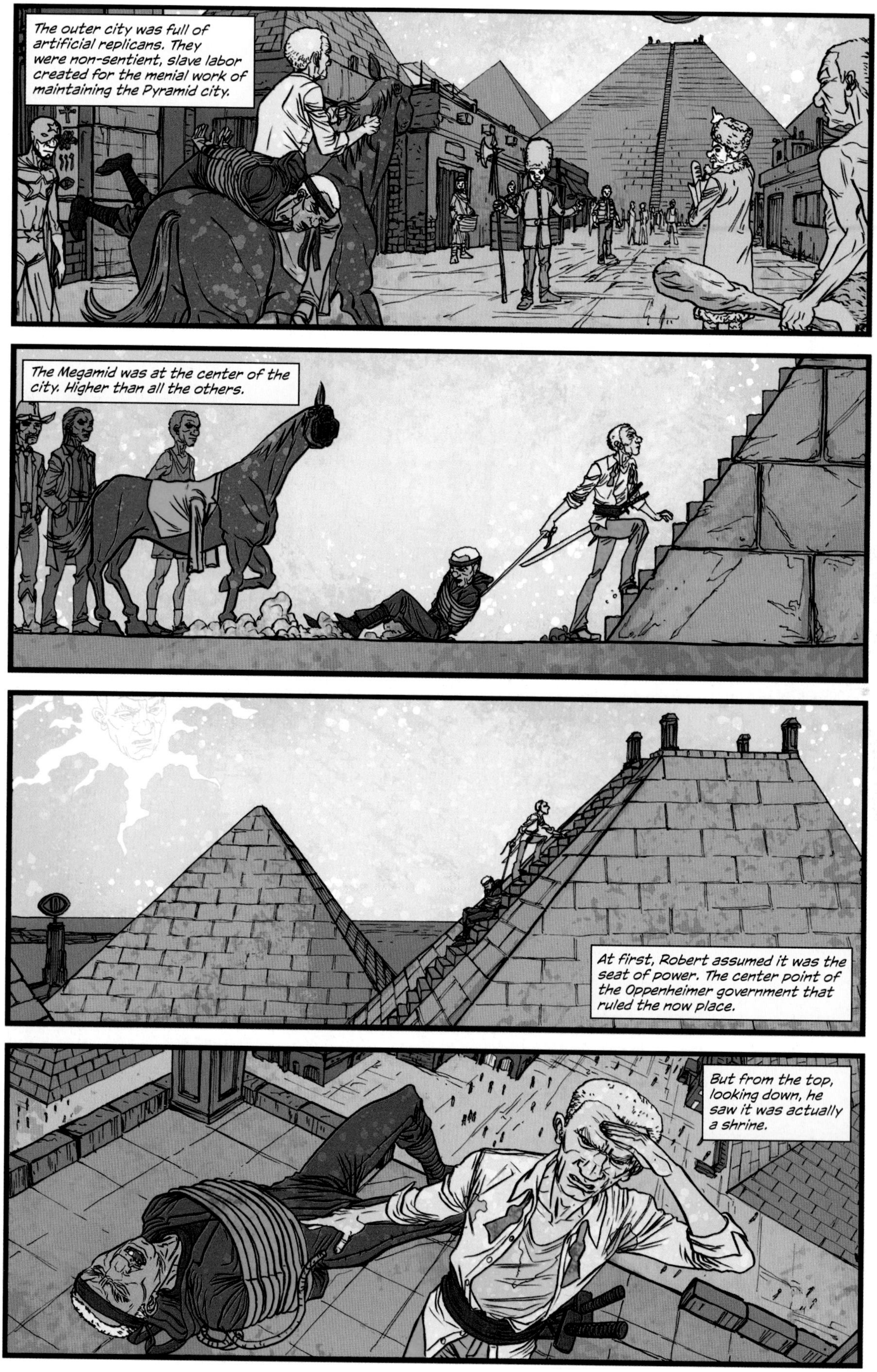
The outer city was full of artificial replicans. They were non-sentient, slave labor created for the menial work of maintaining the Pyramid city.
The Megamid was at the center of the city. Higher than all the others.
At first, Robert assumed it was the seat of power. The center point of the Oppenheimer government that ruled the now place.
But from the top, looking down, he saw it was actually a shrine.

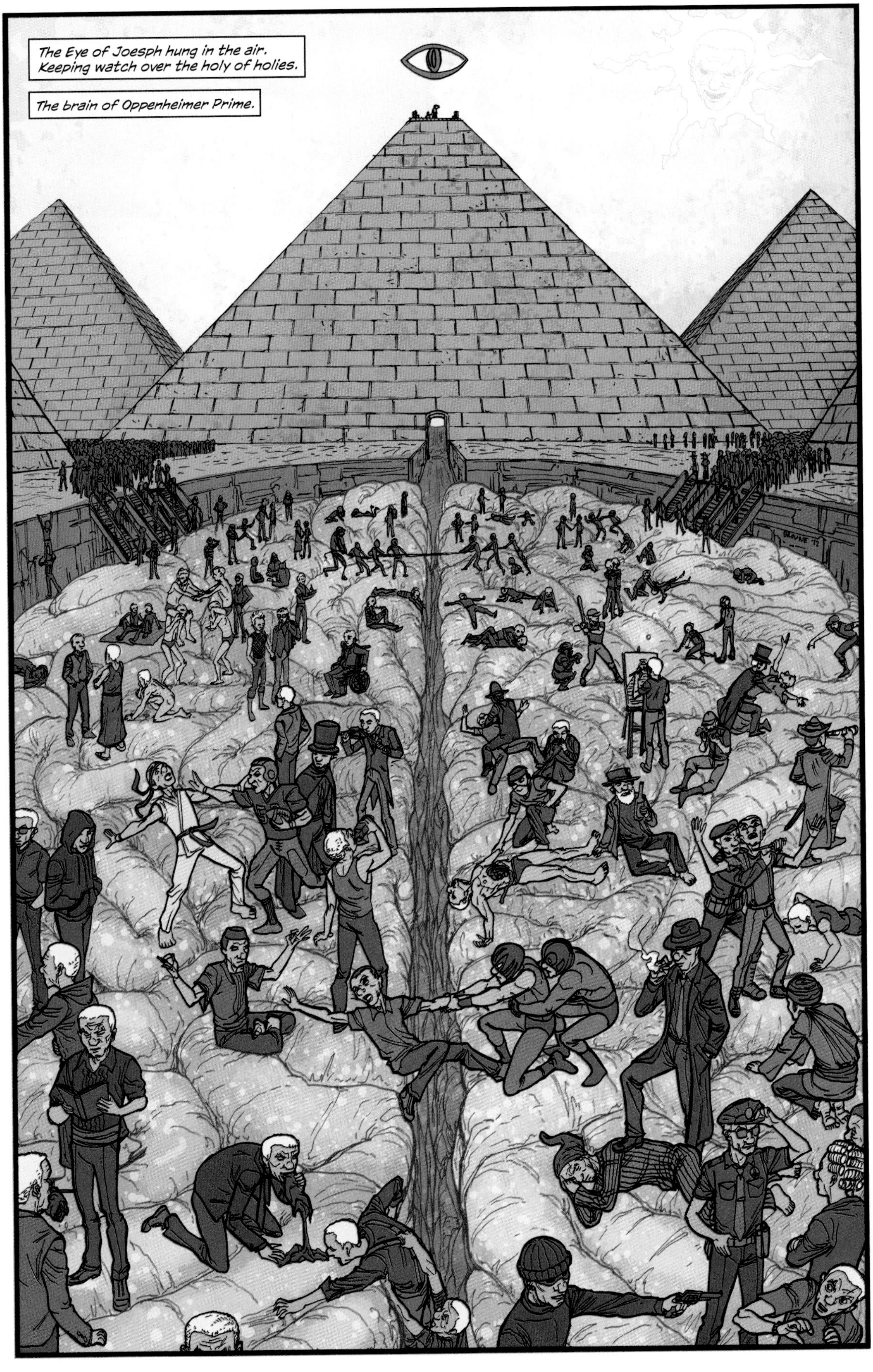
The Eye of Joesph hung in the air. Keeping watch over the holy of holies.
The brain of Oppenheimer Prime.

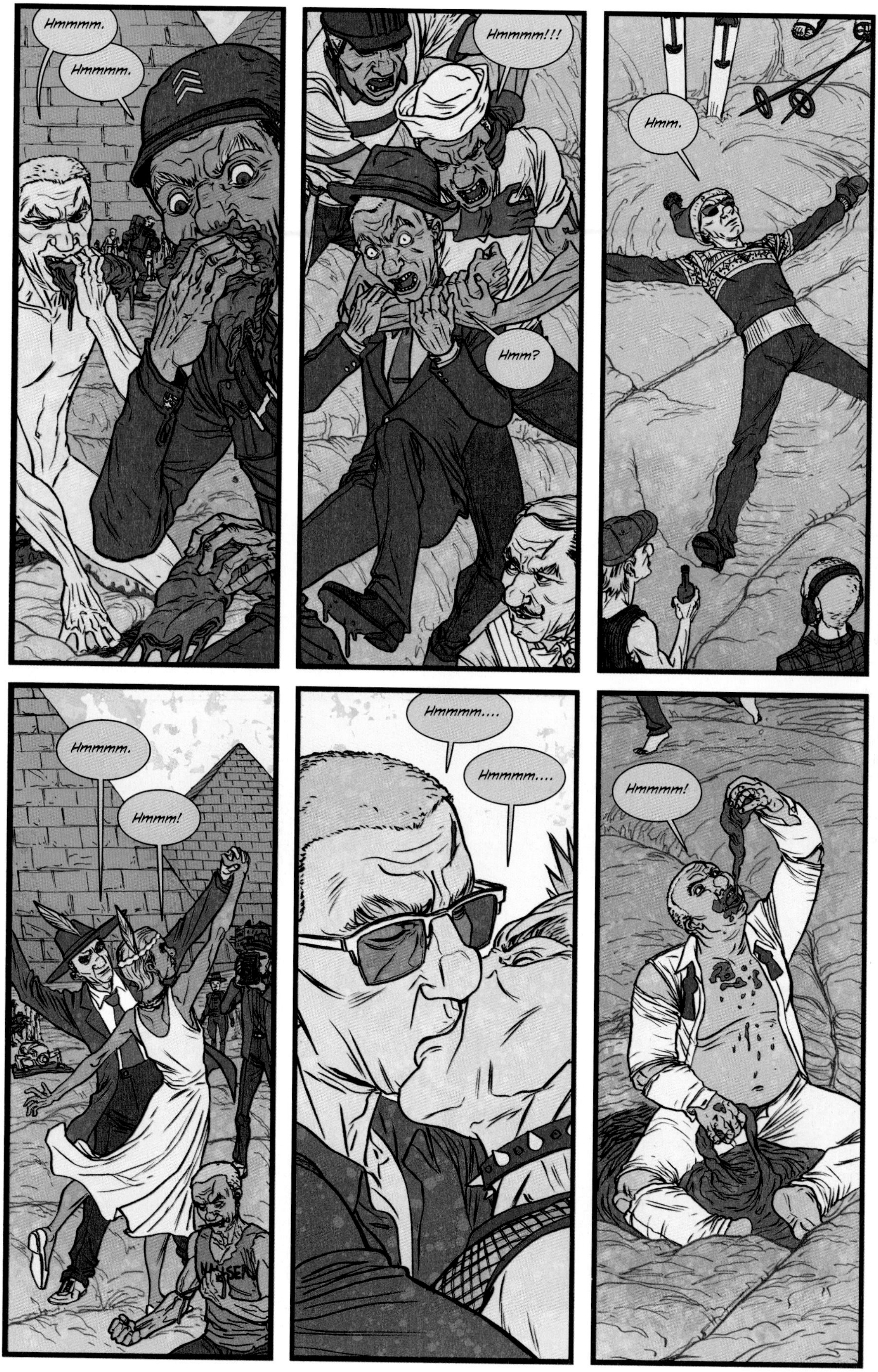
Hmmmm.
Hmmmm.
Hmmmm!!!
Hmm?
Hmm.
Hmmmm.
Hmmm!
Hmmmm....
Hmmmm....
Hmmmm!

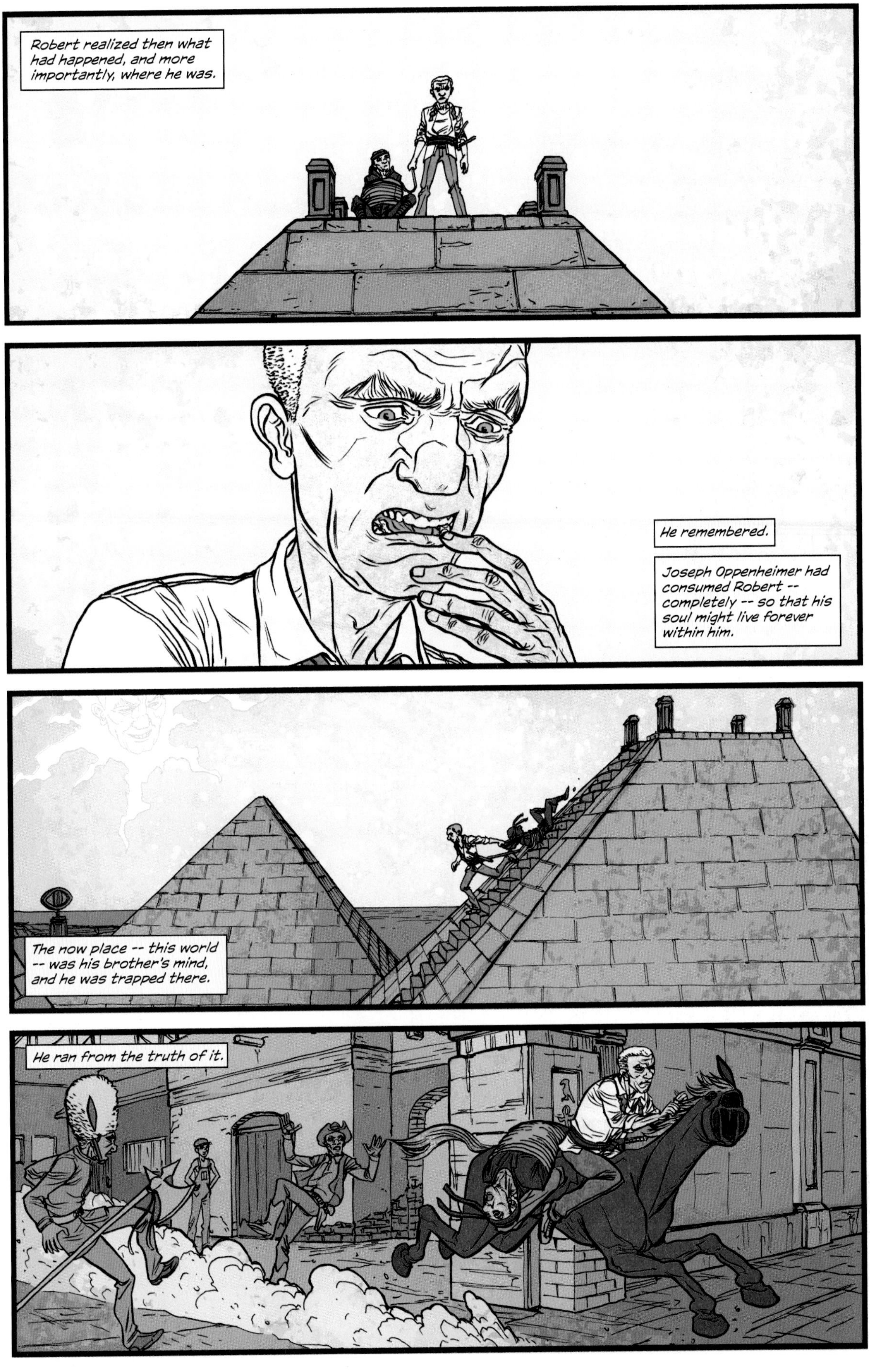

Robert realized then what had happened, and more importantly, where he was.
He remembered.
Joseph Oppenheimer had consumed Robert -- completely -- so that his soul might live forever within him.
The now place -- this world -- was his brother's mind, and he was trapped there.
He ran from the truth of it.

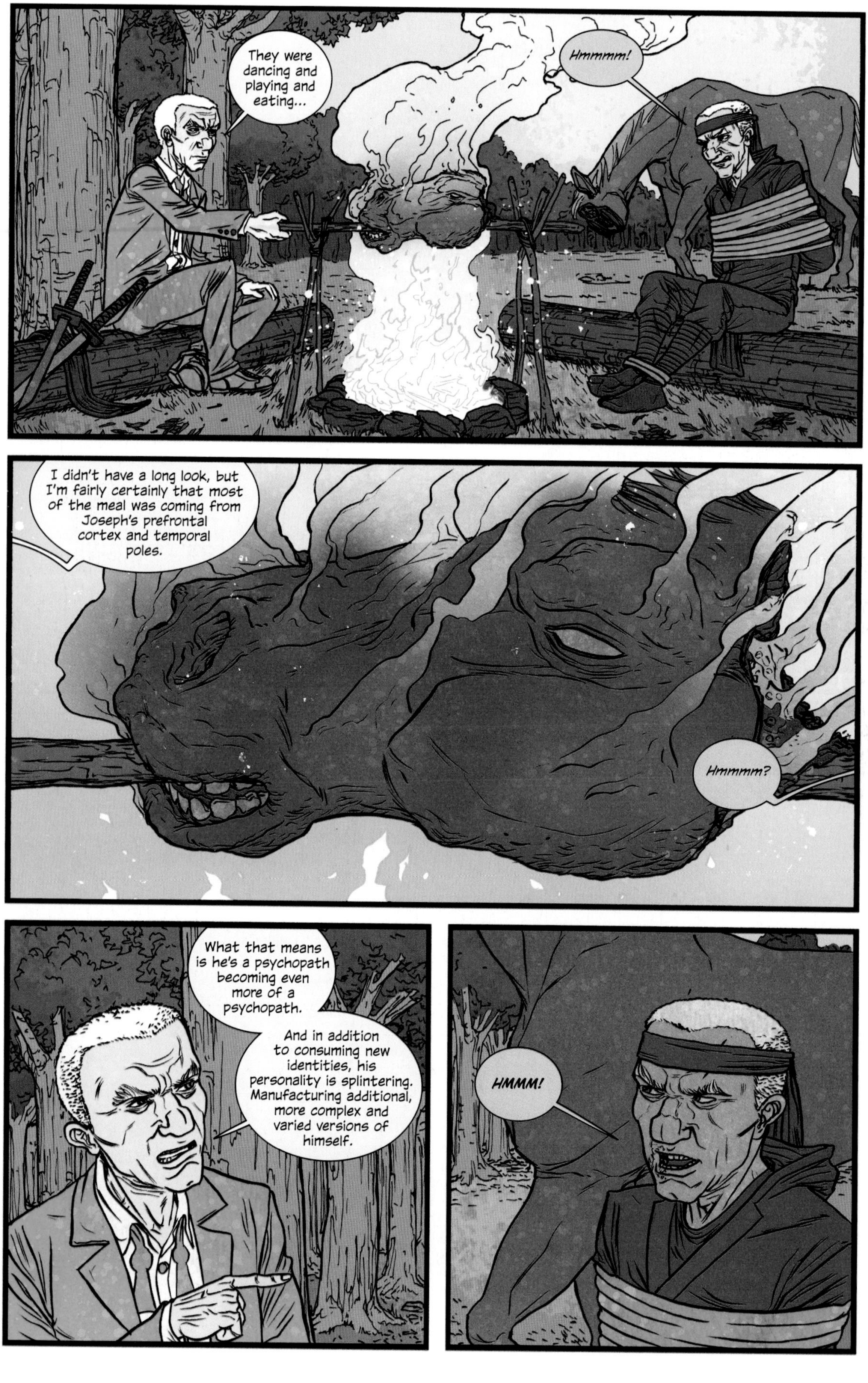
They were dancing and playing and eating...
Hmmmm!
I didn't have a long look, but I'm fairly certainly that most of the meal was coming from Joseph's prefrontal cortex and temporal poles.
Hmmmm?
What that means is he's a psychopath becoming even more of a psychopath.
And in addition to consuming new identities, his personality is splintering. Manufacturing additional, more complex and varied versions of himself.
HMMM!

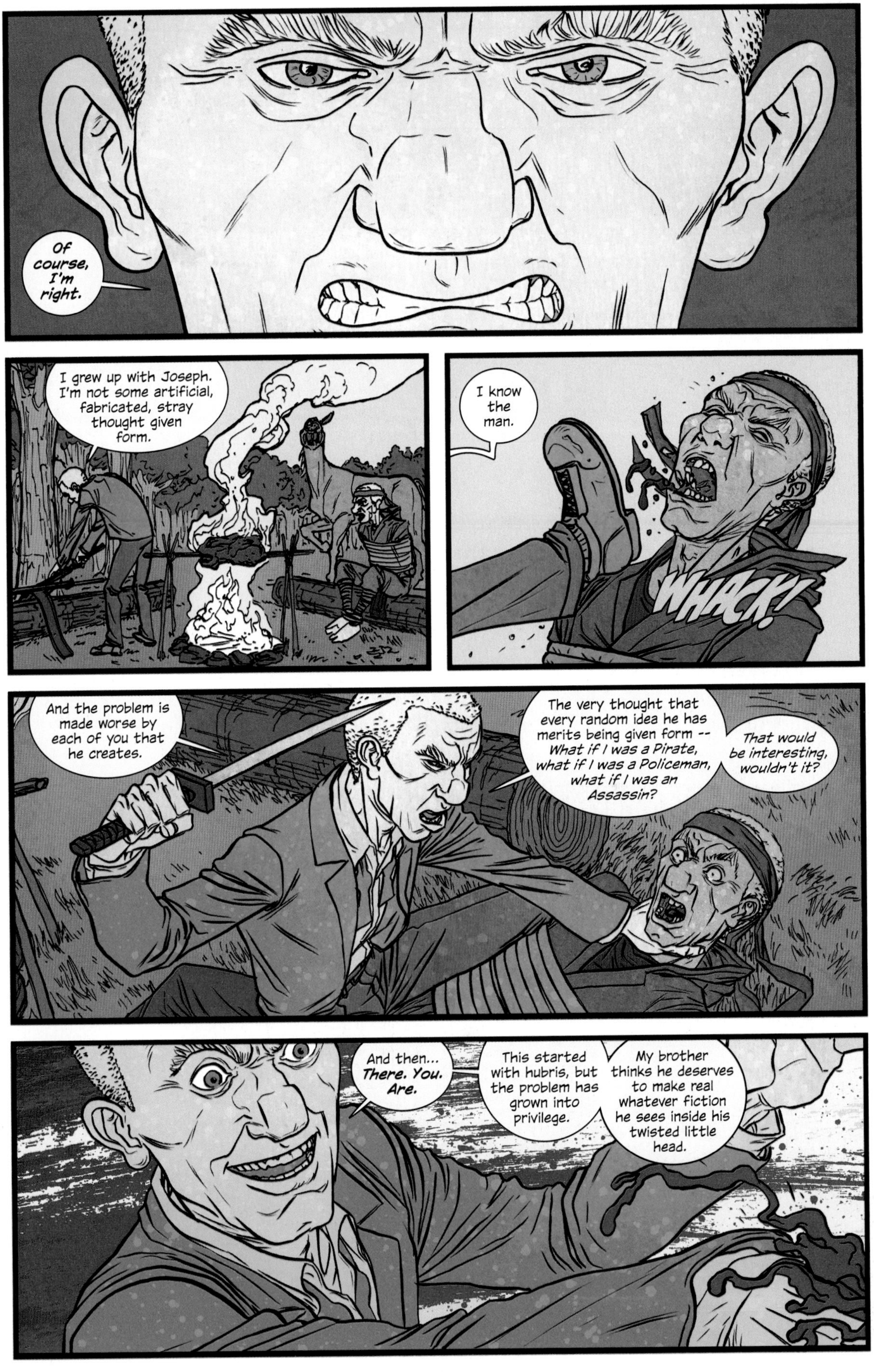
Of course, I'm right.
I grew up with Joseph. I'm not some artificial, fabricated, stray thought given form.
I know the man.
WHACK!
And the problem is made worse by each of you that he creates.
The very thought that every random idea he has merits being given form -- What if I was a Pirate, what if I was a Policeman, what if I was an Assassin?
That would be interesting, wouldn't it?
And then... There. You. Are.
This started with hubris, but the problem has grown into privilege.
My brother thinks he deserves to make real whatever fiction he sees inside his twisted little head.

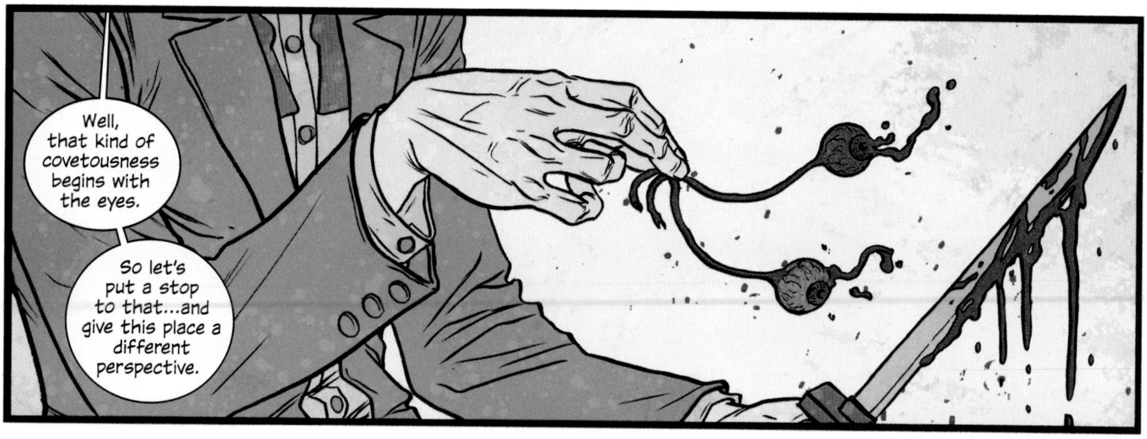
Well, that kind of covetousness begins with the eyes.
So let's put a stop to that...and give this place a different perspective.

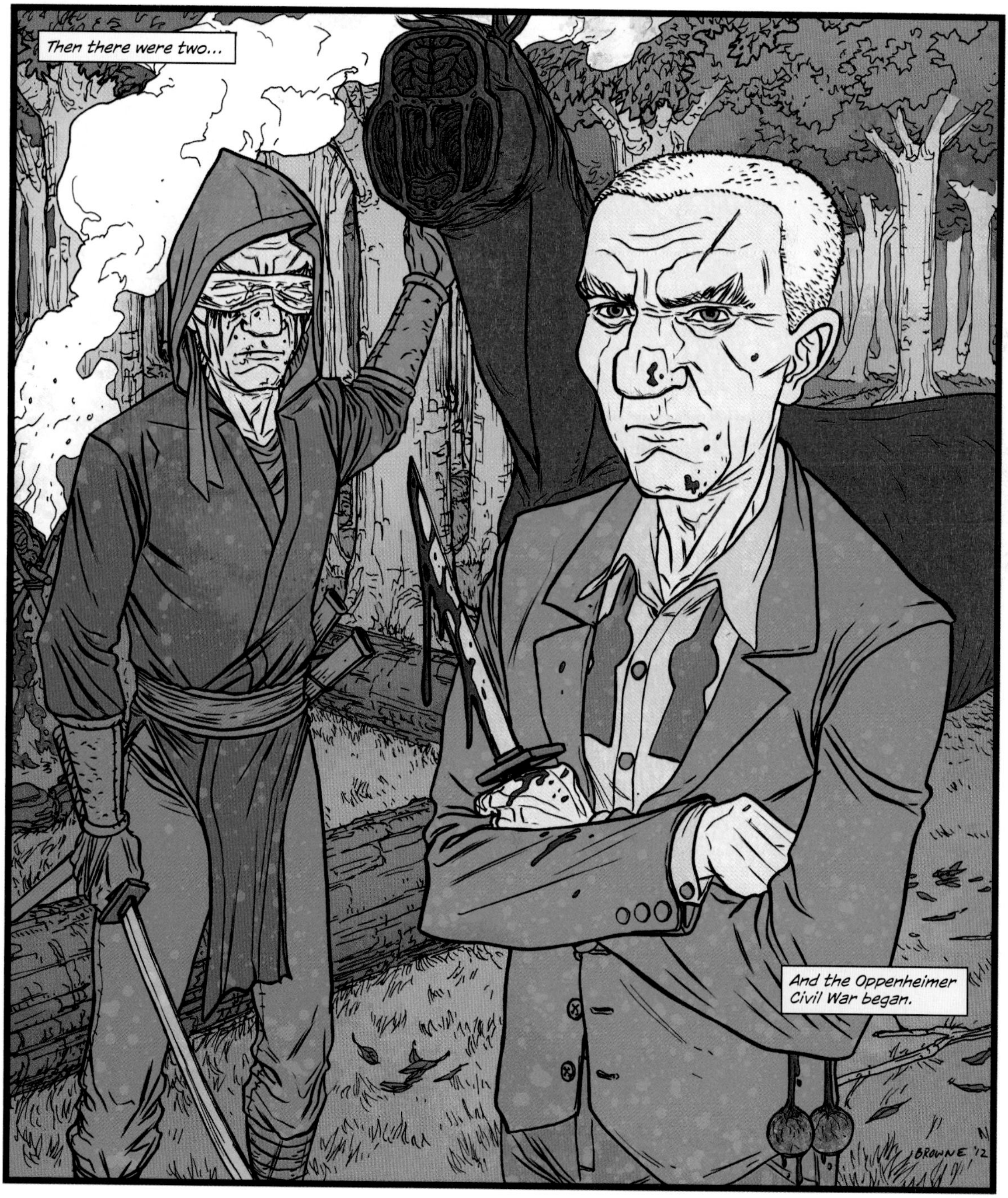
Then there were two...
And the Oppenheimer Civil War began.
BROWNE '12

"WE LOOKED UP, AND FROM THE MEGAMID, IT LOOKED DOWN. THE GREAT EYE OFFENDED, SO WE PLUCKED THEM OUT.

AGAIN, AND AGAIN, AND AGAIN."

- OPPENHEIMER

CLAVIS AUREA
THE RECORDED FEYNMAN | **VOL. 3**

THE CAST

JOSEPH OPPENHEIMER

Super genius.
American. Physicist.
Multiple personalities.

ALBRECHT EINSTEIN

Highly intelligent.
German. Physicist.
Drinks.

RICHARD FEYNMAN

Super genius.
American. Physicist.
Wormholer.

ENRICO FERMI

Super genius.
Italian. Physicist.
Not human.

HARRY DAGHLIAN

Super genius.
American. Physicist.
Irradiated.

WERNHER VON BRAUN

Super genius.
German. Rocket scientist.
Robot arm.

LESLIE GROVES

Not a genius.
American. General.
Smokes. Bombs.

FDR: A.I.

Computational super genius.
American. President.
Dead.

HARRY S. TRUMAN

Not a genius.
American. President.
Freemason.

THE CAST

YURI GAGARIN

Not a genius.
Russian. Cosmonaut.
Hero.

LAIKA

Way smarter than thought.
Russian. Space Dog.
Speaks.

HELMUTT GRÖTTRUP

Super genius.
German. Rocket scientist.
Slave.

DMITRIY USTINOV

Not a genius.
Russian. Minister.
Master.

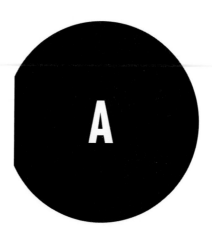

Jonathan Hickman is the visionary talent behind such works as the Eisner-nominated **NIGHTLY NEWS**, **TRANSHUMAN** and **PAX ROMANA**. He also plies his trade at MARVEL working on books like **FANTASTIC FOUR** and **THE AVENGERS**.

His twin brother, Marc, won the Gold in Fencing at the 2012 Olympics.

Jonathan lives in South Carolina surrounded by immediate family and in-laws, which he plans on leaving unless they start showering him with the love and affection he deserves.

This includes his wife.

You can visit his website:***www.pronea.com***, or email him at:***jonathan@pronea.com***.

•

Nick Pitarra is a native Texan and all around nice guy. As a senior in high school he was kicked out of honors English, and subsequently fell in love with comic illustration while doodling with a friend in his new class.

Sometimes it pays not to do your homework.